11/05

AT HOME WITH
MICHAEL CHIARELLO

AT HOME WITH
MICHAEL CHIARELLO

easy entertaining | recipes • ideas • inspiration

BY MICHAEL CHIARELLO | PHOTOGRAPHS BY KARL PETZKE

CHRONICLE BOOKS
SAN FRANCISCO

Library of Congress Cataloging-in-Publication Data available.

ISBN 0-8118-4048-4

Manufactured in China.

Designed by Level, Calistoga, CA

Prop styling by Alessandra Mortolla

Food styling by Dan Becker

The photographer wishes to thank Michael for the opportunity to create the imagery for his beautiful book,
At Home with Michael Chiarello. I would also like to thank my two assistants, Paul Hammond and Dawn Pavli,
for their tireless hours of work. Food styling is an art and Dan Becker is that artist who makes my job that much
more enjoyable. For her amazing props and vision Alessandra Mortolla as our stylist, and her assistant Brooke,
thank you both. As always books are a labor of love, but also a collaboration of talented individuals.

Distributed in Canada by Raincoast Books

9050 Shaughnessy Street

Vancouver, British Columbia V6P 6E5

10 9 8 7 6 5 4 3 2 1

Chronicle Books LLC

85 Second Street

San Francisco, California 94105

www.chroniclebooks.com

introduction

Living, farming, and cooking in California's Napa Valley since 1986 has opened my eyes to the possibilities of entertaining. Nowadays, I am blessed to be on both sides of the stove: the host of the party—at home and on my television shows—and the guest of world-class entertainers. When I met my wife, Eileen, the joke between us was, "Hey, you seem like a nice enough guy, but why is it that we never get invited to anyone's house for dinner?" Since I am a pretty good guy and always help clean up, I figured it was because our friends were intimidated to cook for a chef. Those friends' fear of entertaining is one inspiration for this book. Another inspiration came when, after twenty-five years of cooking professionally, I started entertaining more at home.

In the past, I could never understand why the home cook was nervous about throwing a dinner party. It was always easy for me. Whenever I entertained, I would write a menu and hand it off to a sous-chef, who would pull together the ingredients and prep them. Then the restaurant staff would help me load up my car, and I'd take along a cook or two for the evening who wanted to cook with me. Throw the party, sit down with my guests, and enjoy the last glass of red wine—it was as simple as that. Meanwhile, my apprentices cleaned the kitchen and loaded the car with all the dirty plates, glasses, pots, pans, and linens. It worked out beautifully for me. I was always in bed by eleven.

But for you, and for me when I remove my professional apron, the dynamics are much different. You know the drill: You get excited about throwing the party. You spend a leisurely Sunday morning over coffee with your favorite cookbooks and develop an ambitious menu of seven courses minimum, which yields a monster shopping list and an even larger prep list. You prep for two solid days, and then you scramble to get the table set, the wine at the right temperature, and your clothes changed before your guests arrive, only to find yourself one hour behind schedule when the first people show up thirty minutes early. And someone always does. You keep your best host smile going while trying to enjoy dinner without jumping up what seems like more than a hundred times to stir, plate, and serve. You finally say goodnight, only to be left with hours of cleanup. During the haze that follows, as you try to decide whether to have a beer and go to bed or have a coffee and watch the sun come up (because your cleaning task is monumental), you register the firm decision not to do this again any time soon.

But despite that vow, you do it again soon. That's because deep down, perhaps now more than ever in our recent past, we yearn to bring people close and care for them through food. We need to share a laugh, to feel cozy in our homes and comfortable in our abilities. We need to celebrate our gifts, to be proud of our lives and of ourselves. This book is for all of us who love great food, adore our friends and family, want to share our love for them by entertaining, and still want a life.

Times have changed, and how we want to live, entertain, and be entertained is always a reflection of the times. Our priorities have shifted back to caring for people with handcrafted foods and casual gatherings that happen more often. Most important, as hosts, we require that we enjoy throwing the party as much as our guests love coming. To put the *entertain* back into entertaining you have to open your mind and look way beyond the seven-course meal for creativity. Six basic rules will help you do just that.

RULE NUMBER ONE: TAKE SOMETHING THAT EVERYONE UNDER-STANDS AND PRESENT IT IN A WAY THEY WOULD NEVER IMAGINE
For example, think outside the box when choosing serving pieces. I like to call them props—think theater—and have been known to serve hors d'oeuvres out of a napkin-lined tool chest for a car enthusiast's birthday or appetizers in a Sunday offering basket for a church social. Use that same thinking with recipes. Choose a recipe, and then go small for drama or supersize for impact when serving it. For instance, make one of my main courses, such as Grilled and Braised Short Ribs, Brasciole Style (page 130), and offer it in individual bites on oversized spoons served over polenta as an appetizer. Or, make Grilled Salmon and Spinach Salad with Corn Juice "Zabaglione" (page 73) and serve it in a lettuce cup. How you serve, the whimsy you add, will flavor the memory your guests have for a lifetime.

RULE NUMBER TWO: PLAY WITH THE ELEMENT OF SURPRISE. *I am always looking for ways to enhance the social interaction of my guests, which often means breaking up the traditional sit-down meal. Think about putting together a menu that requires no plate and/or utensils. Grilled Gaucho Steak with Blue Cheese and Pita (page 126) could be the centerpiece. Eating with their hands puts people at ease and allows them permission to see the humor in life. Look backward for inspiration to re-create some retro favorites, such as Melon and Prosciutto "as Soup" (page 77) or Twice-Baked Stuffed Pea Potatoes (page 150). Use creative names for your dishes that will set your guests' minds and taste buds in motion, such as Tomato "Carpaccio" (page 52). Don't be afraid to show your guests that food doesn't always need to be serious.*

RULE THREE: LOCATION, LOCATION, LOCATION. *No matter where you live or how big your house is, always consider all your space when planning a get-together. A bologna-and-cheese sandwich eaten at the top of a beautiful mountain can often be more satisfying than a seven-course meal served in a cold, stuffy restaurant. Get out of the dining room. Serve up Brunch Piadina with Spicy Basted Eggs and Spinach (page 174) on the coffee table in front of the fireplace, or carry the television into the garden, slide in a movie, and serve Pop Culture Popcorn (page 47) and Parmesan French Fries (page 151). Or, on a cold winter day, dig out the picnic table, put on parkas, and throw a barbe-cue in the snow. Experiment. The unexpectedness of an unlikely location adds flavor to any meal.*

RULE FOUR: WHEN WRITING YOUR MENU, EXPLOIT YOUR STRENGTHS. *To do that, you must first get to know a recipe well—to perfect it. Then, only after perfecting it, think, "How can I turn this into an appetizer for twenty, a side dish for eight, or a buffet-table offering for twelve?" Make it several ways over the course of a few months. Do this and you will come to understand the mindset of a chef. Your parties will become as much for you as for your guests because making the dishes will have become second nature, freeing you from worry about their success.*

At Home with Michael Chiarello is filled with scores of tips and pointers that I've learned over twenty-five years of entertaining. In those years, I have literally created and cooked at more than three thousand parties and events of all types, from a dinner for Senator Hillary Rodham Clinton to a birthday party for a crowd of octogenarians, from a pig roast to an all-caviar meal, from a romantic marriage-proposal party for two to the Napa Valley Wine Auction for two thousand. I have experienced firsthand what excites people and what works. Hosting a successful party, be it for four friends around the kitchen counter or for one hundred friends at a New Year's Day seafood boil, is all about planning. What can be done ahead, which techniques allow for last-minute finishing, how to use your butcher to save you time and money, what equipment you need in your kitchen, and how to choose a party style suitable for the occasion are just some of the many questions answered in these pages, in both the Cooking Notes and Entertaining Notes that accompany the recipes and in Entertaining 101, which follows the recipe chapters.

I wrote this book to crack the code for the home entertainer. It's packed with simple dishes that will dazzle your guests without dizzying you. This is not a book of menus for every holiday of the year. It is instead a book that shares my approach to party giving, so you will begin to think like an entertainer. You'll surprise yourself, give your friends and family unforgettable memories, and, most of all, have a ton of fun doing it. Now, go put the *entertain* back into your entertaining!

RULE FIVE: CHEFS COLLECT IDEAS AND TECHNIQUES, AND THEN APPLY THEM TO THE OCCASION, AND YOU SHOULD, TOO. *You have a much larger repertoire than you might initially think. Once you turn that favorite main dish into a new favorite appetizer, your options grow. Ten good ideas can be turned into fifty different dishes. I will act as your coach while you're developing this way of thinking, giving you my suggestions on variations for the recipes in this book: how to change ingredients to suit the season, what to prepare and cook ahead, what to save for putting together at the last moment. For example, I let you know that you can fully assemble Giant Bean Cassoulet with Fennel-Spiced Chicken and Roasted Vegetables (page 128) a day in advance and then simply slip it into the oven when your guests arrive.*

RULE SIX: ALWAYS KEEP IN MIND THAT A PARTY DOES NOT THRIVE ON FOOD ALONE. *A creative beverage—often an afterthought and almost never the center of attention—can start the party off with a bang. From a Tomato Water Martini (page 198) to a Mint Julep (page 199), let drinks be the heroes occasionally, and be just as whimsical about how you serve them as how you serve the food. Then, too, there's wine. Indeed, every great meal deserves a great wine. I have made suggestions for which wine varietals to serve with many of the recipes, and sometimes I talk about glassware, too, such as when to bring out the fine crystal and when to bring out the jelly jars. More important than the glasses, however, is the need to serve the wine at the correct temperature (see page 230).*

pantry

A well-stocked pantry is the first step to effortless entertaining, saving

you time when you need it most. I divide the pantry into two sections,

store-bought items and homemade items. The purchased pantry should

be chock-full of the ingredients you use often. These are the basics,

the building blocks for all the dishes you prepare. Buy the best quality

you can afford, and their superior character will be evident in whatever

you serve.

My purchased pantry always includes a trio of what I consider indispensable ingredients. The first is French gray salt, a coarse-grain salt gathered on the coast of Brittany. It is a whole salt, only minimally processed, free of additives, and with all the micronutrients nature provided still intact. I believe that by changing to this exceptional salt, you can increase the quality of almost everything you cook by 10 percent, so I have used it in all the recipes in this book.

The second item is olive oil, and you'll need at least three types. First, find a good-quality extra-virgin oil to keep on hand for using in everyday cooked and uncooked dishes, from pasta sauces to tossed green salads. Second, look for a special-occasion unfiltered extra-virgin oil to use sparingly as a condiment, such as drizzling on bruschetta; finishing a veal chop just off the heat; or dressing a plate of sliced heirloom tomatoes. This might be a deep green, peppery Tuscan oil; a lighter, buttery Ligurian oil; or an intensely fruity Californian oil. Finally, you need pure olive oil, which is typically labeled simply "olive oil." It is oil that has been extracted from olives that were first cold-pressed for making extra-virgin oil. This second pressing is done with heat and sometimes chemicals, and it yields a lightly flavored, colorless oil that is good for making flavored oils, such as the "Infused" Basil Oil on page 20, and, because it can be heated to a relatively high temperature before it begins to smoke, for deep-frying. Store all your olive oils in a cool, dark place; light and heat will shorten their life.

My third pantry necessity is dried pasta. Not all pastas are created equal, and I regularly pay twice as much for an artisanal Italian product made from organic wheat. These pastas are extruded through bronze dies, which yields a rougher surface that encourages a sauce to cling to it. They also have a more distinctive taste and texture. Simply put, they are worth the extra cost.

There are a number of other ingredients I always have on hand as well because I use them so often. The first is canned whole tomatoes, which I turn to whenever I can't get good ripe plum (Roma) tomatoes. I rarely buy canned diced tomatoes because it's so easy to dice them myself, and I very seldom use tomato paste, though when I do use it, I prefer the paste sold in tubes, rather than cans. The one canned tomato product I never buy is tomato puree, which is usually reconstituted tomato paste. If I need puree, I put tomatoes in a blender or through a food mill myself, using canned whole tomatoes in winter and peeled and seeded plum tomatoes in summer. You'll need about 1 1/2 pounds fresh plum tomatoes to yield

2 cups puree, and a 28-ounce can of whole tomatoes will yield 3 to 3 1/2 cups puree. Finally, I'm a big fan of Muir Glen brand canned organic tomato products. The company packs the tomatoes in an enameled tin, rather than in an unlined one, so you don't get any off flavors.

Growing up in a southern Italian family, chilies were a big part of our cooking. My favorite is a Calabrian chili paste (facing page); there is a very unique flavor to the local pepperoncini that is unparalleled to any I have found in the United States. Pepperoncini are worth seeking out, but if you cannot find them, this is a great substitute recipe.

Balsamic vinegar is an essential pantry ingredient. What you need to know is that traditional *aceto balsamico* is aged a minimum of twelve years in a variety of different barrels and is both expensive and rare. Over the years vinegar makers have improvised, producing both lower-cost and -quality vinegars to give to a broader audience the flavor they crave at a price they can afford. I keep two types of balsamic vinegar on hand: a small bottle of exquisite traditional balsamic and a younger version of the same. The Cavalli family makes my personal favorite. They produce both traditional balsamic and a younger version they call balsamic condimento. I suggest you skip the four-dollar versions altogether, which are nothing more than caramel-flavored red wine vinegar and need to be reduced by half to get any flavor at all. At that point the cost per ounce is the same as the above condimento and not nearly the quality.

Finally, Spanish paprika, commonly labeled *pimentón de La Vera,* is a specialty of the area around the town of La Vera in Spain's Estremadura Province. The peppers are smoke-dried over a wood fire, yielding a smoky powder when ground. The paprika comes in three basic varieties, sweet, medium-hot, and hot. There are a few brands on the market, though I like Ramos brand best.

The other part of my pantry is reserved for homemade ingredients, all of which go together quickly and help to make a good dish great. I usually make the recipes in big batches, so I always have them on hand for adding personal flavor to my menus whenever I entertain. Among them are a perfect pesto, a rice coating for ensuring crisp fried foods, and a full-flavored citrus vinaigrette. Some cooks won't have the time to make these recipes. If that's you, you can order shelf-stable versions of most of them from NapaStyle (see Sources, page 233).

FINELY GROUND SEA SALT—A lot of cooks find that the sea salt they buy is too coarse for many uses, preferring finer grains that melt more easily. This technique solves the problem.

1 pound coarse sea salt, preferably gray salt

Preheat the oven to 200°F. Spread the sea salt on a baking sheet in a layer ¼ inch thick. Place in the oven until dry, about 2 hours. Remove from the oven, let cool, and then pulse the salt in a food processor until it is the texture of fine-ground cornmeal or polenta.

MAKES ABOUT 4 CUPS

CITRUS SALT—You won't have trouble using up this aromatic salt. It is delicious sprinkled on everything from fish fillets to whole chickens to steaks. For the best flavor, seek out locally grown citrus fruits—or harvest them from your own garden if you have a citrus thumb. You will be rewarded with superfresh flavors. Serve a small dish of this salt on the table for those of us who can't resist an extra pinch.

COOKING NOTES: For an herbal accent, add 1 tablespoon minced fresh herb of choice to the ground mixture.

1 tablespoon minced lemon zest
1 tablespoon minced lime zest
1 tablespoon minced orange zest
½ cup coarse sea salt, preferably gray salt

Preheat the oven to 200°F. In a small bowl, stir together all the ingredients, then spread the mixture on a small rimmed baking sheet. Place in the oven to dry for 2 hours. Remove from the oven and let cool completely.

Pour the cooled mixture into a mini processor and process until finely and evenly ground. Store in a tightly covered jar in the refrigerator for up to 2 months.

MAKES ABOUT ⅔ CUP

CALABRIAN CHILI PASTE—One fact often not known of southern Italian cooking is that we eat SPICY. You have to think of it more like Mexican cooking with Italian flavors. The one condiment always on our table is this chili paste. If you cannot find a prepared chili paste, this will fill the bill.

COOKING NOTES: I use this on inexpensive meats like flank and skirt steaks as they come off the grill. Also with Butterflied Chicken Diablo al Mattone (page 117), drizzled on Super-Quick Minestrone (page 63), or simply brushed on a bruschetta that has been grilled and served alongside a simple salad.

You can make a cup of this and keep it in the refrigerator for up to 2 months.

1 tablespoon red pepper flakes
6 tablespoons extra-virgin olive oil
1 clove garlic, finely minced
1 teaspoon finely ground sea salt

In a mortar and pestle, pulverize the red pepper flakes or mince fine with a knife. In a medium saucepan, over medium heat, add 2 tablespoons of the olive oil, the garlic, pulverized pepper flakes, and salt. Sauté for 30 seconds and let stand until it reaches room temperature. Add the final 4 tablespoons of olive oil and serve or refrigerate until needed.

MAKES ABOUT ½ CUP

FENNEL SPICE RUB — This simple spice mixture complements a wide range of foods, from pork ribs and chicken breasts to a bowl of lentil soup or a plate of grilled eggplant. At holiday time, make a big batch, pack it into small jars, and give the jars as gifts.

COOKING NOTES: If you have a spice mill, you can cut the recipe in half. If you have only a blender, you need a minimum of 1 cup to grind evenly.

1 cup fennel seeds

3 tablespoons coriander seeds

2 tablespoons white peppercorns

3 tablespoons finely ground sea salt, preferably gray salt

In a small, heavy skillet, combine the fennel seeds, coriander seeds, and peppercorns over medium heat. Watching carefully, toss the seeds frequently so that they toast evenly. When they are light brown and fragrant, pour them onto a plate to cool. (They must be cool before grinding, or they will gum up the blender blades.)

Pour the cooled seeds into a blender and add the salt. Process until the spices are finely and evenly ground. You may need to remove the blender from its stand and shake it occasionally to redistribute the seeds. Store in an airtight container away from light and heat for up to 4 months, or freeze for up to 1 year.

MAKES ABOUT 1¼ CUPS

TOASTED SPICE RUB — I like to use this spice mix on chicken, lamb, fish, and shrimp. It's also delicious stirred into beans or a pot of rice and mixed into scrambled eggs. Don't be put off by the amount of chili powder. California chili powder is almost sweet, not hot. It is not a blend of chilies and other seasonings, like the powder you use in Texas-style chili. Instead, it is pure ground chilies.

COOKING NOTES: Toasting spices releases their aromatic oils, resulting in more complex flavors. Taste your chili powder, and if it's hot, use less than the recipe indicates.

¼ cup fennel seeds

1 tablespoon coriander seeds

1 tablespoon black peppercorns

1½ teaspoons red pepper flakes

¼ cup California chili powder

2 tablespoons finely ground sea salt, preferably gray salt

2 tablespoons ground cinnamon

In a small, heavy skillet, combine the fennel seeds, coriander seeds, and peppercorns over medium heat. Watching carefully, toss the seeds frequently so that they toast evenly. When the fennel seeds turn light brown, work quickly. Turn on the exhaust fan, add the red pepper flakes, and toss, toss, toss, always under the fan. Immediately turn the spice mixture out onto a plate to cool. (They must be cool before grinding, or they will gum up the blender blades.)

Pour the cooled spices into a blender and add the chili powder, salt, and cinnamon. Process until the spices are finely and evenly ground. If you have a small spice mill or a coffee grinder dedicated to grinding spices, grind only the fennel, coriander, pepper, and red pepper flakes, then pour the ground spices into a bowl and toss with the remaining ingredients. Store in an airtight container away from light and heat for up to 4 months, or freeze for up to 1 year.

MAKES ABOUT 1 CUP

TOASTED SPICE RUB, FACING PAGE

WHOLE-CITRUS VINAIGRETTE — For a long time, I felt that lemon vinaigrettes never had enough depth. They simply fell flat. Then I learned a valuable trick from famed chef Alain Ducasse, who taught me the secret of juicing citrus fruits, peel and all, for the acid. This is now my go-to vinaigrette. I make a big batch and store it in a jelly jar in the refrigerator. All it needs before using is a quick shake. It is complex enough to serve as a sauce on a piece of flaky white fish or as dressing for a pasta salad made with asparagus and peas.

COOKING NOTES: For each 1 cup vinaigrette, you can whisk in 2 tablespoons minced fresh basil or tarragon with the salt and pepper, or you can whisk in 2 ounces blue cheese, mashed, and 1 teaspoon minced fresh thyme with the salt and pepper. Add these flavors just before using the vinaigrette, and save any leftover flavored vinaigrette for only 3 days. If you don't own a heavy-duty juicer, ask your local natural-foods grocer to juice the citrus fruits for you.

2 lemons, preferably Meyer
1 large navel orange
2 tablespoons roughly chopped shallots
1½ cups extra-virgin olive oil
Finely ground sea salt, preferably gray salt
Freshly ground black pepper

Cut a thin slice off the stem and blossom end of each lemon and the orange, and cut the fruits crosswise into ½-inch-thick slices. Remove the seeds with a knife tip, then roughly chop the slices into ½-inch pieces. You should have about 3 cups chopped fruit. Pass the fruits and shallots through a heavy-duty juicer. You should have about 1 cup juice.

Pour the juice into a bowl. Slowly whisk in the olive oil to form a smooth emulsion. (If you want a sturdier emulsion, whirl the juice and oil together in a blender.) Season with 1 teaspoon salt and ¼ teaspoon pepper. Use at once, or store tightly covered in the refrigerator for up to 2 weeks.

MAKES ABOUT 2½ CUPS

MARINARA SAUCE — A simple tomato sauce like this one demands the best and freshest ingredients available. Use them and you will be rewarded with perfect flavor and color. I use this sauce whenever a basic tomato sauce is called for in a recipe. It is also what I sometimes turn to when I need to make a quick pasta supper.

COOKING NOTES: The fresh tomato puree is easy to make (see page 14) and is far superior to canned. Be sure to take the time to sauté the onion until it is translucent. It is the foundation of flavor for the sauce. If you decide to use the sauce for pasta, the yield is sufficient for dressing 1½ pounds.

2 tablespoons extra-virgin olive oil
½ cup minced yellow onion
1 tablespoon chopped fresh Italian (flat-leaf) parsley
1 large clove garlic, minced
4 cups fresh tomato puree
1 large fresh basil sprig, leaves discarded
1 teaspoon sea salt, preferably gray salt
Pinch of baking soda or sugar, if needed

In a large nonreactive pan, heat the olive oil over medium heat. Add the onion and sauté until translucent, about 8 minutes. Add the parsley and garlic and cook briefly to release their fragrance. Add the tomato puree, basil stem, and salt and simmer briskly, stirring occasionally so nothing sticks to the bottom of the pan, until reduced to a saucelike consistency. The timing will depend on the ripeness and meatiness of your tomatoes and the size of your pan. If the sauce thickens too much before the flavors have developed, add a little water and continue cooking.

Taste and adjust the seasoning. If the sauce tastes too acidic, add the baking soda and cook for 5 minutes longer. If it needs a touch of sweetness, add the sugar and cook for 5 minutes longer. Remove the basil stem before serving.

MAKES 2 TO 2½ CUPS

PROSCIUTTO BITS — These crispy, meaty bits were born during my days as chef at Tra Vigne restaurant in St. Helena. We were curing a lot of prosciutto, and we would serve the main part of the leg in large, paper-thin slices. But we would end up with all the shanks—hundreds of pounds of meat each year we couldn't slice. We soon solved the problem by grinding up the shank meat and using it in pasta sauces and other dishes. One day, while I was sautéing the ground prosciutto, it got too crisp. It proved a fortunate accident. The crisped pieces were like the ultimate bacon bits, so I started sprinkling them on everything from salads to buttered asparagus. Nowadays, I find them the perfect addition to any dish that benefits from some crunch and a little meaty flavor.

COOKING NOTES: Ask the counterperson at your local deli to save the prosciutto shanks for you, and to grind them on medium grind if you want to save yourself time. If you end up chopping the meat by hand or putting it through your meat grinder, freeze it partially to make the task easier.

2 tablespoons olive oil
1 pound prosciutto, preferably from the shank, very finely minced or
    ground in a meat grinder fitted with the medium blade

In a large skillet, heat the olive oil over medium-high heat. Add the prosciutto and cook, stirring. The meat will give off steam for about 5 minutes while it releases its moisture. When the hiss of steam turns to a sizzle, reduce the heat to low and cook, stirring occasionally, until the prosciutto bits are crisp, about 30 minutes.

Using a slotted spoon, transfer the bits to paper towels to drain. The bits will crisp even more as they cool. Use the bits immediately, or freeze for up to 6 months and warm in a skillet as needed.

MAKES ABOUT 1½ CUPS

QUICK CHICKEN STOCK — There are plenty of good vacuum-packed stocks on the market now, but they lack the freshness I look for in a stock. I came up with this method of getting the necessary flavor in 3½ hours less cooking time than for a traditionally made stock. You can use it in any of the recipes in this book that call for chicken stock.

COOKING NOTES: After you have strained the stock, you can pull the chicken wings from the sieve, season them with a little salt and pepper, and save them for a snack.

4 cups canned or vacuum-packed broth
6 cups water
1 pound chicken wings
1 carrot, unpeeled, quartered crosswise
1 yellow onion, quartered through the stem end
1 bay leaf

In a saucepan, combine all the ingredients and bring to a simmer over medium heat, skimming once or twice to remove any foam that collects on the surface. Reduce the heat to low and cook, uncovered, for 45 minutes.

Remove from the heat, let cool briefly, and then strain through a fine-mesh sieve into a clean container. If using immediately, skim off any fat from the surface with a large spoon. Or, store in a tightly covered jar in the refrigerator for up to 5 days or in the freezer for up to 2 months. Before using, lift off and discard any congealed fat on the surface.

MAKES ABOUT 2¼ QUARTS (9 CUPS)

ROASTED-GARLIC SPICE — You can use this quick and easy spice mixture to season potato chips, popcorn, or even chops or steaks for grilling. Double or triple the recipe when you need a larger amount, such as when Backyard Lobster Bake (page 104) is on the menu.

COOKING NOTES: I use a good-quality compound chili powder here, typically a mixture of ground dried chilies, garlic, cumin, coriander, oregano, and sometimes other spices.

8 cloves garlic, sliced paper-thin
2 teaspoons finely ground sea salt, preferably gray salt
4 black peppercorns
½ teaspoon dry mustard
Pinch of chili powder

Preheat the oven to 350°F. Line a baking sheet with parchment paper, and arrange the garlic slices in a single layer on top. Cover with a second sheet of parchment. Bake until the garlic is dry and crisp, about 15 minutes. Remove from the oven and let cool completely.

In a spice mill or a coffee grinder dedicated to grinding spices, combine the garlic slices, salt, peppercorns, dry mustard, and chili powder and grind to a powder. Store in an airtight container away from light and heat for up to 2 months.

MAKES ABOUT ¼ CUP

"INFUSED" BASIL OIL — This aromatic oil is good for drizzling on dishes—steamed vegetables, sliced tomatoes, grilled meats, poached fish—just before serving. Never use it for sautéing or other cooking, as heat will destroy its fragrance. You also need to start with a bland pure olive oil, or the flavor of the oil will compete with the flavor of the herb.

4 cups tightly packed fresh basil leaves
2 cups olive oil

In a blender, combine the basil and olive oil and process until a completely smooth puree forms. (Don't be tempted to use a food processor; the basil won't be finely ground enough.) Pour the mixture into a saucepan and bring to a simmer over medium heat. Simmer for 45 seconds, then pour through a fine-mesh sieve into a heatproof bowl. Don't press on the mixture in the sieve. You can, however, tap the sieve against your hand to encourage the oil to flow faster.

Immediately strain the oil again, this time through a flat-bottomed paper coffee filter. The filter will clog partway through, in which case you'll need to change it. It's okay to pick the filter up and squeeze it gently to force the oil out faster, but be careful not to break the filter. Sometimes a little dark liquid comes through the filter first. Don't worry; it's only water. It will settle to the bottom because it is heavier than the oil. Let the filtered oil settle for a few hours, then pour off the clear oil into a clean jar or bottle, leaving the dark liquid behind. Cap tightly and store in a cool, dark place. The oil will stay lively for at least 1 month. Put it in the refrigerator for longer storage.

MAKES ABOUT 1⅓ CUPS

patience gains clarity
Don't force the filtering process for a pristine oil.

"BLANCHED" BASIL PESTO — If you have ever made a basil pesto and then suffered as you watched it turn black before your eyes, this recipe is for you. Blanching helps keep the green color bright. So, too, does a little ascorbic acid, which keeps the pesto from oxidizing. I include parsley because I like the sweetness and good color it contributes. Here, basil is the primary flavor, but pesto is a basic technique that can be used for preserving other herbs as well. However, the flavor of some herbs, such as rosemary and sage, is too strong when concentrated this way. In those cases, parsley helps to dilute that sharpness.

COOKING NOTES: Always start with cold tap water when blanching. Hot water has been sitting in the water heater, where it has gotten stale, flat, and tired. Remember, water is an ingredient, so how it tastes makes a difference. Blanching and squeezing the herbs removes most of their natural water, thus concentrating the flavor and reducing the oxidation.

You can double the recipe and freeze it. Add everything but the cheese (the texture of the cheese suffers in extreme cold), spoon into ice-cube tray(s), and freeze. Pop the frozen pesto cubes out of the tray(s), wrap them individually in plastic wrap, and seal them in a lock-top plastic bag. (Or, freeze the pesto in 1 or more plastic containers.) When ready to use, thaw as much pesto as needed and gradually stir in the cheese, tasting to get the right amount.

3 cups lightly packed fresh basil leaves

1 cup lightly packed fresh Italian (flat-leaf) parsley leaves

½ cup olive oil

1 tablespoon pine nuts, lightly toasted

1 teaspoon minced garlic

Finely ground sea salt, preferably gray salt

Freshly ground coarse black pepper

⅛ teaspoon powdered ascorbic acid (vitamin C) (optional)

¾ cup freshly grated Parmesan cheese

Ready a bowl of ice water. Bring a saucepan filled with water to a boil over high heat. Put the basil and parsley in a sieve and plunge it into the boiling water, pushing the leaves down into the water and stirring them so they blanch evenly. Blanch for 15 seconds, then plunge the herbs into the ice water to cool quickly. Drain immediately, squeeze the herbs dry, and chop them roughly.

In a blender, combine the blanched herbs with the olive oil, pine nuts, garlic, ¼ teaspoon salt, ⅛ teaspoon pepper, and ascorbic acid, if using. Process until well blended. Add the cheese and whirl briefly just to mix. Transfer to a bowl, taste, and adjust the seasoning. Store the pesto in a small, covered container in the refrigerator for up to 1 week or in the freezer for up to 1 month.

MAKES ABOUT 1 CUP

ARBORIO RICE COATING — I originally created this coating for deep-frying calamari, testing dozens of combinations in the process of coming up with the best formula. The natural sugars in the ground rice help the coating caramelize nicely, and the crust, whether on seafood, vegetables, or meats, stays crispy for a long time. You may as well make a large amount. The coating keeps well in the freezer, and less than 1 cup rice is hard to grind in a blender. *COOKING NOTES:* If you have a spice mill, you can halve the recipe. Unlike the blender, the mill will successfully grind ½ cup rice.

1 cup Arborio rice

3 cups unbleached all-purpose flour

1 cup semolina flour

2 tablespoons finely ground sea salt, preferably gray salt

1 teaspoon freshly ground black pepper

Grind the rice in a blender until very fine. Put it in a bowl and add the all-purpose flour, semolina flour, salt, and pepper. Toss until well blended. Store the coating in a tightly sealed container in the freezer for maximum freshness. It will keep for several months.

MAKES ABOUT 5 CUPS

PIADINA DOUGH — A *piadina* is an unleavened Italian flat bread that is traditionally cooked on the stove top. But I have adapted the recipe, adding yeast to yield a result that is more like pizza dough. I like to shape the dough into rounds, cook them on the stove top, on a grill, or in the oven, and use them for sandwiches and as a base for salads.

FOR THE SPONGE:

2 ¼ teaspoons (1 envelope) active dry yeast

½ cup lukewarm water

½ cup all-purpose flour, plus more for dusting

About 3 ½ cups all-purpose flour, plus more for dusting

1 cup cool water

2 tablespoons extra-virgin olive oil

2 teaspoons finely ground sea salt, preferably gray salt

Make the sponge: In the bowl of a stand mixer, whisk together the yeast, lukewarm water, and flour. Dust the top of the mixture lightly with flour, cover the bowl with a kitchen towel, and leave the mixture to rise until the flour dusting "cracks," showing the yeast is alive and well, about 20 minutes.

Add 3 cups of the flour, the cool water, the olive oil, and the salt to the sponge. Fit the mixer with the dough hook attachment and start kneading at low speed. Increase the speed to medium as the flour is incorporated. Add up to ½ cup more flour as needed to produce a slightly moist, soft dough. Continue to knead the dough until it is smooth and silky and adheres to the hook, about 2 minutes.

Dust the dough lightly with flour and move it onto a lightly floured work surface. Knead lightly for about 1 minute, folding the dough over onto itself a few times. Shape into a ball, flatten slightly, dust lightly with flour, cover with a kitchen towel, and leave the dough to rise on the floured surface (or in a bowl) until doubled in size, about 1 hour. The dough should be in a spot slightly warmer than room temperature, if possible.

Proceed as directed in individual recipes. Or, punch down the dough, wrap it airtight in plastic wrap, and freeze for up to 1 month. Thaw and let rise in a large bowl in the refrigerator, about 4 hours, then continue with the chosen recipe.

MAKES ABOUT 2 POUNDS DOUGH, ENOUGH FOR EIGHT 8- OR 9-INCH ROUNDS, 4 OUNCES EACH

SPICED CANDIED WALNUTS—This technique for frying and candying nuts was developed by Cindy Pawlcyn, the famed Napa Valley chef. I use the nuts on salads and as an accompaniment to a cheese course, but they are also wonderful out of hand, enjoyed with a glass of Champagne.

COOKING NOTES: This same technique can be used for pecan halves or almonds.

Peanut or canola oil for deep-frying

Finely ground sea salt, preferably gray salt

Freshly ground black pepper

½ teaspoon ground cinnamon

½ teaspoon cayenne pepper

4 cups walnut halves

1 cup confectioners' sugar, sifted

Pour the oil to a depth of at least 3 inches into a deep fryer or a heavy, 8-inch-deep stockpot and heat to 350°F. While the oil is heating, bring a large saucepan filled with water to a boil over high heat. In a small bowl, combine 1 teaspoon salt, ½ teaspoon pepper, the cinnamon, and the cayenne and mix well.

When the water is boiling, place the nuts in a sieve and dip them into the boiling water, about 1 minute for large halves, less time for smaller halves. Transfer the nuts to a large bowl with a little water clinging to them. (Blanching removes some of the tannins, making the walnuts sweeter.) While the nuts are still hot, add the sugar and toss well to coat evenly. The sugar will melt on contact with the hot nuts. Keep stirring and tossing until all the sugar has melted. If bits of unmelted sugar remain on the nuts, the nuts will not fry properly.

Stir the nuts again before frying. Using a large slotted spoon, transfer a few nuts to the hot oil, allowing the foam to subside before adding another spoonful. (Otherwise, the oil could foam over and burn you.) Fry the nuts until medium brown, about 1 minute for large halves, less time for smaller halves. Be careful not to overcook. Lift them out with the spoon and scatter them on a rimmed baking sheet to cool slightly. Fry the remaining nuts in the same way, always working in small batches.

While the nuts are still warm, transfer them to a bowl and sprinkle evenly with about half of the spice mix. Toss well to distribute the spices and then taste a nut. Add more spice mix to taste and toss well after each addition. Let cool completely, then store in a tightly capped jar. They will keep at room temperature for about 2 weeks.

MAKES 4 CUPS

In the traditional Italian kitchen, cooks put considerable effort into the first two courses of a meal, the antipasto and *primo piatto* (first course), and follow them with a simpler *secondo piatto* (main course). That same formula works great for entertaining. You can make three of these recipes and arrange them on big platters for serving family style. For example, Crispy Risotto Balls with Warm Mozzarella Centers (page 40), Bruschetta Tart (page 29), and Old-World Antipasti (page 26) would make a palette of interesting and contrasting tastes, while passing the platters helps to set a casual and convivial mood at the table. And because people are helping themselves and one another, you will have a few extra minutes in the kitchen to ready the rest of the meal.

appetizers

You will also find a handful of casual snacks in this chapter. They are based on foods—almonds, popcorn, potato chips, pasta—popular with nearly everyone, young and old alike. You can set these snacks out for a casual cocktail hour, an afternoon ballgame on television, or an evening of movie watching at home. They can also join up with other dishes. Pop Culture Popcorn (page 47) makes a wonderful garnish for seafood gazpacho (page 57), Toasted Marcona Almonds (page 49) are a nice addition to an Artisanal Wine and Cheese Party (page 190), and "Speed Scratch" Roasted Garlic Potato Chips (page 48) slip in nicely alongside Smoked Salmon Rillette (page 28).

cocktail party

OPPOSITE: CRISPY SAUSAGE-STUFFED OLIVES, PAGE 37

OLD-WORLD ANTIPASTI—Here is my favorite answer to the problem of inviting too many friends over for a Sunday afternoon meal. The whole idea is to have everything done before the first guest arrives. Dishes like this one are a mainstay in Italy and have served me well for myriad events, from bocce ball tournaments and Italian-style tailgate parties to cross-country plane flights (each element packs nicely into a Chinese to-go box). Put out plenty of country-style bread for eating with the antipasti.

COOKING NOTES: Bocconcini are small balls of fresh mozzarella, perhaps an inch in diameter, usually sold packed in water in small plastic tubs. You will find them in cheese shops, Italian delicatessens, and better supermarkets.

ENTERTAINING NOTES: You can prepare the peppers (except for the mint garnish), zucchini, fennel, and chickpeas the day before serving. They taste even better with this added marinating time. Remember to bring them to room temperature before serving. If you are short of time, make a trip to a local delicatessen or other specialty-food store to buy roasted peppers and other roasted vegetables and/or ready-made salads and then personalize them at home with olive oil, vinegar, the mint garnish, and/or pesto. The cheese, tomatoes, and salami can be arranged on platters and left at room temperature for up to 1 hour before serving.

WINE NOTES: On a hot day, room-temperature antipasti and jet-cold Pinot Grigio are a good match. If you have half a dozen or more guests, serve a magnum of wine. The added drama is well worth the price.

FOR THE PEPPERS:

6 large red or yellow bell peppers

1 tablespoon extra-virgin olive oil

½ teaspoon red wine vinegar

1 tablespoon finely shredded fresh mint

FOR THE ZUCCHINI:

1½ pounds medium zucchini, ends trimmed

Extra-virgin olive oil

Finely ground sea salt, preferably gray salt

¼ cup basil pesto, homemade (page 21) or purchased

1 tablespoon pine nuts, lightly toasted

FOR THE FENNEL:

4 fennel bulbs

Finely ground sea salt, preferably gray salt

½ cup Kalamata olives, pitted and halved

¼ cup lightly packed torn fresh basil leaves

2 tablespoons extra-virgin olive oil

Grated zest of ½ lemon

Freshly ground black pepper

FOR THE CHICKPEAS:

2 cans (15½ ounces each) chickpeas (garbanzo beans),
    rinsed and drained

¼ cup extra-virgin olive oil

¼ cup roughly chopped fresh Italian (flat-leaf) parsley

2 tablespoons minced red onion

1 tablespoon red wine vinegar

1 tablespoon Fennel Spice Rub (page 16)

Finely ground sea salt, preferably gray salt

Freshly ground black pepper

FOR THE MOZZARELLA:

¾ pound fresh mozzarella *bocconcini*

3 tablespoons extra-virgin olive oil

1 tablespoon finely chopped fresh basil

½ teaspoon Calabrian Chili Paste (page 15) or ¼ teaspoon
    red pepper flakes

Finely ground sea salt, preferably gray salt

FOR THE TOMATOES:

2 pounds ripe tomatoes, cored and cut crosswise into ½-inch-thick slices

2 tablespoons extra-virgin olive oil

Finely ground sea salt, preferably gray salt

Freshly ground black pepper

1 tablespoon thinly sliced red onion

FOR THE SALAMI:

1½ pounds assorted hard salamis, sliced or diced as you like them

Preheat the oven to 450°F. Line 2 large baking sheets, each about 13 by 18 inches, with aluminum foil.

Prepare the bell peppers: Put the bell peppers on a prepared baking sheet and roast in the oven until blackened and blistered on all sides, about 30 minutes, turning every 10 minutes. Transfer the peppers to a bowl and cover the bowl with plastic wrap so they steam as they cool. When they are cool, peel them, using your fingers, perhaps aided by a small knife. Split them lengthwise and remove and discard the stems, seeds, and ribs. Do not rinse them with water, or you will wash the flavor away. Cut the peppers lengthwise into ½-inch-wide strips. In a bowl, combine the peppers with the olive oil and vinegar and toss to coat evenly. Arrange the pepper strips on a serving plate. Scatter the mint on top.

Prepare the zucchini: Trim the ends of the zucchini and then cut the zucchini crosswise into 1½-inch-long sections. Cut each section lengthwise into sixths so that you have little wedges. In a bowl, toss the zucchini pieces with enough olive oil to coat lightly. Season with a little salt and spread the zucchini in a single layer on the second prepared baking sheet. Roast in the oven, turning occasionally, until fork-tender and just beginning to brown, 12 to 15 minutes. Remove from the oven, let cool for 5 minutes, and then transfer to a bowl. Add the pesto and pine nuts and mix to distribute evenly. Arrange the zucchini on a serving plate.

Prepare the fennel: Bring a saucepan filled with water to a boil.

Meanwhile, cut off the stalks and feathery leaves from the fennel bulbs (if still attached), remove any bruised outer leaves, and then cut each bulb in half lengthwise so some core is still attached to each half. Cut each half lengthwise into ½-inch-wide wedges, making sure a little of the core is attached to each wedge. Add a little salt to the boiling water, then drop the fennel into the water. When the water returns to a boil, cook for 1 minute, then drain the fennel into a colander. Spread the fennel on a work surface and let cool to room temperature. Transfer the fennel to a bowl, add the olives, basil, olive oil, and lemon zest, and toss to mix well. Season to taste with salt and pepper. Arrange the fennel on a serving plate.

Prepare the chickpeas: In a bowl, combine all the ingredients, including 1 teaspoon salt and ¼ teaspoon pepper, and mix well. Transfer to a serving bowl.

Prepare the mozzarella: In a bowl, combine all the ingredients, including salt to taste, and mix well. Transfer to a serving bowl.

Prepare the tomatoes: Gently coat the tomato slices with the olive oil and season to taste with salt and pepper. Arrange the tomato slices on a serving plate. Scatter the onion slices on top.

Prepare the salamis: Arrange the salami slices on a serving plate.

To serve the antipasti, arrange all the serving plates and bowls on a buffet table. Serve at room temperature.

SERVES 6 TO 8

2 days before	1 day before	morning of	1 hour before	service
shop	roast peppers, cut salami	roast zucchini, blanch fennel, prepare ingredients for chickpeas and mozzarella	rest	sit back and enjoy

SMOKED SALMON RILLETTE— This is a play on the classic French *rillette*, which is a smooth, savory well-seasoned moist paste made by slowly cooking pork, duck, goose, or other meat in its own fat. I use this salmon version whenever I want to impress guests. It is always a hit, and never expected.

COOKING NOTES: For the most luscious texture, poach the salmon over the lowest heat setting on your stove top, with the water just gently steaming the fish.

ENTERTAINING NOTES: This dish has countless uses. Serve it with homemade flavored potato chips (page 48) or baguette slices, or spoon it on raw vegetables, such as celery, endive, romaine, or radicchio. For an elegant main course, drape it over sautéed halibut. Or, drop a spoonful in the center of a bowl of chilled pea soup for a first course. You can make the mayonnaise up to 3 days in advance and store it tightly covered in the refrigerator. The finished *rillette* will keep for up to two days in the refrigerator.

WINE NOTES: Chardonnay is wonderful with this dish. Ask your wine merchant for one with little or no oak, so the wine does not clash with the woodsy flavor of the smoked salmon.

FOR THE MAYONNAISE:

1 large egg yolk

1½ tablespoons fresh lemon juice

1 tablespoon Dijon mustard

¾ cup olive oil

1½ teaspoons drained capers

1½ teaspoons brine from caper jar

Dash of Tabasco sauce or other hot-pepper sauce

Dash of Worcestershire sauce

Finely ground sea salt, preferably gray salt

Freshly ground black pepper

1 skinless salmon fillet, ½ pound and ¾ inch thick

Finely ground sea salt, preferably gray salt

Freshly ground black pepper

1 cup water

1 tablespoon fresh lemon juice

4 ounces smoked salmon, cut into strips about
     1 inch long and ¼ inch wide

Make the mayonnaise: In a blender, combine the egg yolk, lemon juice, and mustard and blend until well mixed. With the machine running, add the olive oil, at first by drops and then, as the mixture emulsifies, in a thin, steady stream until all the oil is incorporated. Add the capers, caper brine, Tabasco sauce, Worcestershire sauce, ½ teaspoon salt, and ¼ teaspoon pepper and process briefly to mix. Taste and adjust the seasoning. You will have about 1 cup. Scrape into a bowl or jar, cover, and refrigerate until needed.

Generously season the salmon fillet on both sides with salt and pepper. Place the salmon in an 8-inch skillet. Add the water and the lemon juice (the liquid should be about ¾ inch deep). Bring the water to a simmer over high heat. Reduce the heat to low, cover the pan tightly, and poach the salmon until medium-rare, 5 to 6 minutes. Remove the pan from the heat and allow the salmon to cool to room temperature in the liquid, with the lid on. Remove the salmon from the liquid and break it apart with your fingers into small pieces.

In a bowl, combine the poached salmon, smoked salmon, and mayonnaise and mix well. Cover tightly and refrigerate until serving. Serve cool but not cold.

MAKES ABOUT 2 CUPS

BRUSCHETTA TART — Carmen Quagliata, one of the most talented chefs I ever worked with at Tra Vigne, came up with this tart as an offensive maneuver against all the California vegetarians who would come into the restaurant with great red wines and needed a dish to go with them.

COOKING NOTES: In the fall, replace the zucchini and eggplant with 3 cups fresh wild mushrooms, sliced and sautéed in extra-virgin olive oil, and 1 cup cubed butternut squash (½-inch cubes), tossed with extra-virgin olive oil, finely ground sea salt (preferably gray salt), and freshly ground black pepper and then roasted in a 375°F oven until tender and light brown, about 20 minutes.

ENTERTAINING NOTES: At the restaurant, we always made this tart the day before serving and reheated it in a 375°F oven until hot in the middle, about 15 minutes. You can serve it topped with an arugula salad dressed with Whole-Citrus Vinaigrette (page 18) for a dramatic presentation. You can also make individual servings by using eight 1½-cup soufflé dishes in place of the cake pans; reduce the cooking time to 40 minutes when the tarts are covered and to 10 minutes when the foil has been removed. The tart is also a great side to Double-Cut Bistecca alla Fiorentina (page 124), Forever-Roasted Lamb with Herbes de Provence (page 125), or Grilled and Braised Short Ribs, Brasciole Style (page 130).

WINE NOTES: A California Zinfandel or Syrah pairs beautifully with this robust tart.

¼ cup extra-virgin olive oil

Peanut oil for deep-frying

2 cups diced, peeled eggplant (¾-inch dice; 1 medium eggplant)

Finely ground sea salt, preferably gray salt

1 cup all-purpose flour

8 round slices country-style bread, each ¼ inch thick

8 cups cubed country-style bread (½-inch cubes, about 1 pound)

1 cup diced zucchini (½-inch dice, about 2 small)

½ cup freshly grated Parmesan cheese

1 tablespoon finely chopped fresh basil

1 tablespoon finely chopped fresh oregano

1½ teaspoons minced garlic

1 teaspoon red pepper flakes

3 cups Marinara Sauce (page 18) or good-quality jarred tomato-basil pasta sauce

2 large egg yolks, lightly beaten

1 cup heavy cream

Freshly ground black pepper

Preheat the oven to 300°F. Using 2 tablespoons for each pan, brush the bottom of 2 round cake pans each 9 to 10 inches in diameter with the olive oil.

Pour the peanut oil to a depth of at least 3 inches into a deep fryer or a heavy, 8-inch-deep stockpot. While the oil is heating, in a bowl, toss the eggplant with a little salt. Then add the flour to the eggplant and toss to coat evenly. Remove the eggplant from the bowl, lightly patting off the excess flour.

Working in 2 batches, add the eggplant to the hot oil and fry until light brown, about 2 minutes. Using a slotted spoon, transfer to paper towels to drain.

Cover the bottom of each prepared pan with 4 bread slices. It is okay if there are spaces between the slices. In a large bowl, combine the eggplant, cubed bread, zucchini, cheese, basil, oregano, garlic, red pepper flakes, 1 cup of the tomato sauce, egg yolks, and cream

and mix well. Add 1 teaspoon salt and ¼ teaspoon pepper and mix again. Divide the mixture evenly between the 2 pans, packing it lightly and making sure there are no large gaps in the pan.

Cover the pans with aluminum foil and bake for 1 hour. Raise the oven temperature to 375°F, remove the foil, and continue baking until the top is medium brown, 15 to 20 minutes longer. Remove from the oven, place on racks, and let rest for 15 minutes. While the tarts are resting, gently heat the remaining 2 cups tomato sauce until hot.

Run a knife around the inside edge of 1 pan to loosen the sides of the tart, invert a serving plate over the pan, invert the pan and plate together, and lift off the pan. Repeat with the second tart. Cut into wedges with a serrated knife and serve immediately. Pass the hot tomato sauce at the table.

SERVES 8 TO 10

WHITE BEAN AND CORN "CANNOLI" WITH HERB SALAD AND TOMATOES—Take a dish every-

one understands and present it in a way they would never imagine . . . that's entertaining! What could be more fitting than a classic Italian dessert method, cannoli, turned into a whimsical celebration of two heroes of summer, tomatoes and corn?

COOKING NOTES: If you do not have cannoli molds, which are sold at most cookware shops, you can buy ¾-inch wooden dowels and cut them into 5-inch lengths. Fill the cannoli shells no more than 15 minutes before serving, or the shells will lose their crispness.

ENTERTAINING NOTES: If you are facing a time crunch, buy fresh pasta dough sheets and fold and reroll them by hand or through the pasta machine with some Parmesan cheese between the layers. You can make the cannoli shells a couple days in advance and store in an airtight container at room temperature. For a fun hors d'oeuvre, omit the herb salad and tomatoes, cut the cannoli shells in half with a serrated knife, fill them, and then pass the mini-cannoli on a tray or in a cigar box.

WINE NOTES: Look for a bottle of good rosé.

FOR THE CANNOLI SHELLS:

2 cups all-purpose flour, plus more for dusting

⅓ cup freshly grated Parmesan cheese

¼ teaspoon finely ground sea salt, preferably gray salt

3 tablespoons Champagne vinegar

3 tablespoons water

3 large eggs

2 tablespoons unsalted butter, melted, plus
    room-temperature butter for molds

Canola oil for deep-frying

FOR THE FILLING:

3 tablespoons unsalted butter

2 tablespoons finely chopped yellow onion

2 teaspoons minced garlic

1 tablespoon finely chopped fresh thyme

4 cups corn kernels (from 6 ears)

1 cup heavy cream

Finely ground sea salt, preferably gray salt

2 cups rinsed, drained canned white beans or drained, home-cooked
    beans (see "Super-Tuscan" White Bean Soup, page 76)

4 large, ripe tomatoes

3 tablespoons extra-virgin olive oil

Finely ground sea salt, preferably gray salt

Freshly ground black pepper

2 cups assorted fresh herb leaves such as basil, Italian (flat-leaf) parsley,
    and tarragon, whole or roughly chopped

1 teaspoon fresh lemon juice

½ cup freshly grated Parmesan cheese

Make the cannoli shells: Sift the flour into the bowl of a stand mixer fitted with the paddle attachment. Add the cheese and salt. In a small bowl, whisk together the vinegar, water, and 2 of the eggs just until blended. With the mixer on low speed, pour the vinegar mixture into the flour mixture. Add the melted butter in a thin stream. Stop the mixer and scrape down the sides of the bowl and the paddle as necessary. Continue to mix on low speed for about 3 minutes. The dough should be soft, slightly sticky, and begin to come away from the sides of the bowl.

Transfer the dough to a clean work surface, dust it lightly with flour, form it into a ball, and flatten slightly. Wrap in plastic wrap and chill for at least 2 hours or up to overnight.

In a small bowl or cup, beat the remaining egg just until blended. Lightly butter 16 cannoli molds each 5 inches long and $3/4$ inch in diameter. On a lightly floured surface, roll out the dough about $1/16$ inch thick. (You can instead roll out the dough on a hand-cranked pasta machine, as you would fresh pasta dough.) Using a 4-inch plate or other template as a guide, cut out 16 circles. Wrap each dough circle around a prepared cannoli mold. Brush a little of the beaten egg between the 2 edges of the circle where they meet and overlap, then press together to seal.

Pour the canola oil to a depth of a least 3 inches into a deep fryer or a heavy, 8-inch-deep stockpot and heat to 375°F. Add the cannoli shells, a few at a time, and fry until lightly browned, about 1 minute. Using tongs, transfer to papers towels to drain. Before the shells cool, pick each one up with a clean towel and gently knock the mold out from the shell. Set the shells aside on a baking sheet to cool completely.

Make the filling: In a skillet, combine the butter, onion, and garlic over medium-high heat. Cook, stirring often to prevent browning, until the onion is translucent, about 4 minutes. Add the thyme and cook for 10 seconds to release its fragrance. Add the corn and cook, stirring, for 1 minute. Add the cream and 1 teaspoon salt and bring the mixture to a boil. Reduce the heat to medium and simmer until the corn is tender, 4 to 5 minutes. Remove from the heat.

In a food processor, combine two-thirds of the corn mixture with the white beans and puree until smooth. Return the puree to the corn mixture remaining in the skillet, stir to mix, and let cool to room temperature. Using a pastry bag fitted with a $1/2$-inch plain tip, fill the cannoli shells by piping the filling into both ends of each shell.

Core each tomato and then cut crosswise into 4 slices. Place the slices in a bowl, add 2 tablespoons of the olive oil, and turn gently to coat lightly. Season to taste with salt and pepper. Arrange 2 tomato slices on each plate, overlapping them slightly. Arrange 2 cannoli on each plate, propping 1 cannoli up against the tomato slices and positioning the other one so that it crosses over the first cannoli. In the same bowl, lightly coat the herbs with the remaining 1 tablespoon oil and the lemon juice. Arrange a small cluster of herbs between the tomatoes and the cannoli on each plate. Sprinkle the Parmesan cheese evenly over the plates. Serve at once.

SERVES 8

2 days before	1 day before	morning of	1 hour before	service
shop, make dough, buy cannoli molds	roll and fry cannoli shells (store in airtight container)	make filling, pick herbs	slice tomatoes	fill shells and arrange over tomatoes

broken cork tip

Don't fret over a broken cork; simply tie a good-size knot in a piece of string, push the knot past the cork with a skewer, and lift the string. While holding the string taut and the cork back against the neck, make another attempt with a corkscrew. If that fails, simply push the cork all the way in. Pour and enjoy.

goes great with ...

My favorite wine for fried foods is Champagne.
It has plenty of fruit and acid to stand along-
side the richness of the food.

CECI WITH GARLIC AND SAGE — In America, chickpeas, known as *ceci* in Italy, have been unfairly exiled to the salad bar. This dish draws on the Italian kitchen's tradition of celebrating the ability of these everyday legumes to carry rich flavors. Here, they are transformed into a great fried snack to serve before dinner.

COOKING NOTES: This technique lends itself to other beans, such as cooked runner beans and fava beans, and to fresh English peas.

ENTERTAINING NOTES: You can fry the chickpeas 1 hour in advance of serving. If you want to serve them warm, you can heat them up for a few minutes on a rimmed baking sheet in a 300°F oven. Most Italians serve fried foods close to or at room temperature, believing they taste better that way, so the choice is yours. For an eye-catching presentation, serve the fried *ceci* in a paper cone inside a cocktail glass.

2 cans (15½ ounces each) chickpeas (garbanzo beans)

¾ cup buttermilk

¾ cup olive oil

1½ cups Arborio Rice Coating (page 22)

¼ cup thinly sliced garlic

15 fresh sage leaves

2 teaspoons thin serrano chili slices (optional)

Finely ground sea salt, preferably gray salt

Zest of 1 lemon, cut into julienne

Freshly ground black pepper

Drain the chickpeas in a colander, then rinse well under running cold water and pat dry with a paper towel. In a bowl, combine the chickpeas and buttermilk, stirring to coat evenly. Drain the chickpeas again in the colander, then place the colander over a clean bowl.

In a large sauté pan, heat the olive oil over high heat. While the oil is heating, sprinkle the rice coating over the beans and shake the colander to coat the beans evenly. Repeat the process, using the coating that collects in the bowl. Don't worry if the beans don't absorb all the coating.

When the oil is very hot but not smoking, carefully add the beans, spreading them in an even layer. Cook, without stirring, until they are browned and crisp on the bottom, 3 to 5 minutes. Turn once with a spatula and add the garlic. When the garlic turns brown, add the sage. When the sage turns crispy, add the chili slices, if using, and season with 1 teaspoon salt. At the last moment, add the lemon zest and pepper to taste.

Using a slotted spoon, transfer the beans to paper towels to drain. Serve warm or at room temperature.

MAKES ABOUT 3½ CUPS

ROASTED-ARTICHOKE PESTO — During late spring and early fall, when artichokes are wonderfully sweet, I like to make artichoke pesto. The combination of the roasted oil from the artichokes and the fresh oil from the bottle is spectacular. Serve the pesto on crostini or artisanal crackers topped with a slice of fresh mozzarella—an ultrasimple yet memorable appetizer.

COOKING NOTES: Look for artichokes with tightly closed heads, and be sure to trim away any dark green areas, or the pesto will be bitter.

ENTERTAINING NOTES: This puree is one of the most versatile in my pantry. It is incredible in risotto, or stirred into hot pasta with a small amount of the pasta cooking water to bridge the ingredients. You can also sear a lamb loin or a piece of swordfish, smear some of the pesto on one side, cover the pesto coating with bread crumbs, and then finish the lamb or fish in the oven. To stretch this recipe for a crowd, drain a small can (12 ounces) of white beans, rinse the beans under running cold water, and then puree them with the artichokes. Spread the artichoke–white bean puree on crostini and top each one with a slice of mozzarella and a fresh basil leaf.

WINE NOTES: It's true that artichokes can be problematic with wines, but if you roast them thoroughly, their bitterness fades away until it is almost impossible to detect. I like to serve this pesto with a fruity white.

⅓ cup fresh lemon juice

6 medium or 4 large artichokes

¾ cup extra-virgin olive oil

3 large cloves garlic, quartered lengthwise

1 teaspoon finely chopped fresh thyme

1 bay leaf

Finely ground sea salt, preferably gray salt

Freshly ground black pepper

½ cup tightly packed fresh basil leaves

Preheat the oven to 325°F.

Select a nonreactive bowl large enough to hold all the artichokes once they are trimmed and pour the lemon juice into it. Working with 1 artichoke at a time, bend the tough outer leaves backward until they break at the point where the tough leaf becomes part of the tender base; stop when you reach the more tender interior leaves that are at least half yellow-green. With a serrated knife, cut across the leaves at the point where the color changes from yellow-green to dark green. Trim the stem of its outer layer, then trim the base to 1 to 2 inches, removing any dark green bits. Quarter the artichokes lengthwise and scoop out the hairy choke. As the artichokes are trimmed, drop them into the bowl and turn to coat with the lemon juice.

When all the artichokes are trimmed, transfer them and the lemon juice to a large ovenproof skillet along with 5 tablespoons of the olive oil, the garlic, thyme, bay leaf, 1 teaspoon salt, and ¼ teaspoon pepper. Bring to a boil over medium heat, tossing to coat the artichokes with the seasonings, cover with aluminum foil, transfer to the oven, and cook until the artichokes are browned in spots and tender when pierced, about 35 minutes. Remove from the oven and let the artichokes cool in the liquid.

Remove the bay leaf and discard. Transfer the contents of the skillet to a food processor and process until completely smooth. Add the remaining 3 tablespoons olive oil and the basil and again process until smooth.

Taste and adjust the seasoning. Spoon into a small bowl and serve.

MAKES ABOUT 2 CUPS

CRISPY SAUSAGE-STUFFED OLIVES—This appetizer packs a lot of southern Italian attitude in every bite. I love to catch my guests off guard with a flavor they don't expect. The idea is to wake up their palates with some big tastes and textures. This dish does just that.

COOKING NOTES: Look for large, pitted green Sicilian-style olives for this dish. They come packed in cans and jars, or buy them loose from a local deli. If you can only find already-stuffed olives—with pimientos, onions, anchovies, almonds—you can just remove the stuffing.

ENTERTAINING NOTES: Pass these olives in a typical ceramic olive boat, just as you would plain olives. If you know the fancy artichoke napkin fold (if not, and you have a few minutes, you can track it down online), serve the olives on a folded napkin–lined plate. They are also a great partner for a platter of Italian cheeses.

WINE NOTES: A cool, fruity red such as a Beaujolais nicely complements these crisp green olives. Or, for a fun presentation, serve them alongside jet-cold martinis.

1 sweet fresh Italian sausage, about ¼ pound, casing removed

1 teaspoon minced garlic

¼ to ½ teaspoon red pepper flakes (optional)

1 can or jar (12 ounces) large pitted green olives

½ cup all-purpose flour

1 large egg

½ cup fine dried bread crumbs

2 teaspoons extra-virgin olive oil

Peanut oil for deep-frying

In a bowl, combine the sausage meat, garlic, and red pepper flakes, if using, and mix to distribute the ingredients evenly. Drain the olives and rinse them under running cold water. Stuff each of the olives with ¼ to ½ teaspoon of the sausage mixture.

Spread the flour on a dinner plate. Break the egg into a shallow bowl and beat lightly. Spread the bread crumbs on another dinner plate. Moisten the bread crumbs with the olive oil, and stir to distribute the oil evenly. One at a time, roll the olives in the flour, coating them evenly and shaking off the excess. Then dip them in the egg, letting any excess drip back into the bowl. Finally, coat the olives evenly with the bread crumbs. As each olive is finished, place it on a tray. Cover and refrigerate the olives for at least 10 minutes or up to 2 hours before frying.

Pour the peanut oil to a depth of at least 3 inches into a deep fryer or a heavy, 8-inch-deep stockpot and heat to 375°F. Working in batches, add the olives to the hot oil and fry until golden brown and the sausage stuffing is cooked through, about 3 minutes. The olives will bubble vigorously until they are nearly done, so be careful to avoid splatters. Using a slotted spoon, transfer to paper towels to drain.

Arrange the olives in a ceramic dish. Serve warm or at room temperature.

MAKES ABOUT 35 OLIVES; SERVES 6 TO 8

POLENTA BITES WITH CARAMELIZED MUSHROOMS — The soft polenta I made at Tra Vigne was so good that customers were always asking me for the recipe. I was almost embarrassed to give it to them because it called for an amazing amount of cream. But what a delicious indulgence! This is the same recipe, but since you eat only a small bite when it is an appetizer, the amount of cream doesn't seem so extreme.

COOKING NOTES: Each spoonful gets only a little bit of the mushrooms, so they need to pack a punch, which means it's important to caramelize them well. That involves patience. Let the oil get hot in the skillet, then add the mushrooms and leave them alone. They will release their moisture first and it will evaporate. Turn them only when they are deep brown on the bottom. If you stir the mushrooms too early, all the liquid comes out and floods the pan with water, resulting in mushrooms that boil and thus never develop intense flavors.

ENTERTAINING NOTES: Think about serving other foods on spoons, too, such as a little chopped salad, a tiny nest of noodles, or a few crispy gnocchi. Chinese flat-bottomed porcelain spoons or larger tablespoons are best for serving.

WINE NOTES: Select a big, ripe luscious red such as Barolo or Petite Sirah.

FOR THE POLENTA:

3 cups heavy cream

2 cups chicken stock

Finely ground sea salt, preferably gray salt

½ teaspoon freshly grated nutmeg

1 cup polenta

1 cup freshly grated Parmesan cheese

Additional ¼ cup chicken stock or heavy cream, warmed, if needed

FOR THE MUSHROOMS:

3 tablespoons extra-virgin olive oil

½ pound fresh cremini mushrooms, roughly chopped into ¼-inch pieces

Finely ground sea salt, preferably gray salt

Freshly ground black pepper

1 tablespoon unsalted butter

1 tablespoon minced garlic

½ teaspoon finely chopped fresh thyme

1 tablespoon fresh lemon juice

½ cup dry white wine

1 tablespoon finely chopped fresh Italian (flat-leaf) parsley

---

Cook the polenta: In a heavy saucepan, combine the cream, stock, 1 teaspoon salt, and nutmeg and bring to a boil over medium heat. Add the polenta gradually, whisking constantly. When the mixture thickens, after about 2 minutes, switch to a wooden spoon and adjust the heat to maintain a bare simmer. Cook, stirring often, until the polenta is thick, smooth, and creamy and begins to pull away from the sides of the pan, about 15 minutes. Add the Parmesan cheese and stir until thoroughly combined. Keep the polenta warm over very low heat, stirring occasionally. If the polenta gets dry as it sits, stir in the ¼ cup warmed stock.

Cook the mushrooms: In a skillet, heat the olive oil over high heat. When the oil is hot and just starting to smoke, sprinkle in the mushrooms in a single layer. Don't stir them! Let them sizzle until they caramelize on the bottom, about 2 minutes. When they are ready, toss them once and season to taste with salt and pepper. Continue to cook over high heat without stirring for about 5 minutes. Add the butter and cook until it begins to brown, then add the garlic. Continue to cook until the garlic begins to brown, about 1 minute. Add the thyme and cook for about 10 seconds. Add the lemon juice and cook until the liquid evaporates. Add the wine and simmer until the mushrooms are glazed with the pan sauce, about 3 minutes. Add the parsley, stir, and remove the pan from the heat. You should have about ¾ cup.

Using a pastry bag fitted with a ½-inch plain tip, pipe about 1 tablespoon warm polenta onto each spoon (or place it in the spoon using another spoon). Put about ½ teaspoon of the mushroom mixture on top of each polenta serving. Serve immediately.

MAKES ABOUT 50 SPOONFULS

loving spoonfuls

This appetizer must be served piping hot, so have the polenta and mushrooms cooked and ready to go as guests arrive, then create spoonful-size bites as you need them.

CRISPY RISOTTO BALLS WITH WARM MOZZARELLA CENTERS — Sicilians call these crisp and delicious rice balls *arancine*, or "little oranges," because they turn golden in the hot oil. Romans make a similar dish they call *supplì al telephono*. Its name comes from the fact that when you bite into a ball and pull one-half of it away from the other half, the molten cheese center forms a long string that recalls the cord suspended between the base and the handset of a phone. No matter which name they travel under, these are heavy hors d'oeuvres, the kind you serve when the entire dinner menu is made up of an assortment of hors d'oeuvres.

COOKING NOTES: Spinach is the primary flavor in this dish. Don't cloud the picture with strong stock. Instead, I thin out the stock with water to leave room for other flavors. The biggest problem with risotto is that people don't sweat the onions long enough. This is the foundation of the flavor. Caramelizing would be too much for the delicate spinach and lemon flavors, but you need to cook the onions until they are soft and translucent. Also, never cook the risotto over high heat. If the liquid boils too hard, it evaporates before it can be absorbed into the rice.

ENTERTAINING NOTES: You can save time by cooking the risotto the day before. Note, too, the fried risotto balls can be kept warm in the oven for up to 2 hours before serving. Or, if you are serving a large group and want to skip shaping the small balls, omit the mozzarella, pour the risotto into a baking dish, sprinkle fine dried bread crumbs and freshly grated Parmesan cheese over the top, and heat in a 400°F oven until the risotto bubbles, about 30 minutes. Spoon it onto small plates for a delicious sit-down first course.

WINE NOTES: Open a cool, light, fruity Beaujolais or similar wine.

oozing flavor

When your guests bite into these risotto balls they will be rewarded with oozing Mozzarella in the center.

Finely ground sea salt, preferably gray salt

½ pound baby spinach

3½ cups water

⅛ teaspoon powdered ascorbic acid (vitamin C) (optional)

2 cups chicken stock

¼ cup extra-virgin olive oil

1 cup finely chopped yellow onion

1 tablespoon minced garlic

1 tablespoon minced fresh thyme (optional)

2 cups Arborio rice

1 cup dry white wine

2 cups freshly grated Parmesan cheese

1 tablespoon freshly grated lemon zest

Freshly ground black pepper

Peanut oil for deep-frying

½ pound fresh mozzarella cheese, cut into ½-inch cubes

1 cup all-purpose flour

2 or 3 large eggs

1½ cups fine dried bread crumbs

Peanut oil for deep-frying

Bring a large pot of salted water to a boil, add the spinach, and blanch for 10 seconds. Drain the spinach in a colander. Rinse under running cold water, then squeeze well to remove most of the water. Place the spinach in a blender with ½ cup of the water and the ascorbic acid, if using (it sets the bright green color). Process until smooth. Set aside.

In a saucepan, combine the chicken stock and the remaining 3 cups water over medium-high heat and bring to a boil. Reduce the heat to low to keep the diluted stock at a bare simmer.

In a skillet, heat the olive oil over medium heat. Add the onion, garlic, and 2 teaspoons salt and cook until the onion sizzles, then reduce the heat to low. Cook, stirring occasionally, until the onion is translucent and soft, about 10 minutes; do not let the onion color. Add the thyme, if desired, and let it crackle for about 10 seconds. Stir in the rice, coating it evenly with the oil, and cook, stirring, until hot, about 2 minutes. Adjust the heat to maintain a simmer. Add the wine and simmer, stirring, until almost all the wine is absorbed. Begin adding the hot stock 1 cup at a time, stirring often and adding more liquid only when the previous addition has been absorbed. It should take about 20 minutes for the rice to be just shy of al dente, with a little starchiness left in the center of each grain. You may not need all the liquid; if you need a little more, use boiling water.

Remove the risotto from the heat, stir in the Parmesan cheese and lemon zest, and then stir in the spinach puree. Season to taste with salt and pepper. Immediately pour the risotto onto a rimmed baking sheet. It should form a thin layer. Place uncovered in the refrigerator for about 1 hour to chill.

To form each ball, spread about 2 tablespoons of the cooled risotto in the palm of your hand. Place a cube of mozzarella cheese in the center. Shape the risotto into a sphere about the size of a golf ball, with the cheese cube in the center. Repeat with the remaining risotto and mozzarella, placing the balls on a baking sheet as they are formed.

Spread the flour on a dinner plate. Break 2 eggs into a shallow bowl and beat lightly. Spread the bread crumbs on a second dinner plate. Roll the risotto balls first in the flour, coating them evenly and shaking off the excess. Then dip them in the eggs, letting any excess drip back into the bowl. Finally, coat the risotto balls evenly with the bread crumbs. As the balls are ready, place them on a clean baking sheet. If you run short of beaten egg, use the remaining egg. Cover the balls and refrigerate for at least 30 minutes or up to 3 hours to firm the coating before frying.

Pour the peanut oil to a depth of at least 4 inches into a deep fryer or a heavy, 8-inch-deep stockpot and heat to 350°F. Working in small batches, add the risotto balls to the hot oil and fry until golden brown, 2 to 2½ minutes. Do not crowd the pan. Using a slotted spoon or tongs, transfer the balls to paper towels to drain for 1 to 2 minutes, then place on a baking sheet and keep warm in a 200°F oven. They will keep for up to 2 hours.

To serve, cover a large platter with a cloth napkin (to keep the balls from rolling around) and arrange the balls on top. Serve warm.

MAKES ABOUT 50 BALLS

GIANT CROSTINI — I created these oversized crostini when I was working at Tra Vigne. I wanted croutons to serve with my whole-leaf Caesar salad, but I didn't want those tiny croutons that get lost in a mix of large leaves. In fact, these crostini are about the same size as the inner leaves of a romaine head. Don't be afraid to season them generously. They are meant to be standouts. Here, I have provided a trio of toppings. If you decide to make more than one topping, or all three, you will need a loaf of bread for each one.

COOKING NOTES: It's important that the bread slices be no more than about 1/3 inch thick. Either ask someone in your local deli to cut fresh bread with a meat slicer, or use day-old bread, which is easier to slice. You could also freeze fresh bread for 15 or 20 minutes to firm it before slicing. You'll need a serrated knife to get the best results.

ENTERTAINING NOTES: An assortment of these crostini makes a beautiful centerpiece at a cocktail party. Alternatively, float one on top of a bowl of soup, spread with the pulp squeezed from roasted garlic cloves and serve under a steak, or set them out with a cheese course. If you have leftover crostini, break them into small pieces and combine them with fresh tomatoes, red onions, garlic, olive oil, and herbs for a summer *panzanella* salad.

WINE NOTES: Any fruity, light white wine you like is a good choice.

1 loaf country-style bread such as Pugliese,
   1 pound and at least 12 inches long

FOR COUNTRY CROSTINI:
Extra-virgin olive oil for brushing
Finely ground sea salt, preferably gray salt
Freshly ground black pepper
3/4 cup freshly grated Parmesan cheese

FOR ANCHOVY AND GARLIC CROSTINI:
4 olive oil–packed anchovy fillets
3 cloves garlic

1 teaspoon fresh thyme leaves
1/4 teaspoon red pepper flakes
2 teaspoons balsamic vinegar
1/4 cup extra-virgin olive oil
Freshly ground black pepper

FOR BROWN BUTTER AND TOASTED SPICE CROSTINI:
1/2 cup (1 stick) unsalted butter
1/2 teaspoon Toasted Spice Rub (page 16)

Preheat the oven to 375°F. Cut the loaf of bread in half crosswise, then cut each half lengthwise into 1/3-inch-thick slices. You should have 10 to 12 slices. Lay the slices in a single layer on rimmed baking sheets, then choose *one* of the toppings to make.

If making the country topping: Brush the top side of each slice with the olive oil and season with salt and pepper. Sprinkle about 1 tablespoon Parmesan evenly over each slice. Toast in the oven until golden brown, about 12 minutes.

If making the anchovy and garlic topping: Mince the anchovies, garlic, and thyme together on a cutting board to create a paste. Scoop the paste into a small bowl, add the remaining ingredients, including 1/8 teaspoon pepper, and stir to combine evenly. Smear the mixture on the top of each bread slice, dividing it evenly. Toast in the oven until golden brown, about 12 minutes.

If making the brown butter and toasted spice topping: Put the butter in a cold skillet and place it over medium heat. Cook, stirring occasionally to prevent it from burning in spots but without moving the pan, until it browns evenly, about 2 minutes. Remove from the heat and strain through a fine-mesh sieve to remove any brown bits, if desired. Add the spice mixture and mix well. Brush the butter mixture on the top side of each bread slice. Toast in the oven until golden brown, about 12 minutes.

The crostini can be served warm or at room temperature. Leftovers can be stored in a tightly covered container at room temperature for up to 1 week.

MAKES 10 TO 12 CROSTINI

POTATO AND SAGE FRITTERS — This is a master recipe that can be flavored dozens of different ways. You can mix nearly any dry flavoring you like—grated cheese, other herbs or spices, chopped dried tomato—into the dough. Don't try mixing in "wet" ingredients, however, or the fritters will not hold together properly. Remember, too, don't be afraid to deep-fry foods at home. When done correctly, little oil is absorbed and the flavors are fantastic.

COOKING NOTES: Whenever you deep-fry, be sure not to overload the oil. If you add too many fritters—or too many of whatever you are frying—the oil temperature will drop dramatically and the fritters will absorb the oil, producing a greasy, leaden result. Also, wait a minute or so between batches to allow the oil to come back up to temperature before adding the next batch.

ENTERTAINING NOTES: You can fry up a couple of batches of these fritters an hour before your guests arrive and reheat them for about 5 minutes in a 300°F oven before serving. Or, you can keep the freshly fried fritters warm in a 250°F oven for about 1 hour before serving. I like these fritters served alone, but they are equally good with a couple of dipping sauces, such as Roasted-Artichoke Pesto (page 36) or "Green Goddess" Dressing (page 68).

WINE NOTES: Pour a Chardonnay or White Burgundy.

FOR THE SPONGE:

¼ cup warm water

2 tablespoons all-purpose flour

1⅛ teaspoons (½ envelope) active dry yeast

1 pound russet potatoes, peeled and cut into 1-inch cubes

Finely ground sea salt, preferably gray salt

2 cups (10 ounces) all-purpose flour

1 tablespoon finely chopped fresh sage

2 teaspoons grated lemon zest

Freshly ground coarse black pepper

2 large eggs

½ cup extra-virgin olive oil

Peanut oil for deep-frying

Make the sponge: In a small bowl, combine the water, flour, and yeast. Mix well and set aside in a warm place until yeasty-smelling and covered in very small bubbles, about 45 minutes.

Meanwhile, in a saucepan, combine the potatoes with water to cover by 1 inch. Bring to a boil over high heat and add 1 tablespoon salt. Reduce the heat to medium and simmer, uncovered, until the potatoes are very tender, 15 to 20 minutes. Drain the potatoes in a colander, transfer to a bowl, and mash with a fork. Let cool completely.

In a large bowl combine the cooled potatoes with the sponge, flour, sage, lemon zest, ½ teaspoon pepper, and 2 teaspoons salt. Mix to distribute the ingredients evenly. In a small bowl, whisk together the eggs and olive oil until thoroughly combined. Add the egg mixture to the potato mixture and stir until thoroughly com-

bined. Use a rubber spatula to scrape down the sides of the bowl. You should have a thick, sticky batter. Add a bit more flour, if needed. Cover the bowl with a kitchen towel and let the dough rise in a warm place until doubled in size, 1½ to 2 hours.

Pour the peanut oil to a depth of at least 3 inches into a deep fryer or a heavy, 8-inch-deep stockpot and heat to 375°F. For each fritter, scoop up 1 tablespoon of the risen batter and, using a second spoon, push it into hot oil. Repeat to add more fritters to the oil, but be careful not to crowd the pan. Fry the fritters, turning them over occasionally, until golden brown, 2 to 3 minutes. Using tongs or a slotted spoon, transfer to paper towels to drain briefly.

Arrange the fritters on a warmed platter and serve at once.

MAKES ABOUT 50 FRITTERS

POLENTA CROSTINI—These crisp, golden rectangles are incredibly delicious just as they are, so although you may never want to stray from the recipe, I urge you to get creative. Imagine them as croutons in a salad. Or, top them with Roasted-Artichoke Pesto (page 36) or marinated sun-dried tomatoes for a light lunch. A stinky cheese and some sausage on top would make a fantastic adult mini-pizza as well. Nutmeg and polenta is a strictly northern Italian pairing. If my late grandmother, a proud southern Italian, was still alive, she would be chasing me with her polenta spoon for ruining her recipe with a northern ingredient.

COOKING NOTES: You need fine-grain polenta for the mixture to bind together sufficiently for crostini. If you cannot find fine-grain polenta, grind coarse polenta in a food processor. The crostini are pretty soft when they first come out of the broiler, but they will firm up in about 5 minutes. You can use chicken stock instead of water for cooking the polenta, but do not use milk, which would make the crostini greasy.

ENTERTAINING NOTES: This recipe is an entertainer's friend. Save yourself time the day of the party by making the polenta a day in advance. Simply stop once you have poured the polenta onto the baking sheet and refrigerated it. Then, the day of the party, remove the baking sheet from the refrigerator and continue with the recipe.

WINE NOTES: Open a soft, sexy Merlot.

4 cups water

Finely ground sea salt, preferably gray salt

½ teaspoon freshly grated nutmeg

1 cup fine-grain polenta

1 cup freshly grated Parmesan cheese

Freshly ground coarse black pepper

2 tablespoons minced fresh thyme

In a heavy saucepan, bring the water to a boil over high heat. Add 2 teaspoons salt and the nutmeg and reduce the heat to medium. Add the polenta gradually, whisking constantly. Continue to whisk for 5 minutes as the mixture bubbles. Reduce the heat to low and cook, stirring occasionally, until the mixture begins to come away from the sides of the pan, about 10 minutes. Add ½ cup of the Parmesan cheese and ½ teaspoon pepper and stir to combine thoroughly.

Invert a rimmed baking sheet on a countertop and cover the surface with parchment paper. Spoon the polenta over the parchment paper and spread it out with a spatula into a smooth, even layer. Cover the polenta with another sheet of parchment paper. Place another baking sheet, right side up, on top of the parchment. With two hands, press down evenly on the top baking sheet until the polenta is ¼ inch thick. The idea is to sandwich the polenta between 2 flat surfaces. Refrigerate for at least 1 hour or up to overnight.

Preheat the oven to 400°F. Invert the baking sheets together. Remove the top baking sheet and the top layer of parchment paper. The smoother side of the polenta will be facing up. Cut the polenta into rectangles about 2 inches long by 1½ inches wide. Transfer the rectangles to 1 or more baking sheets, spacing them ½ inch apart. Sprinkle about ½ teaspoon of the remaining Parmesan cheese and ⅛ teaspoon of the thyme on top of each rectangle.

Bake the crostini until hot throughout and starting to brown, about 12 minutes. Turn the oven to broil and broil the crostini about 8 inches from the heat source until crispy and golden brown on top, about 3 minutes. Serve warm or at room temperature.

MAKES ABOUT 48 CROSTINI

ROASTED EGGPLANT AND WHITE BEAN SPREAD — Most folks simply do not cook enough eggplant at home. Peter Forni, an organic farmer in the nearby town of Calistoga, showed me how sweet a truly fresh eggplant can be when he convinced me to eat one raw, right off the vine. Like many people, I am trying to reduce the amount of red meat in my diet, and I am looking to vegetables like the eggplant to take its place. The rich, smoky flavor that distinguishes this recipe always makes me feel satiated. The idea in this dish is to capture an intense flavor like eggplant and dilute it with something smooth and mellow like white beans.

COOKING NOTES: Don't stir the eggplants in the skillet, or they will release all their water, absorb all the oil in the pan, and never caramelize. Because eggplants can get bitter, especially the females, we salt them to draw out the bitterness. The recipe has a large yield, but the spread also has many uses (see below). Plus, leftovers can be stored in a covered container in the refrigerator for up to 1 week.

ENTERTAINING NOTES: A list of ways to use this spread whenever you are entertaining could go on for pages, but here are my top suggestions. Spread it on grilled bread with fresh ricotta and serve as part of an appetizer assortment. Spread it over halibut, sprinkle bread crumbs on top, and roast for a main course. Layer it along with feta cheese and fresh oregano leaves on country-style bread or focaccia for a midday sandwich. Place a spoonful alongside seared lamb loin as a condiment. It even makes a wonderful ravioli filling.

WINE NOTES: Eggplant can be rough on wine, so keep it simple, cool, and white.

---

2 globe eggplants, about 1 pound each

Kosher salt

½ cup extra-virgin olive oil

¼ cup thinly sliced garlic (about 6 cloves)

1 tablespoon minced fresh oregano

1 teaspoon red pepper flakes

1 tablespoon drained capers

1 tablespoon brine from caper jar

1 can (28 ounces) whole tomatoes, drained

Finely ground sea salt, preferably gray salt

Freshly ground black pepper

1 can (15 ounces) cannellini beans, drained and rinsed

Peel the eggplants and cut them crosswise into ½-inch-thick slices. Sprinkle 4 teaspoons kosher salt over both sides of each slice and place the slices in a colander to drain for 1½ hours. Rinse the eggplant slices, pat them dry with paper towels, and cut them into ½-inch dice.

Preheat the oven to 425°F.

In a large skillet, heat the olive oil over high heat. When the oil is hot, add the eggplant pieces in a single layer. Do not stir. After 1 minute, stir once, add the garlic, and put the pan in the oven. Roast the eggplant pieces until golden brown all over, about 20 minutes.

Remove the pan from the oven and add the oregano, red pepper flakes, capers, and caper brine. Crush the tomatoes in your hands and let them fall into the pan. Season the mixture to taste with sea salt and pepper and stir well. Return the pan to the oven and roast until the eggplant mixture is beginning to brown on top, about 25 minutes.

Remove from the oven and let cool slightly. Spoon two-thirds of the eggplant mixture into a food processor, add the cannellini beans, and process until smooth. Spoon the eggplant puree into a bowl. Add the remaining eggplant mixture and stir to combine.

Serve warm or at room temperature.

MAKES ABOUT 6 CUPS

POP CULTURE POPCORN — Is there anything worse than when a food you have loved for years suddenly turns up on the if-you-eat-too-much-it-will-kill-you list? Or, perhaps just as bad, what do you do when the flavors of the world have evolved, but a classic food has not. Don't fret. I have just reinvented popcorn so that it is both better for you and tastes amazing.

COOKING NOTES: Making brown butter is an important technique to master. Always add the butter to a cold pan and then place it over the heat. As the butter melts, do not move the pan for about 2 minutes, or the butter may brown prematurely. Keep a close eye on it, too. The butter will foam and then the foam will subside. When that happens, the butter will be nicely browned and have a nutty aroma. Remove the pan from the heat before adding the other ingredients.

ENTERTAINING NOTES: You can pop the popcorn an hour in advance and then rewarm it in an ovenproof bowl in a 300°F oven for 5 minutes before tossing it with the flavoring. The toasted spice popcorn also makes a great garnish. Pass the popcorn for guests to float on top of butternut squash soup, just like croutons.

WINE NOTES: Serve Chianti with the basil oil and Parmesan popcorn, Guinness with the sage and toasted spice popcorn, Cabernet Sauvignon with the rosemary and lemon popcorn, a good pilsner beer with the roasted garlic popcorn, and some port or sparkling wine with the chocolate and orange zest popcorn. Or, Blood Orange White Sangria (page 194) goes well with all of the flavored popcorns.

½ cup unpopped popcorn

1½ tablespoons extra-virgin olive oil or canola
   or other bland vegetable oil

FOR BASIL OLIVE OIL AND PARMESAN FLAVORING:

3 tablespoons "Infused" Basil Oil (page 20)

½ cup freshly grated Parmesan cheese

Finely ground sea salt, preferably gray salt

Freshly ground coarse black pepper

FOR BROWN BUTTER, SAGE, AND TOASTED SPICE FLAVORING:

3 tablespoons unsalted butter

1 tablespoon finely chopped fresh sage

Finely ground sea salt, preferably gray salt

2 teaspoons Toasted Spice Rub (page 16)

FOR BROWN BUTTER, ROSEMARY, AND LEMON FLAVORING:

3 tablespoons unsalted butter

1 tablespoon finely chopped fresh rosemary

1 tablespoon grated lemon zest

Finely ground sea salt, preferably gray salt

FOR ROASTED GARLIC FLAVORING:

3 tablespoons extra-virgin olive oil

2 teaspoons Roasted-Garlic Spice (page 20)

Finely ground sea salt, preferably gray salt

FOR CHOCOLATE AND ORANGE ZEST FLAVORING:

3 tablespoons unsalted butter

¼ cup grated semisweet chocolate

1 tablespoon grated orange zest

Finely ground sea salt, preferably gray salt

Select *one* of the flavoring mixtures and have all the ingredients for it assembled before you begin to pop the corn. Then, to pop the corn, combine the unpopped kernels and the oil in a heavy 4-quart saucepan. If you will be using a savory flavoring, use olive oil, and if you will be using the chocolate and orange zest flavoring, use vegetable oil. Place the pan over medium-high heat and when the kernels start to pop, cover tightly and continue to cook, shaking the pan occasionally, until all the kernels pop, 2 to 3 minutes. Pour the popcorn into a large bowl, and then make the flavoring.

To flavor the popcorn with basil olive oil and Parmesan: Add the oil to the hot popcorn, toss well, and then add the cheese and again toss well. Finally, add 1 teaspoon each salt and pepper and mix well.

RECIPE CONTINUED ON PAGE 48

RECIPE CONTINUED FROM PAGE 47

To flavor the popcorn with brown butter, sage, and toasted spice: Put the butter in a cold skillet and place it over medium heat. Cook, stirring occasionally to prevent it from burning in spots but without moving the pan, until it browns evenly, about 2 minutes, then remove from the heat. Immediately add the sage to the butter. When it stops crackling, after a few seconds, pour the butter mixture over the hot popcorn and toss well. Add 2 teaspoons salt and the spice mixture and toss again.

To flavor the popcorn with brown butter, rosemary, and lemon: Put the butter in a cold skillet and place it over medium heat. Cook, stirring occasionally to prevent it from burning in spots but without moving the pan, until it browns evenly, about 2 minutes, then remove from the heat. Immediately add the rosemary and lemon zest to the butter. Pour the butter mixture over the hot popcorn and toss well. Add 2 teaspoons salt and toss again.

To flavor the popcorn with the garlic spice: Heat the olive oil in a sauté pan over high heat until hot but not smoking. Pour the oil over the hot popcorn and toss well. Add the garlic spice and 2 teaspoons salt and toss again.

To flavor the popcorn with chocolate and orange zest: Put the butter in a cold skillet and place it over medium heat. Cook, stirring occasionally to prevent it from burning in spots but without moving the pan, until it browns evenly, about 2 minutes, then remove from the heat. Pour the butter over the hot popcorn and toss well. Add the chocolate, orange zest, and 1/2 teaspoon salt and toss again. Taste and adjust with more salt if needed.

Serve the popcorn at once.

MAKES ABOUT 4 CUPS

"SPEED SCRATCH" ROASTED GARLIC POTATO CHIPS — Okay, I admit it. I love potato chips. I have made them from scratch my entire professional career. But it is just as satisfying, and really fun for the kids, to use artisanal potato chips from the store and flavor them yourself.

COOKING NOTES: I prefer the taste of potato chips cooked in olive oil, if you can find them. You can easily cut this recipe in half, but the leftovers keep well in an airtight container at room temperature for a few days (if they last that long!). For a different flavoring, use 1 1/2 tablespoons Toasted Spice Rub (page 16) in place of the garlic mixture.

ENTERTAINING NOTES: You can make the recipe a day ahead and store the chips in an airtight container. You should probably tuck the container away in a closet to keep hungry preparty snackers from discovering it. Most people like potato chips, which means that this simple recipe is particularly versatile. You can put the chips out when friends come over to watch a ballgame or a movie, or they are wonderful for guests to nibble as they arrive for a dinner party.

WINE NOTES: Champagne and potato chips . . . can it get any better?

2 large bags favorite salted potato chips
Roasted-Garlic Spice (page 20)

Preheat the oven to 350°F.

Spill the potato chips onto 2 rimmed baking sheets in an even layer and place in the oven. When oil is visible on the chips, after 3 to 5 minutes, remove from the oven and sprinkle evenly with the garlic mixture. Let cool completely.

Pile the potato chips in 1 or more big bowls or baskets and serve.

SERVES 10

TOASTED MARCONA ALMONDS — My new favorite nut, heralding from Spain, is the Marcona almond. It is flat, almost round, and has a wonderful rich flavor. Spice up these tasty almonds a little and watch the bowl empty before your eyes.

COOKING NOTES: If you cannot find Marcona almonds, you can substitute blanched whole almonds. Toss them with 1 teaspoon water and ½ teaspoon finely ground sea salt (preferably gray salt), spread them on a rimmed baking sheet, and toast in a 350°F oven until they take on color and are fragrant, about 8 minutes. Remove from the oven and proceed as directed for the Marcona almonds.

ENTERTAINING NOTES: You don't need to limit these delicious nuts to the appetizer or snack realm. They are also good tossed in salads, sprinkled over grilled swordfish, or served with a cheese course. During the holidays, make up a big batch and use them as host gifts.

WINE NOTES: I love pouring fortified wines like sherry, port (if serving after dinner), or Madeira with these nuts.

¼ cup extra-virgin olive oil

2 cups salted toasted Marcona almonds

¼ cup Toasted Spice Rub (page 16)

Preheat the oven to 350°F. In an ovenproof skillet, heat the olive oil over medium heat. Add the almonds, stir to coat them with the oil, sprinkle with the spice mixture, and toss to coat evenly.

Place the skillet in the oven and toast the almonds until lightly browned, 6 to 7 minutes. Remove from the oven, pour into a bowl, and let cool before serving. Store any leftovers in an airtight container at room temperature.

MAKES 2 CUPS

FUSILLI SNACK MIX — Who doesn't like Chex mix? Well, we have a new favorite in the neighborhood—one with grownup flavors.

COOKING NOTES: You can substitute other snacks that you love to vary the mix, but keep the crispy *fusilli* as your base. Don't use heavily seasoned snacks. They will overpower the seasoning.

ENTERTAINING NOTES: Serve this irresistible mix in a big, old-fashioned bowl, or make parchment-paper envelopes and pass the packets around at a ballgame or movie theater. College students (like my daughter Margaux) love this snack, too.

WINE NOTES: Whip up a batch of Bloody Marys (page 202).

Finely ground sea salt, preferably gray salt

½ pound *fusilli* pasta (cork screw)

Peanut oil for tossing and deep-frying

3 tablespoons freshly grated Parmesan cheese

2 teaspoons finely minced fresh thyme

Freshly ground black pepper

1½ cups (2¼ ounces) bite-sized pretzels

1 cup (2 ounces) Parmesan Goldfish

1 cup (2 ounces) wasabi-coated dried peas

½ cup (1½ ounces) sesame worms (small Asian crackers)

½ cup (2½ ounces) dry-roasted peanuts

Bring a large pot of salted water to a boil. Add the *fusilli* and cook until al dente. Drain thoroughly in a colander and transfer to a large bowl. Add about 2 tablespoons of the peanut oil and toss to prevent sticking. Let the pasta cool completely, tossing occasionally.

Pour the peanut oil to a depth of at least 4 inches into a deep fryer or a heavy, 8-inch-deep stockpot and heat to 350°F. Working in batches, add the pasta to the hot oil and fry until lightly golden brown, about 2 minutes. While frying each batch, use a slotted spoon to pull the pasta out of the oil a couple of times to make sure the oil doesn't boil over. Using the spoon, transfer the pasta to paper towels to drain briefly, then place in a large bowl.

When all the pasta is in the bowl and is still hot, add the cheese, thyme, ⅛ teaspoon salt, and ½ teaspoon pepper. Mix well to coat the pasta evenly. Add the pretzels, goldfish, dried peas, sesame worms, and peanuts and again mix well.

Serve at room temperature. Store leftover snack mix in an airtight container in a cool, dry place for up to 2 weeks.

MAKES ABOUT 8 CUPS

Soups and salads are invaluable gifts to every overworked cook. Soups can usually be made hours ahead and finished at the last moment, while salads nearly always go together quickly and can often be a satisfying and tasty main course for a midweek supper. So, whenever my guest list grows large, I slip a soup or a salad into the first-course slot on my menu, or sometimes I put one of each on the table.

soups & salads

On a hot summer day, who wouldn't appreciate a chilled melon and prosciutto soup (page 77)? Follow the soup with Grilled Avocado and Tomato Salad with "Green Goddess" Dressing (page 68) and your guests will be applauding the chef. Or on a cold winter night, who can resist a steaming bowl of "Super-Tuscan" White Bean Soup (page 76)? It is like a hug for your stomach. Serve Sliced Orange Salad with Sautéed Olives and Ricotta Salata (page 74) after the soup and the feast is nearly complete—except for perhaps a handful of biscotti (page 206) and some sweet wine for dipping.

Unless I am sipping a glass of sherry along with lobster bisque, I don't serve wine with soup. For me, two liquids of different temperatures don't mesh well, so my soup recipes do not include wine suggestions.

out by the pool

TOMATO "CARPACCIO" WITH ARUGULA AND HERB SALAD—Entertaining does not have to mean three days in the kitchen and three days to clean up. Here, I take what is typically thinly sliced raw meat, or carpaccio, and apply it to thinly sliced tomatoes. Your guests will love the wordplay and the dish.

COOKING NOTES: You can use whatever herbs you like for the vinaigrette, but I recommend 50 percent basil. The vinaigrette can be prepped but not assembled ahead, as it does not benefit from long maceration time. You can use *ricotta salata*, aged goat cheese, or Manchego cheese in place of the Parmesan. And if you can find them, this is the perfect recipe for heirloom tomatoes. The funky colors and varied flavors are visually stunning, and you are often introducing your guests to something new.

ENTERTAINING NOTES: Slide a few slices of grilled steak or a piece of grilled salmon under the herb salad to turn this simple dish into an equally simple main course. Or, serve some paper-thin slices of raw beef along with the tomato slices for a "two-carpaccio salad."

WINE NOTES: Serve an Italian Vernaccia or a Pinot Blanc.

FOR THE VINAIGRETTE:

2 tablespoons fresh lemon juice

1 tablespoon minced shallot

1 teaspoon minced garlic

½ cup extra-virgin olive oil

2 cups diced red and/or yellow tomatoes (½-inch dice; 2 to 3 tomatoes)

1 cup (about 5 ounces) Sweet 100 tomatoes, stemmed and halved through the stem end

1 tablespoon finely chopped fresh tarragon

1 tablespoon finely chopped fresh Italian (flat-leaf) parsley

1 tablespoon finely chopped fresh chives

3 tablespoons finely chopped fresh basil

Finely ground sea salt, preferably gray salt

Freshly ground black pepper

4 large red and/or yellow tomatoes, about ½ pound each

6 cups (about 6 ounces) lightly packed baby arugula

2-ounce wedge Parmesan cheese

Freshly ground black pepper

Make the vinaigrette: In a bowl, stir together the lemon juice, shallot, and garlic. Slowly whisk in the olive oil to form an emulsion. Add the remaining vinaigrette ingredients, including salt and pepper to taste, and mix well.

Cut a ½-inch-thick slice from the stem end and blossom end of each tomato. Discard the trim (or trim away edible portion and reserve for another use) and cut each tomato crosswise into ¼-inch-thick slices. On a round platter, arrange the tomatoes in concentric circles, slightly overlapping the slices and alternating colors if using both red and yellow.

Spoon the tomatoes from the vinaigrette over the sliced tomatoes, along with some, but not all, of the vinaigrette. In another bowl, toss the arugula with just enough of the reserved vinaigrette to coat the leaves lightly. Save any vinaigrette in the bowl for another use.

Arrange the arugula in the middle of the tomato-covered platter. Using a vegetable peeler, shave thin slices of Parmesan cheese over the platter. Serve at room temperature. Pass the pepper mill.

SERVES 6 TO 8

BRIGHT GREEN ASPARAGUS SOUP WITH PARMIGIANO-REGGIANO "ZABAGLIONE"—

I have always believed that capturing the peak flavors of a season has to be one of a cook's highest priorities. This dish does exactly that for spring. When asparagus spears are filling the markets, dazzle your guests with this satisfying soup finished with a surprise—a normally sweet dessert sauce turned into a savory garnish.

COOKING NOTES: The keys to achieving a brilliant green color for this soup are blending the cooked asparagus with fresh spinach, adding a bit of ascorbic acid, and cooling the soup as quickly as possible. You can also exchange the asparagus for broccoli for a fall variation.

ENTERTAINING NOTES: You can make both the soup and the zabaglione the day before serving them. Add the whipped cream to the zabaglione up to 8 hours ahead, but no longer, or it will deflate and not float as beautifully on top of the soup. Or, you can make the soup and store it in the freezer for up to 1 month. The soup can be served at a variety of temperatures. If it is cold outside, serve it piping hot; on cool days, serve it warm; and if it's a hot day, serve it at room temperature.

FOR THE SOUP:

2 tablespoons extra-virgin olive oil

1½ cups finely chopped yellow onion

Finely ground sea salt, preferably gray salt

1 large russet potato, about ¾ pound, peeled and cut into 1-inch cubes

6 cups chicken stock

1 bay leaf

Freshly ground black pepper

2 pounds asparagus, tough ends removed and cut crosswise into ¼-inch-thick slices

2 teaspoons finely chopped fresh thyme

2 cups tightly packed fresh spinach leaves

1 cup heavy cream

2 teaspoons freshly grated lemon zest

¼ teaspoon powdered ascorbic acid (vitamin C) (optional)

FOR THE ZABAGLIONE:

2 large egg yolks

2 tablespoons dry white wine

Finely ground sea salt, preferably gray salt

½ cup freshly grated Parmigiano-Reggiano cheese

Freshly ground black pepper

¼ cup heavy cream, whipped to soft peaks

Make the soup: In a large saucepan, heat the olive oil over high heat. Add the onion, stir briefly, and reduce the heat to medium. Add a pinch of salt to draw moisture out of the onion. Cook the onion, stirring occasionally, until soft and translucent, about 4 minutes. Do not allow it to brown. Add the potato, chicken stock, and bay leaf, raise the heat to high, and bring the stock to a boil. Reduce the heat to medium, then taste the stock and season with salt and pepper if needed. Cook the potato until tender, about 10 minutes. Add the asparagus and thyme, return the stock to a simmer, and cook until the asparagus is barely tender, about 5 minutes.

Remove the bay leaf and discard. Working quickly, ladle some of the soup into a blender and add the spinach, cream, lemon zest, and the ascorbic acid, if using. Process until perfectly smooth. To cool quickly, pour into a large bowl and set the bowl inside a larger bowl filled with ice water or a sink partially filled with ice water. Puree the remaining soup in batches and add to the bowl floating in the ice water. Stir often until the soup is no longer steaming.

Make the zabaglione: Pour water to a depth of about 2 inches into a saucepan and bring to a simmer. In a nonreactive bowl, whisk together the egg yolks and wine. Season with a little salt. Set the bowl over—but not touching—the simmering water and whisk the yolk mixture constantly until it is very thick, 3 to 5 minutes. To test, draw the whisk through the center of the mixture; it should leave a clean trail on the bottom of the bowl. Remove the bowl from over the water and whisk in the cheese. Set the bowl back over the simmering water and whisk the mixture just until the cheese is thoroughly melted, about 1 minute. Remove the bowl from the heat and season to taste with pepper. Let cool to room temperature.

Add one-third of the whipped cream to the egg mixture and whisk until smooth. Gently fold in the remaining whipped cream, being careful to keep the mixture light and airy. You should have about ¾ cup.

The soup can be served hot, warm, or at room temperature. Ladle into bowls and spoon about 1 tablespoon zabaglione atop each serving.

SERVES 10 TO 12

CAPELLINI SOUP WITH RICH CHICKEN BRODO — Imagine a cold, sleet-filled winter night and friends over for a fireplace meal. The coffee table is set with dinner linens and wineglasses, and the entire menu is cooked in the hearth. As the guests arrive, they peel off the layers, slip out of their boots, and settle next to the fire. When you walk into the room with a tray topped with bowls of this soup, you will be welcoming them with a warm hug. Now that's entertaining at its best!

COOKING NOTES: Two tips will guarantee success in this simple preparation. First, you want a clear broth, so never allow it to boil, which can turn it cloudy. Second, use cold water in the broth to give it the freshest flavor. Capellini, sometimes labeled angel hair pasta, are long, fine dried noodles. To turn this soup into a main course for supper, add grated vegetables to the broth just before serving.

ENTERTAINING NOTES: The broth can be made a day in advance. The next day, you can cook the pasta and finish the soup in about 15 minutes. Come winter, I love this soup before a main course of *bistecca alla fiorentina* (page 124) and a green salad. Serve the soup in clear glass bowls to show off its rich color and texture.

1 whole chicken, about 4 pounds	1 bay leaf
Finely ground sea salt, preferably gray salt	¼ ounce (¼ cup) dried porcini mushrooms (optional)
Freshly ground black pepper	2½ quarts (10 cups) water
¼ cup extra-virgin olive oil	¼ cup roughly chopped fresh Italian (flat-leaf) parsley
2 yellow onions, quartered lengthwise	1 pound capellini
2 celery stalks, cut on the diagonal into 2-inch lengths	¾ cup freshly grated Parmesan cheese
2 carrots, peeled and cut on the diagonal into 2-inch lengths	Red pepper flakes or Calabrian Chili Paste (page 15) for serving
1 cup dry red wine	

Rinse the chicken under cold running water, pat dry, and then cut into 8 pieces: 2 breasts, 2 thighs, 2 drumsticks, and 2 wings. (Reserve the back and neck for making stock.) Cut each breast in half crosswise. Generously season each piece with salt and pepper.

In a large, wide, heavy pot, heat the olive oil over high heat until it begins to smoke. Carefully add the chicken pieces, skin side down and in a single layer, and brown for about 10 minutes. Turn the pieces and brown them on the second side, about 8 minutes longer. When the chicken pieces are deeply browned on both sides, remove to a plate. Add the onions, celery, and carrots to the pot and cook, stirring occasionally, until deeply browned, about 15 minutes.

Add the wine, bay leaf, and the mushrooms, if using. Cook over high heat until about ¼ cup of the wine remains, about 7 minutes. Using a wooden spoon, scrape the bottom of the pot to remove any browned bits. Return the chicken pieces to the pot, add the water, and bring to a simmer, skimming any foam or impurities that rise to the top. Reduce the heat to maintain a slow, steady simmer; do not let the broth boil. Simmer the broth uncovered, occasionally skimming any foam and impurities that rise to the top, for 2½ to 3 hours. The liquid will have reduced by about one-fourth and have a rich flavor.

Using tongs or a slotted spoon, transfer the chicken pieces to a plate. Line a sieve or colander with a tea towel or a triple thickness of cheesecloth, place over a large, clean pot, and pour the broth through it. Discard the contents of the sieve. You should have about 8 cups broth. Using a large spoon, skim off the fat from the surface. (You can make the broth a day in advance and refrigerate it; the next day, the fat will have solidified on the surface and is easily lifted off.) Taste the broth and season it well. This is a simple dish that requires plenty of salt and pepper. Keep the broth just below a simmer over low heat.

When the chicken is cool enough to handle, remove the meat from the bones and discard the bones and skin. Shred the meat into 1-inch pieces with your fingers and place it in a large bowl. Add the parsley to the chicken and season with salt and pepper.

Bring a large pot of salted water to a boil over high heat. Add the capellini and cook until just shy of al dente. Drain in a colander, then add to the bowl holding the chicken meat and mix well.

Divide the chicken and capellini evenly among 8 warmed individual bowls. Ladle 1 cup of hot broth into each bowl. Scatter some Parmesan cheese over each serving. Pass chili paste at the table. Serve at once with both a spoon and a fork.

SERVES 8

CRISPY SEAFOOD SALAD WITH WHOLE-CITRUS VINAIGRETTE — Contrasting textures and temperatures create layers of flavor that I rely on in my cooking. Here, I am serving warm, crispy calamari with a cool arugula salad and tangy dressing. The calamari are so good, my family often stands around the kitchen counter and eats them as soon as they come out of the hot oil, and then follow them with the simple salad.

COOKING NOTES: Rock shrimp, appreciated for their sweet flavor and a texture reminiscent of lobster, have rock-hard shells and so are typically sold already peeled and deveined. You can use medium-sized regular shrimp in their place. Buy them in the shell—increase the amount to 10 ounces—and peel and devein them. Most fishmongers sell already-cleaned calamari (squid), which will save you time. Ask for only the tubular bodies, not the tentacles.

ENTERTAINING NOTES: The vinaigrette can be made up to 2 weeks in advance and stored in the refrigerator. The greens can be rinsed, dried, and placed in the refrigerator up to 1 day before serving. You can fry the seafood 30 minutes before the guests arrive. Toss the seafood with the greens and dressing at the last moment, just before you carry the salad to the table.

WINE NOTES: A crisp Sauvignon Blanc is just the ticket here.

3 navel oranges

1 red onion, thinly sliced

Finely ground sea salt, preferably gray salt

Freshly ground black pepper

Peanut oil for deep-frying

6 ounces cleaned squid (calamari) tubes

1 cup buttermilk

½ pound rock shrimp

1 cup Arborio Rice Coating (page 22)

12 cups (about ¾ pound) lightly packed baby arugula or spinach

6 tablespoons Whole-Citrus Vinaigrette (page 18)

Working with 1 orange at a time, cut a slice off the stem and blossom end, revealing the flesh. Place the orange upright on a cutting board and, using a sharp knife, cut off the peel and pith, following the contour of the fruit. Holding the fruit in one hand over a bowl, cut along both sides of the membrane holding each segment, freeing the segments and capturing them and any juices in the bowl. Add the onion slices to the orange segments and juices and toss together gently. Season to taste with salt and pepper. Set aside.

Pour the peanut oil to a depth of at least 3 inches into a deep fryer or a heavy, 8-inch-deep stockpot and heat to 375°F. While the oil is heating, cut the calamari tubes in half lengthwise on the diagonal. Put half of the buttermilk in one small bowl, and the other half in another. Add the calamari to one bowl and the rock shrimp to the other and let soak until the oil is ready.

Spread the rice coating on a dinner plate. Drain the calamari in a sieve, then dredge it in the coating, shaking off the excess. Working in batches, add the calamari to the hot oil and fry until golden brown, about 3 minutes. Using a slotted spoon, transfer to paper towels to drain. Then drain the rock shrimp in the sieve and dredge it in the rice coating. Working in batches, add the rock shrimp to the hot oil and fry until golden brown, about 3 minutes. Using a slotted spoon, transfer to paper towels to drain. Season the calamari and rock shrimp to taste with salt and pepper.

Put the arugula in a large bowl. Add the fried calamari and shrimp and lightly drizzle the vinaigrette over the top (you may not need all the vinaigrette). Toss to coat the ingredients evenly with the vinaigrette. Taste and adjust the seasoning with salt and pepper.

Divide the salad among individual plates. Spoon an equal amount of the orange-onion mixture over each salad. Serve immediately.

SERVES 6

SEAFOOD GAZPACHO COCKTAIL WITH FLAVORED POPCORN — I love gazpacho and ceviche separately. Here, I've put them together, turning two simple dishes into a lasting memory. On a trip through South America, I enjoyed ceviche topped with roasted corn kernels. I borrowed that idea here, finishing this cocktail with highly flavored homemade popcorn. As the heat of the summer turns up, turn up the chill and thrill with this dish.

COOKING NOTES: Commercial tomato juice can be salty, so if you can buy—or harvest—flavorful fresh tomatoes, use the tomato puree option. If you do use the juice and find the mixture is too salty, squeeze in some lime or lemon juice. If you like the heat of a jalapeño chili, use the larger amount.

ENTERTAINING NOTES: Have the seafood gazpacho and popcorn ready to go, and when your guests arrive, just ladle them up. The gazpacho is cold, the popcorn is warm. Simply add a handful to each bowl and mix together. It's a mind-blowing pair that's sure to get your guests talking!

WINE NOTES: Serve ice-cold white sangria (page 194) in glasses that have been dipped in water and set in the freezer for 30 minutes to frost.

---

2 cans (11½ ounces each) tomato juice or 3 cups peeled, seeded, and
    pureed fresh tomatoes

2 tablespoons fresh lemon juice

1 cup finely diced fennel (½ bulb)

1 cup peeled, seeded, and finely diced cucumber (1 medium cucumber)

½ cup finely diced red onion (½ small)

½ cup finely diced celery (2 medium stalks)

Finely ground sea salt, preferably gray salt

Freshly ground coarse black pepper

3 tablespoons extra-virgin olive oil

½ pound skinless halibut fillet, cut into ½-inch pieces

½ pound medium shrimp, peeled and deveined

1 tablespoon minced garlic

2 to 3 tablespoons minced, seeded jalapeño chili

1 can (6½ ounces) clams, drained, with clams and
    juice reserved separately

¼ cup dry white wine

1 pint Sweet 100 or other small cherry tomatoes (preferably Sweet 100s),
    stems removed and quartered through the stem end

2 tablespoons finely chopped fresh Italian (flat-leaf) parsley

1 tablespoon finely chopped fresh basil

1 tablespoon sherry vinegar

Pop Culture Popcorn flavored with basil oil and
    Parmesan cheese (page 47)

In a bowl, combine the tomato juice, lemon juice, fennel, cucumber, onion, celery, and 1 teaspoon each salt and pepper. Cover and place in the refrigerator to chill.

In a 10-inch skillet, heat 2 tablespoons of the olive oil over high heat. Season the halibut and shrimp with salt and pepper and, when the oil is hot but not smoking, add the halibut to the pan. Cook, without stirring, until the halibut is browned on the first side, 2 to 3 minutes. Stir the halibut briefly and cook for 30 seconds longer on the other side. Using a slotted spoon, transfer the halibut to a plate.

Add the remaining 1 tablespoon oil to the pan over high heat. When the oil is hot but not smoking, add the garlic and cook, stirring, until light brown, 1 to 2 minutes. Add the chili (use the smaller amount if you want a milder dish) and cook, stirring, for 15 sec-

onds. Add the shrimp, stir, and cook until barely done, about 1½ minutes. Add the juice from the can of clams along with the wine and bring to a boil. Return the halibut to the pan and add the drained clams. Cook and stir gently for just 5 seconds, then remove the pan from the heat.

Pour the seafood mixture into the bowl holding the chilled vegetable mixture, re-cover, and refrigerate until cold, 1 to 2 hours. Just before serving, add the tomatoes, parsley, basil, and vinegar and toss to mix. Spoon the seafood-vegetable mixture into oversized martini glasses and top with a little of the hot popcorn. Serve at once, with the remaining hot popcorn on the side.

SERVES 6 TO 8

popcorn for dinner?

Traveling through South America I fell in love with the dry roasted corn served with ceviche. I have adapted to use flavored popcorn . . . Incredible! Serve with Blood Orange White Sangria (page 194).

the right temperature

The definition of "room temperature" should say cellar temperature, as all good red wines taste twice as good at 58°F–60°F. Repurposed decanters like this are perfect for keeping your wines the right temperature.

when to decant

If you're opening an expensive, top-drawer red wine that is meant to age, and you're serving it young, giving it some air will oxidize it, thus accelerating the aging process.

OPPOSITE, CLOCKWISE FROM TOP: SEAFOOD GAZPACHO COCKTAIL WITH FLAVORED POPCORN, PAGE 57;

BLOOD ORANGE WHITE SANGRIA, PAGE 194; POP CULTURE POPCORN, PAGE 47

NAPA NIÇOISE SALAD—As a chef I can either build upon a classic recipe or deconstruct it and put it back together with a new identity. In this case, I have taken all the things I have always liked about a Niçoise salad and presented them in a completely different way.

COOKING NOTES: You need plenty of oil to cook the potatoes correctly. If you end up with too much oil, you can easily pour it off, but be sure to start with a lot. And get it hot. You want to sear the outside of the potatoes right away, or they will absorb too much oil. Don't be frightened by the length of this recipe. Simply make it the entire meal and enjoy.

ENTERTAINING NOTES: Party food should have a "wow factor." When you bring this beautiful array to the table, you are offering guests an element of surprise. When you tell the story of how it evolved from a classic southern French salad to an elegant mousse, they will remember the tale. And finally, when they take their first bite of the tuna mousse, you'll see the wow factor at work in their faces. Busy hosts will be happy to know that the mousse can be made up to 4 days in advance and stored, tightly covered, in the refrigerator. Bring it to room temperature before serving. The potatoes can be boiled up to 4 hours in advance, left at room temperature, and then browned just before serving.

WINE NOTES: Pour a crisp, cool Sauvignon Blanc.

FOR THE POTATOES:

16 small yellow-fleshed new potatoes, about 2 ounces each, unpeeled

Finely ground sea salt, preferably gray salt

½ cup extra-virgin olive oil

8 cloves garlic, peeled but left whole

Freshly ground black pepper

1 teaspoon minced fresh thyme

FOR THE TUNA MOUSSE:

2 cans (7 ounces each) imported Italian olive oil–packed tuna, drained

4 teaspoons fresh lemon juice

4 teaspoons soy sauce

4 teaspoons balsamic vinegar

2 tablespoons plus 2 teaspoons unsalted butter, at room temperature

Finely ground sea salt, preferably gray salt

Freshly ground black pepper

2 tablespoons heavy cream

FOR THE VINAIGRETTE:

¼ cup red wine vinegar

2 tablespoons Dijon mustard

1 teaspoon minced thyme

Finely ground sea salt, preferably gray salt

Freshly ground black pepper

1 cup extra-virgin olive oil

FOR THE ASPARAGUS:

2 pounds asparagus, tough ends removed

1 cup water

¼ cup extra-virgin olive oil

Finely ground sea salt, preferably gray salt

Freshly ground black pepper

1 cup (about 5 ounces) Sweet 100 or other small cherry tomatoes, stemmed

⅔ cup oil-cured olives

⅔ cup caper berries or ½ cup drained capers

Boil the potatoes: In a saucepan, combine the potatoes with water to cover by 1 inch. Add 1 tablespoon salt and bring to a boil over high heat. Reduce the heat to medium and simmer until the potatoes are just tender, 10 to 12 minutes. Drain the potatoes in a colander and let cool to room temperature.

Make the tuna mousse: In a food processor, pulse the tuna to break it up. With the machine running, add the lemon juice, soy sauce, and balsamic vinegar. Add the butter and process until smooth, then stop the food processor and scrape down the sides of the processor bowl. Season to taste with salt and pepper and process again. Check the seasoning, then add the cream and pulse to blend. Be careful not to overblend once the cream is added or the mixture may break. Scrape into a bowl. You should have about 1 1/2 cups.

Make the vinaigrette: In a small bowl, combine the vinegar, mustard, thyme, 1/2 teaspoon salt, and 1/2 teaspoon pepper and whisk to dissolve the salt. Slowly whisk in the olive oil to form an emulsion. Set aside.

Cook the asparagus: In a large skillet, combine the asparagus, water, olive oil, 1 teaspoon salt, and 1/4 teaspoon pepper. Cover the skillet and bring to a boil over high heat. Cook until the asparagus spears are tender but not soft, about 6 minutes. Using tongs, transfer the asparagus in a single layer to a rimmed baking sheet. Pour the liquid in the skillet over the asparagus. Let cool. Drain well and pat dry before serving.

Cut the cooled potatoes into quarters. In 1 or 2 large skillets over high heat, heat the olive oil. Just before the oil begins to smoke, add the potatoes, cut side down, in a single layer. Cook until the potatoes begin to brown on one side, about 10 minutes. Do not stir the potatoes as they brown, but tilt the pan occasionally to distribute the oil evenly. Add the garlic, 1 teaspoon each salt and pepper, and the thyme. Stir the potatoes once, then use tongs to turn each potato so that the unbrowned side is now facedown. Continue to cook until browned on the second side, about 5 minutes longer. Remove from the heat.

In a small serving bowl, combine the tomatoes and olives. Whisk the vinaigrette again and pour into a small serving bowl. On a large platter, arrange the potatoes, asparagus, caper berries, and tuna mousse in separate piles, leaving room for the tomato and vinaigrette bowls. Serve the salad while the potatoes are still warm.

SERVES 8

2 days before	1 day before	morning of	1 hour before	service
shop, make tuna mousse	make vinaigrette, trim asparagus	blanch asparagus, prepare potatoes to first phase, set table	remove tuna from refrigerator, cook potatoes, arrange platter, chill and open wine	season and serve

PLT SALAD — Everybody understands a BLT (bacon, lettuce, and tomato sandwich). My PLT is an Italian second cousin, and two steps removed from a BLT. For the first twist, the bacon is swapped out for pancetta. Second, the sandwich is swapped for a salad. I finish the salad with a roasted garlic basil dressing made from the pancetta drippings . . . *voilà!*

COOKING NOTES: Take this dish from great to awesome by using brilliantly colored heirloom tomatoes. You could also substitute other lettuces or salad greens, but be sure they are pungent. Spring mix, for example, would be too sweet for these big flavors. To keep the basil in the dressing from discoloring, do not add it until just before you add the dressing to the salad.

ENTERTAINING NOTES: You can assemble these salads an hour in advance and refrigerate them until serving. Slip the forks into the freezer at the same time. Your guests will especially appreciate the ice-cold forks on a hot summer day. The salads also look good served in over-sized bowls, rather than on plates.

WINE NOTES: Serve good-quality Pilsner beer in icy glasses.

1 ½ pounds pancetta, sliced ¼ inch thick

Extra-virgin olive oil as needed

2 tablespoons thinly sliced garlic

¼ cup red wine vinegar

Finely ground sea salt, preferably gray salt

Freshly ground black pepper

1 ¼ cups lightly packed torn fresh basil leaves

FOR THE BRUSCHETTA:

6 large slices country-style bread, about ¾ inch thick

Extra-virgin olive oil for brushing

Finely ground sea salt, preferably gray salt

2 ½ to 3 pounds ripe tomatoes

8 to 9 cups thinly sliced hearts of romaine lettuce (from 1 large head)

Unroll the pancetta slices and cut them crosswise into 1-inch lengths. In a large skillet, cook the pancetta over medium heat until it renders much of its fat and the pancetta begins to get crisp, about 20 minutes. Drain the pancetta in a sieve placed over a heat-proof measuring pitcher. Add olive oil to the pancetta fat as needed to total 1 cup.

Return the fat to the skillet and place over high heat. Add the garlic and cook until it begins to brown, 1 to 2 minutes. Immediately add the vinegar, then season to taste with salt and pepper. Remember, the pancetta will add saltiness to the finished salad, so do not oversalt at this point. Remove the skillet from the heat and let cool to room temperature. This will be the dressing for the salad. Measure out ½ cup of the basil and reserve for adding to the dressing just before serving.

Make the bruschetta: Preheat the oven to 500°F. Place the slices in a single layer on a rimmed baking sheet and toast in the oven until golden brown and just beginning to crisp, about 6 minutes. (You can also toast the bread on a stove-top grill.) Remove from the oven and lightly brush the bread slices on both sides with olive oil, then season lightly with salt. Let cool.

Core the tomatoes and quarter them lengthwise through the stem end, then cut each wedge into ½-inch chunks. In a small bowl, combine the tomatoes with the remaining basil. Season to taste with salt and pepper. Mix well.

To serve, arrange a row of lettuce down the center of each plate. Arrange the tomatoes on one side of the lettuce. Cut each bruschetta on the diagonal into 2 or 3 pieces, and arrange the pieces on the other side of the lettuce. Place some pancetta in the center of each plate. Whisk together the dressing in the skillet, add the reserved basil, and whisk briefly again. Spoon an equal amount of the dressing over each plate. Serve at once.

SERVES 6

SUPER-QUICK MINESTRONE — This recipe reveals my secret to making a good minestrone soup in record time. After less than thirty minutes on the stove top, you have it done. As all chefs know, outstanding soup is all about building layers of flavor, one at a time. Here, first you have the pancetta and garlic, then the vegetables and herbs, and finally a good stock with depth. I finish the soup with Parmesan cheese and a drizzle of olive oil. Serve it with grilled or toasted country-style bread brushed with olive oil.

COOKING NOTES: For the best flavor, make the soup the day before you plan to serve it so the flavors have a chance to blend. Add the cooked pasta just before serving. If it sits in the soup too long, it develops a flabby texture. To vary the flavors, use other vegetables such as asparagus or chard, tomatoes or mushrooms. *Tubetti* (little hollow tubes) are the classic pasta for minestrone, but you could substitute another small pasta shape.

ENTERTAINING NOTES: To turn this soup into a meal, serve it with skewers of grilled lamb, beef, and/or chicken sausages.

Finely ground sea salt, preferably gray salt

1 cup (4 ounces) *tubetti*

Extra-virgin olive oil as needed

6 cups chicken stock

¼ pound pancetta, cut into ½-inch pieces

6 cloves garlic, halved lengthwise

2 cups finely chopped yellow onion (2 small onions)

1 cup diced celery (¼-inch dice; 2 medium stalks)

1 cup diced carrot (¼-inch dice; 2 to 3 medium carrots)

1 tablespoon finely chopped fresh thyme or rosemary

4 cups diced green and/or yellow zucchini
  (¼-inch dice; 5 small zucchini)

2 cups diced, peeled russet potato (¼-inch dice; 1 large potato)

1 can (14½ ounces) tomatoes, drained and diced

1 can (14 ounces) cannellini beans, drained and rinsed

Freshly ground black pepper

1 cup freshly grated Parmesan cheese

Bring a large pot of salted water to a boil over high heat. Add the *tubetti* and cook until al dente. Drain thoroughly in a colander and transfer to a rimmed baking sheet. Toss the pasta with a little olive oil to prevent sticking.

In a large saucepan, heat the chicken stock over medium heat. Adjust the heat to maintain a bare simmer.

Meanwhile, in another large saucepan, heat ¼ cup olive oil over high heat. When the oil is hot but not smoking, add the pancetta and cook, turning occasionally, until it begins to brown, 3 to 4 minutes. Add the garlic and cook, stirring occasionally, until it begins to brown, about 1 minute. Reduce the heat to medium and add the onion, celery, and carrot. Cook the vegetables, stirring occasionally to prevent browning, until soft, 8 to 10 minutes.

Season the vegetables with 1 teaspoon salt. Add the thyme and raise the heat to high. Add the zucchini, potato, tomatoes, and beans, and then pour in the hot stock. Taste the stock and adjust with more salt. Cook the soup, skimming off any foam that forms on the surface, until the potato pieces are tender, 12 to 15 minutes. Season generously with pepper. A few minutes before serving, add the cooked pasta and heat through.

Ladle the soup into warmed bowls and serve at once. Pass the Parmesan cheese and olive oil at the table.

SERVES 8 TO 10

ROASTED TOMATO SOUP WITH SUNNY-SIDE-UP CROUTON — This recipe was created to celebrate the tomato in all its summer glory. Too many tomato soups are made with tasteless tomatoes. You need to roast them, and roast them really well until they are black in spots. Use good olive oil and vinegar, plenty of salt and pepper, and, of course, lots of garlic.

COOKING NOTES: When you use tomatoes at the absolute height of their season, their skins are thin, so you don't need to peel them for this soup or strain the skins out of the finished soup.

ENTERTAINING NOTES: Everything here can be made hours ahead except for the eggs. You can use a poached or basted egg, but basted eggs with bright yolks look nicer, and the flavored oil makes a delicious drizzle. I love barely warm soups in summer, and this soup can be served warm or at room temperature.

FOR THE SOUP:

12 large, ripe tomatoes, about 4 pounds total weight

½ cup extra-virgin olive oil

¼ cup balsamic vinegar

12 large cloves garlic, peeled but left whole

Finely ground sea salt, preferably gray salt

Freshly ground black pepper

1 cup finely chopped yellow onion

2 cups water

2 cups lightly packed fresh basil leaves

FOR THE BRUSCHETTA:

1 loaf country-style bread, 1 pound

Extra-virgin olive oil for brushing

Finely ground sea salt, preferably gray salt

FOR THE EGGS:

Extra-virgin olive oil for frying

1 teaspoon red pepper flakes

8 large eggs

1 cup torn fresh basil leaves

Preheat the oven to 500°F.

Prepare the tomatoes for the soup: Core the tomatoes and quarter them lengthwise. In a large bowl, mix the tomatoes, ¼ cup of the olive oil, the vinegar, garlic, 1 teaspoon salt, and ½ teaspoon pepper. Spread the tomatoes on a nonreactive rimmed baking sheet. Roast the tomatoes in the oven until very dark in spots, 35 to 40 minutes. Remove from the oven and let cool. Leave the oven on.

Make the bruschetta: Cut the bread crosswise into slices about 1 inch thick. You will need 8 slices. Place the slices in a single layer on a rimmed baking sheet and toast in the oven until golden brown and just beginning to crisp, about 6 minutes. Remove from the oven and lightly brush the bread slices on both sides with olive oil, then season lightly with salt. Let cool.

In a large saucepan, combine the remaining ¼ cup olive oil, the onion, and a pinch of salt over medium heat. Cook the onion, stirring occasionally, until very soft, 8 to 10 minutes. Raise the heat to high and add the roasted tomatoes and water. Bring to a simmer, adjust the heat to maintain the simmer, and cook for 5 minutes. Season to taste with salt and pepper.

Remove from the heat and let cool slightly. Working in batches, puree the tomato mixture with the basil, starting at a slow speed and increasing the speed gradually. The mixture should be very smooth. Alternatively, you can use an immersion blender right in the pan. You should have about 8 cups. (You can prepare the soup to this point and refrigerate several hours in advance. When ready to serve, bring to room temperature or reheat gently over medium heat.)

Cook the eggs: Over medium-high heat, use 2 skillets large enough for 4 eggs each; add enough oil to cover the bottom of each skillet by ⅛ inch. Divide the red pepper flakes evenly between the skillets, scattering them evenly over the bottom, then crack 4 eggs into each pan. Cook the eggs until the yolks are barely set, about 4 minutes, occasionally tilting each skillet to collect some oil in a spoon and pouring it over the yolks. Remove the eggs from the skillets with a slotted spatula.

To serve the soup, place 1 bruschetta in the center of each of eight shallow soup bowls. Pour the soup around the bruschetta. Place an egg on top of each bruschetta. Garnish with the torn basil. Drizzle the flavored oil from the skillets over each bowl of soup and serve.

SERVES 8

ROASTED TOMATOES WAITING TO BE TURNED INTO SOUP.

pre-cook & chill out

The benefit to poaching the eggs is they can be cooked an hour in advance and put in ice water a little underdone, then simply immersed in simmering water briefly before serving.

OPPOSITE: ROASTED TOMATO SOUP WITH SUNNY-SIDE-UP CROUTON, PAGE 64

GRILLED AVOCADO AND TOMATO SALAD WITH "GREEN GODDESS" DRESSING—I went to university in Miami, where the avocados are gigantic but not nearly as flavorful as the California crop. I resorted to grilling them to add some extra kick and stumbled on a huge flavor. Back in California, the rich avocados are truly spectacular on the grill. Sometimes success in the kitchen is as simple as adding an unexpected technique to an expected ingredient. The dressing here is not your mother's green goddess recipe, which is laden with mayonnaise and green herbs for the color. Here, the richness and much of the color comes from the avocados.

COOKING NOTES: I always toast pine nuts on a baking sheet in a preheated 350°F oven, which takes about 4 minutes. They burn too easily in a sauté pan on the stove top.

ENTERTAINING NOTES: You can also use this versatile dressing as a dip for crudités, on a retro iceberg lettuce salad, or for chicken salad sandwiches.

WINE NOTES: This a good time to serve a flowery and fruity Viognier.

FOR THE DRESSING:

2 avocados, halved, pitted, peeled, and chopped

2 tablespoons roughly chopped fresh basil

1 tablespoon roughly chopped fresh tarragon

1 tablespoon roughly chopped fresh Italian (flat-leaf) parsley

1 teaspoon minced garlic

1/8 teaspoon powdered ascorbic acid (vitamin C) (optional)

2 tablespoons fresh lime or lemon juice

Finely ground sea salt, preferably gray salt

Freshly ground black pepper

1/2 cup extra-virgin olive oil

FOR THE SALAD:

10 tomatoes

4 avocados, halved, pitted, and peeled

5 tablespoons extra-virgin olive oil

2 lemons

Finely ground sea salt, preferably gray salt

Freshly ground black pepper

1 red onion, sliced

1 cup freshly grated Parmesan cheese

1/4 cup pine nuts, lightly toasted

Make the dressing: In a food processor, combine the avocados, basil, tarragon, parsley, garlic, and the ascorbic acid, if using. Process until very smooth. Add the lime juice, 1/2 teaspoon salt, and 1/4 teaspoon pepper and process until well mixed. With the machine running, add the olive oil in a slow, steady stream. If the dressing is very thick, add cold water as needed to create a pourable dressing. Transfer to a bowl, cover, and refrigerate until needed.

Make the salad: Ready a charcoal or gas grill for direct heat grilling over a medium-hot fire. Core the tomatoes, quarter through the stem end, and arrange on a large platter; set aside. Place the avocado halves in a bowl and drizzle with 2 tablespoons of the olive oil and the juice of 1 lemon. Season to taste with salt and pepper and toss gently to coat evenly.

Place each avocado half, flat side down, on the grill and grill until well caramelized, 30 to 45 seconds. Remove and place, flat side up, on top of the tomatoes. Do not grill on the second side.

In another bowl, squeeze the juice from the remaining lemon over the onion slices and mix well. Add the remaining 3 tablespoons olive oil, season to taste with salt and pepper, and toss to coat evenly. Divide the onion slices evenly among the avocado halves, draping them over the hollows left by the pits. Spoon the lemon–olive oil mixture remaining in the bowl over the avocados and onion slices. Top with the dressing, distributing evenly and generously on all sides. Sprinkle with the cheese and pine nuts and serve at once.

SERVES 8 AS A FIRST COURSE, OR 4 AS A MAIN COURSE

chillin' then grillin'

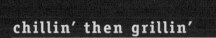

The trick to grilling fruit (really avocado is a fruit) is to chill before grilling and flash grill over a hot flame to keep the inside cool.

SALAD OF QUICK CHICKEN CONFIT—Duck confit is one of my favorite flavors in the fall. The bird's rich meat is deliciously enhanced by this French curing and cooking technique. For a larger group, I substitute chicken to ensure broad appeal, but don't be afraid to try this recipe with duck.

COOKING NOTES: Toasting the spices brings their buried flavors to the surface, and often with surprising results. Do you know that one of the principal flavors in gin comes from the juniper berry? You will taste the echo of gin here.

ENTERTAINING NOTES: The shortcut here is that the chicken gets a quick cure, which busy cooks with guests arriving can appreciate. The traditional French method for confit calls for salting the meat, slowly cooking it in its own fat over low heat, and then packing the meat into jars, covering it with the same fat, and storing it for several months. Here, I am simply adding the flavors, which embed themselves into the meat, and using the chicken right away. The pulled chicken is also good in a salad, with pasta and greens, or even for breakfast.

WINE NOTES: Pour a big, fat California Chardonnay.

FOR THE CHICKEN:

1 tablespoon black peppercorns

1 tablespoon juniper berries

¾ cup kosher salt

7 bay leaves

8 bone-in, skin-on chicken thighs, 3½ to 4 pounds total weight

2 cups olive oil

1 head garlic, split in half crosswise

6 to 8 fresh thyme sprigs

1½ pounds yellow-fleshed potatoes, unpeeled, cut crosswise into ¼-inch-thick slices

1 teaspoon finely chopped fresh thyme

1 teaspoon grated lemon zest

Finely ground sea salt, preferably gray salt

Freshly ground black pepper

¼ cup cider vinegar

2 Granny Smith apples

8 cups roughly chopped frisée

Prepare the chicken: In a small skillet, toast the peppercorns and juniper berries over high heat, shaking the skillet occasionally, until they begin to smoke, about 4 minutes. Pour into a mortar or mini-processor and let cool. Add the kosher salt and 4 of the bay leaves, torn into pieces. Grind the mixture to a medium grind.

Spread the salt mixture on a dinner plate. Dredge each chicken thigh in the salt mixture, coating on all sides and using all of the mixture. Place the thighs in a single layer on a rimmed baking sheet. Cover with plastic wrap and refrigerate for 45 minutes.

Rinse the thighs under running cold water. Pat very dry with paper towels. Pour ¼ cup of the olive oil into a large skillet. Place the garlic halves, cut side down, in the skillet. Set the pan over medium-high heat and cook until the garlic is well browned on the cut side, about 6 minutes. Turn the garlic over. Add the chicken thighs, skin side down, to the skillet and cook until well browned on the skin side, about 12 minutes. Add the thyme sprigs and the remaining 3 bay leaves. Turn the thighs over on top of the herbs. Reduce the heat to low. Add the remaining 1¾ cups oil to the skillet, bring the oil to a low simmer, and cook the chicken, uncovered, for 1½ hours. At this point, the chicken will be very tender and almost falling off the bone. Remove the skillet from the heat and allow the meat to cool in the oil, about 30 minutes.

Preheat the oven to 350°F.

Remove ¾ cup oil from the skillet used to cook the chicken and heat it in another large skillet set over medium-high heat. When it begins to smoke, add the potato slices in a single layer. You may need to cook the potatoes in 2 batches. Be careful, as the oil may splatter because it has chicken juices in it. Cook the potatoes, turning once, until tender and golden brown on both sides, about 20 minutes total. Using a slotted spatula, transfer the potatoes to paper towels to drain. Season to taste with salt.

Return the skillet used to cook the potatoes to medium-high heat. When the fat is hot, using tongs, remove the chicken thighs from the first skillet and add to the hot fat, skin side down. Cook until the skin side is golden brown and crispy, 2 to 3 minutes. Turn the chicken thighs over, reduce the heat to medium, and cook until golden brown on the second side, about 2 minutes. Remove the chicken thighs to a baking sheet. Put the reserved potatoes on another baking sheet. Put the chicken and the potatoes in the oven while you assemble the salad.

Remove ¼ cup of the oil from the skillet used to cook the chicken and pour it into a medium bowl. Add the chopped thyme, lemon zest, ½ teaspoon sea salt, and ¼ teaspoon pepper. Whisk in the vinegar to form an emulsion that will be the dressing.

Quarter and core the apples and cut them lengthwise into ¼-inch-thick slices. In a large bowl, mix the apples and frisée.

Remove the chicken and potatoes from the oven. Pull the chicken meat from the bones and shred into ½-inch-wide strips (be careful—it will be hot). Add the chicken to the apples and frisée. Drizzle enough of the dressing over the salad to coat the ingredients lightly (you may not need all of it) and toss well. Divide the salad among individual plates and garnish each plate with several slices of crisp potato. Serve immediately.

SERVES 8

2 days before	1 day before	morning of	1 hour before	service
shop	make confit and refrigerate	slice and blanch potatoes, clean greens, make vinaigrette	slightly warm chicken, cook potatoes	arrange and enjoy

TRICOLOR SALAD WITH FRICCO CRACKERS AND CAESAR "VINAIGRETTE" —Be quiet, already, about the egg yolk in a Caesar dressing. This one rocks without it. It is basically a broken Caesar dressing, just like a vinaigrette. It is great on this salad that echoes the green, red, and white of the Italian flag, or you can use it on pasta. *Fricco*, sometimes spelled *frico*, is a melted-cheese cracker native to the kitchens of Friuli, in northeastern Italy. It is traditionally made with a local cheese, *monstasio*, but here I have used the easier-to-find Parmesan.

COOKING NOTES: If possible, make the dressing a day ahead and keep it in the refrigerator. It likes to sit, so the garlic and anchovy flavors can bloom. Remove from the refrigerator 1 hour before using, to bring to room temperature. You can also make the *fricco* crackers a day ahead, wrap them in plastic wrap, and keep at room temperature.

ENTERTAINING NOTES: Make extra dressing to send home with your guests. They will be able to relive one aspect of the great meal they ate at your house throughout the week.

WINE NOTES: A Pinot Grigio is a good match.

FOR THE DRESSING:

2 cloves garlic

Finely ground sea salt, preferably gray salt

6 olive oil–packed anchovy fillets, minced

1 tablespoon Champagne vinegar

1 tablespoon Dijon mustard

1½ teaspoons fresh lemon juice

¼ teaspoon Worcestershire sauce

Dash of Tabasco sauce or other hot-pepper sauce

Freshly ground coarse black pepper

½ cup olive oil

2 tablespoons freshly grated Parmesan cheese

FOR THE CRACKERS:

2¼ cups freshly grated Parmesan cheese

3 heads Belgian endive, separated into whole leaves

1 head radicchio, separated into whole leaves

3 cups (about 3 ounces) lightly packed arugula, tough stems removed

1 tablespoon freshly grated Parmesan cheese

Make the dressing: On a cutting board, chop and smear the garlic and ¼ teaspoon salt together until you create a smooth paste. Transfer the paste to a small bowl and add the anchovies, vinegar, mustard, lemon juice, Worcestershire sauce, Tabasco sauce, and ½ teaspoon pepper. Mix well. Gradually whisk in the olive oil. Add the cheese and whisk again. Set the dressing aside for 1 hour or longer. You should have about ¾ cup.

Make the crackers: Heat an 8-inch nonstick skillet over medium heat. Sprinkle 6 tablespoons of the cheese into the pan, creating an even lace-thin layer that fills the bottom of the skillet. The cheese cracker will bubble in the pan. When the top surface of the cracker is pale gold, after 3 to 4 minutes, remove the pan from the heat and allow the cracker to firm up for 1 minute. Carefully turn the cracker over with a spatula, return to medium heat, and cook until the cracker is golden on the second side, about 1 minute longer. Using the spatula, transfer the cracker to paper towels to drain. Wipe the skillet clean with paper towels and repeat the process 5 more times with the remaining cheese, to create 6 crackers in all.

In a large bowl, combine the endive, radicchio, and arugula. Drizzle enough dressing over the top to coat the leaves lightly (you may not need all the dressing). Toss to coat the leaves evenly. Arrange the leaves on 6 individual plates. Sprinkle ½ teaspoon of the grated Parmesan over each salad. Split each cracker into 2 or 3 pieces and garnish the salads with them. Serve immediately.

SERVES 6

GRILLED SALMON AND SPINACH SALAD WITH CORN JUICE "ZABAGLIONE" — Corn juice is one of my secret flavors. I use it in everything from bloody Mary mixes to stews. Here I am once again borrowing a method for a traditionally sweet concoction, the frothy egg zabaglione, and using it for a stellar savory presentation. The key here is to make the zabaglione at the height of corn season, when the flavor will be at its best.

COOKING NOTES: You need a heavy-duty juicer for the corn. If you don't have a juicer, start with about 50 percent more corn, puree in a food processor, and strain the puree to get the juice. Or simply ask your natural grocer to help you out.

ENTERTAINING NOTES: The elements that go into this salad work great for crostini, too. Top each bread slice with some julienned spinach, a little piece of salmon, and some of the sauce. Or, for an amazing brunch, adapt the recipe to eggs Benedict, using the salmon in place of the ham or Canadian bacon and the zabaglione in place of the hollandaise.

WINE NOTES: This is another good match for one of my favorite new white wine varietals, Viognier from France. Ask your wine merchant for his or her favorite.

8 ears corn, shucked

FOR THE ZABAGLIONE:

3 large egg yolks

Finely ground sea salt, preferably gray salt

Freshly ground black pepper

FOR THE SALAD:

6 cups (about 6 ounces) lightly packed baby spinach

1 pint Sweet 100 tomatoes, stems removed and halved through the
    stem end

¼ cup Whole-Citrus Vinaigrette (page 18)

2 tablespoons finely chopped fresh chives

6 skinless salmon fillets, each 5 to 6 ounces and 1 inch thick

Extra-virgin olive oil for brushing

Finely ground sea salt, preferably gray salt

Freshly ground black pepper

With a sharp knife, cut the kernels off the ears of corn. Measure out and reserve 1½ cups kernels and juice the remaining kernels. You should have about 1½ cups corn juice.

Make the zabaglione: Pour water to a depth of about 2 inches into a saucepan or the bottom pan of a double boiler and bring to a bare simmer. In a stainless-steel or other heatproof bowl or the top pan of the double boiler, whisk together the egg yolks, corn juice, 1 teaspoon salt, and ½ teaspoon pepper. Set the pan bowl over—but not touching—the simmering water and whisk the yolk mixture vigorously until frothy and thick, 12 to 15 minutes. Do not let the sauce boil. If it gets too hot, remove the pan or bowl from over the water for a few seconds. To test if the sauce is thick enough, scoop up some of it with the whisk; the sauce should fall back on itself like a ribbon and remain visible on the surface for a few seconds before it dissolves into the whole. Pour the sauce into a thermos or bowl, cover, and keep warm (next to the stove) until ready to serve. It will keep for up to 1 hour.

Preheat a grill pan over medium-high heat.

While the pan is heating, make the salad: In a large bowl, combine the spinach, tomatoes, and reserved corn kernels. Drizzle enough of the vinaigrette over the salad to dress the vegetables lightly (you may not need all of it) and toss well. Arrange the salad on a platter or individual plates. Reserve the chives for adding later as garnish.

Lightly coat the salmon on both sides with olive oil; season with salt and pepper. Place on the hot pan and grill, turning once, until brown on both sides and medium-rare in the center, about 8 minutes.

Remove the salmon fillets from the pan and place them on top of the salad, or divide among the individual salads. Spoon the warm zabaglione over the salmon and sprinkle the chives on top. Serve at once.

SERVES 6

SLICED ORANGE SALAD WITH SAUTÉED OLIVES AND RICOTTA SALATA—One of the tricks of the chef trade is to cook for all the senses. In this dish, I put together sweet orange slices with salty cheese, and warm olives with a cool salad. The results will fill your mouth with contrasting flavors.

COOKING NOTES: Ricotta salata is a snow white, lightly salted Italian sheep's milk cheese with a semifirm, dense texture. It is popular in southern Italy, especially Sicily, where it is often added to pastas.

ENTERTAINING NOTES: The olives can be sautéed hours in advance, and the vinaigrette can be made up to 2 weeks in advance. That leaves only two quick tasks to the last minute, cutting the oranges and tossing them with the spinach.

WINE NOTES: The natural citrus quality of Sauvignon Blanc marries well with the citrus in the recipe.

4 navel oranges

2 tablespoons extra-virgin olive oil

1 tablespoon finely chopped fresh rosemary

½ cup oil-cured black olives, pitted and halved

6 cups (about 6 ounces) lightly packed baby spinach or arugula

¼ cup Whole-Citrus Vinaigrette (page 18)

Finely ground sea salt, preferably gray salt

Freshly ground black pepper

2 ounces *ricotta salata* cheese

Using a vegetable peeler, remove the zest from 1 orange in strips. Cut the strips lengthwise as thinly as possible until you have 1 tablespoon thin slices. Reserve the thin slices and discard the remaining zest. Using a large, sharp knife, place the peeled orange upright on a cutting board and cut off the pith, following the contour of the fruit. Peel the remaining 3 oranges, one at a time, by first cutting off the stem and blossom end, revealing the flesh, and then cutting away the peel and pith, following the contour of the fruit. Cut all 4 oranges crosswise into ¼-inch-thick slices. Cut each slice in half to form half-moons and remove any seeds.

In a 10-inch skillet, heat the olive oil over high heat. When the oil is hot, add the rosemary and cook for a few seconds, then add the olives. Cook for 10 seconds, then add the thinly sliced zest. Cook for a few seconds longer, then remove the skillet from the heat and allow the mixture to cool in the skillet.

Put the spinach in a large bowl. Pour the olive-orange mixture from the skillet over the spinach and add the vinaigrette. Toss gently to coat the spinach evenly. Add the reserved orange slices and toss a bit more to incorporate the oranges, being careful they do not break up. Season to taste with salt and pepper.

Transfer the salad to a serving platter or individual soup plates. Grate the *ricotta salata* over the top. Serve immediately.

SERVES 4 TO 6

WARM PANCETTA, GOAT CHEESE, AND SPINACH SALAD — This salad was on the Tra Vigne menu for many years. When all was said and done, I must have eaten a hundred pounds of it, because each time I made it, I couldn't resist taking a bite.

COOKING NOTES: Laura Chenel began making French-style goat cheese in Sonoma County, California, in the early 1980s, making her a true pioneer in America's artisanal-cheese movement. Many American cheese makers have followed her lead. If you cannot find a good American-made fresh goat cheese, look to the French imports.

ENTERTAINING NOTES: To make the salad ahead of time, make the dressing right up to the point where you add the vinegar, then remove the skillet from the heat. When you are ready to serve, have the spinach and cheese ready, reheat the dressing, and finish as directed. Garnish with big crostini (page 42, using country topping) and you'll have an awesome first course.

WINE NOTES: I developed this salad for Laura Chenel and Dan Duckhorn. Laura makes goat cheese and Dan makes Sauvignon Blanc. The cheese and wine are a classic match, but the challenge was how to incorporate them into a salad with vinegar, which can overwhelm wine. I discovered that if you cook the vinegar, getting the acetic acid down and the flavor of the vinegar up, it works beautifully with wine.

6 cups (about 6 ounces) lightly packed baby spinach

5 ounces fresh goat cheese, preferably Laura Chenel brand

1/3 pound pancetta, thickly sliced

Extra-virgin olive oil as needed

1 tablespoon minced garlic

2 teaspoons minced fresh thyme

1/4 cup sherry vinegar

Finely ground sea salt, preferably gray salt

Freshly ground black pepper

1/2 cup dried sour cherries, dried cranberries, or raisins

Put the spinach in a large bowl. Crumble the cheese over the spinach.

Unroll the pancetta slices and cut into strips about 1 inch long and 1/4 inch wide. Put the pancetta in a skillet over medium heat and cook, stirring occasionally, until crispy, 8 to 10 minutes. Drain the pancetta in a sieve placed over a heatproof measuring pitcher. Add olive oil to the pancetta fat as needed to total 1/4 cup.

Pour the fat back into the pan, add the pancetta, and return the pan to medium-high heat. When the pancetta is warm again, add the garlic and cook, stirring occasionally, until light brown, about 30 seconds. Add the thyme and let it crackle in the fat for about 10 seconds. Add the vinegar and season to taste with salt and pepper. Cook for about 30 seconds to reduce the acidity of the vinegar. You should see tiny drops of vinegar dispersed throughout the fat. Add the dried cherries and stir.

Pour the hot dressing over the spinach and cheese. Toss to coat the leaves evenly and melt the cheese a little. Divide among individual salad plates and serve immediately.

SERVES 4

"SUPER-TUSCAN" WHITE BEAN SOUP—In Tuscany, this type of soup appears during the fall festivals that celebrate the new crop of dried beans. This traditional soup is so popular that I have family friends there who eat it every day for half the year.

COOKING NOTES: In this soup, the bean is the hero. Cook the beans 1 or 2 days before serving the soup, seasoning them well enough to serve them by themselves. You need quite a bit of salt to get the flavor all the way to the center of the beans. Let them cool in their cooking liquid. If made the day before, reheat slowly and add water if it is too thick. For an extra flourish, garnish with Prosciutto Bits (page 19).

ENTERTAINING NOTES: To turn this soup into a casual winter supper, cook ½ pound short tube pasta just short of al dente, drain, and add to the soup a minute before serving. You can also expand the taste profile of the soup by adding a small amount of a highly flavored ingredient, such as sautéed wild mushrooms or butternut squash. Simply sprinkle it on top when serving. I have used a diluted version of the soup as a sauce for fish, too. It's wonderful, especially with the pesto drizzle as a finishing touch.

FOR THE BEANS:

1 pound dried cannellini beans

2 ounces thinly sliced prosciutto

1 yellow onion, quartered lengthwise

1 celery stalk, quartered crosswise

1 carrot, peeled and quartered crosswise

2 cloves garlic, lightly crushed

1 bay leaf

4 cups chicken stock

Finely ground sea salt, preferably gray salt

FOR THE BRUSCHETTA:

6 slices country-style bread, each ¾ inch thick

Extra-virgin olive oil for brushing

Finely ground sea salt, preferably gray salt

¼ cup extra-virgin olive oil

Finely ground sea salt, preferably gray salt

Freshly ground black pepper

1 tablespoon minced garlic

¼ to ½ teaspoon red pepper flakes

¼ cup lightly packed fresh basil leaves

¼ cup basil pesto, homemade (page 21) or purchased

½ cup freshly grated Parmesan cheese

Cook the beans: Rinse the beans, place in a saucepan, and add cold water to cover by 2 inches. Bring to a boil, cover, and remove from the heat. Let stand for 1 hour, then drain.

Return the beans to the saucepan and add the prosciutto, onion, celery, carrot, garlic, and bay leaf. Pour in the chicken stock and then add water as needed to cover the beans by 2 inches. Slowly bring to a simmer over medium-low heat. (If you heat them too fast, the skins may break.) Adjust the heat to maintain a bare simmer and cook, uncovered, until the beans are almost tender, 20 minutes or longer, depending on the age of the beans. Add salt to taste and continue cooking until the beans are tender but not mushy, about 20 minutes longer. Remove from the heat and let the beans cool in the liquid.

Meanwhile, make the bruschetta: Preheat the oven to 500°F. Place the bread slices in a single layer on a rimmed baking sheet and toast in the oven until golden brown and just beginning to crisp, about 6 minutes. (You can also toast the bread on a stove-top grill.) Remove from the oven and lightly brush the bread slices

on both sides with olive oil, then season lightly with salt. Let cool.

Strain the cooled beans and other solids through a sieve, reserving the liquid. In a food processor, puree the beans and other solids in batches with 3½ cups of the cooking liquid and 2 tablespoons of the olive oil. Using a rubber spatula, push the solids through a fine-mesh sieve into a clean saucepan (you should have about 6 cups soup in the pan). Season to taste with salt and pepper, then bring to a simmer over medium heat, stirring occasionally.

Meanwhile, in a small skillet over high heat, warm the remaining 2 tablespoons olive oil. Turn on the fan above your stove. Add the garlic to the skillet and cook, stirring occasionally, until it begins to turn brown. Add the red pepper flakes and cook for a few seconds, then add the basil. Cook until the basil wilts. Add the mixture to the soup. Taste the soup again and adjust the seasoning.

Ladle the hot soup into warmed bowls. Float a bruschetta on top of each bowl. Serve with pesto and Parmesan cheese.

SERVES 6

MELON AND PROSCIUTTO "AS SOUP"—Everyone knows the classic Italian antipasto of melon and prosciutto. But have you ever had the melon turned into a cool soup and the prosciutto finely cut and cooked until crisp like bacon bits? The combination is not only heavenly, but also simple to prepare.

COOKING NOTES: The most important element of this recipe is perfectly ripe melons. You can use almost any variety except watermelon (which makes a soup that's too thin), but the melons must be at the peak of their season. Off-season fruits have traveled too far and don't have sufficient flavor.

ENTERTAINING NOTES: Sometimes, instead of soup plates, I serve this soup in oversized martini glasses that have been dipped in water and slipped in the freezer for at least 10 minutes to frost.

2 cantaloupes, about 10 pounds total weight, halved, seeded, peeled, and
    cut into 1-inch pieces
Finely ground sea salt, preferably gray salt
⅓ cup honey
⅓ cup fresh lemon juice

12 fresh mint leaves
2 tablespoons dark rum (optional)
⅓ cup mascarpone cheese
2 tablespoons Prosciutto Bits (page 19)
Freshly ground black pepper

Put 8 soup plates in the freezer. Working in batches, combine the cantaloupe pieces, 1 teaspoon salt, honey, lemon juice, 10 of the mint leaves, and the rum, if using, in a blender and process until very smooth. Taste and adjust the seasoning. Cover and refrigerate until well chilled, about 2 hours. Alternatively, pour the soup into a stainless-steel bowl, float the bowl in an ice-water bath prepared in a larger bowl or in the sink, and stir until cool enough to serve.

Finely julienne the remaining 2 mint leaves. Ladle the soup into the chilled soup plates. Garnish the center of each bowl with a dollop of the mascarpone. Sprinkle the Prosciutto Bits on the mascarpone. Top each serving with a sprinkle of the julienned mint and a grind of pepper. Serve immediately.

SERVES 8

a dinner with Sinatra

OPPOSITE: PASTINA TIMBALE, PAGE 85

Pasta and rice are made for entertaining: easy to prepare, generally cooked in only one pan, affordable, and, if prepped in advance, on the table in a half hour or less. They also can deliver drama to an evening of entertaining. Imagine a three-foot-wide paella pan being walked around the table, the carrier stopping alongside each guest who helps him- or herself to some fragrant Italian sausage, spicy shrimp, and saffron rice. Washed down with a fine Spanish claret, it's entertaining at its best.

pasta & rice

Let the marketplace help you decide which dish in this chapter to serve. In spring, prepare a beautiful platter of Pea-and-Potato Ravioloni with Sage Brown Butter (page 92), or go decadent with Pappardelle with Asparagus and Gorgonzola Cream (page 83). In fall or winter, consider serving a simple Pumpkin Risotto (page 98) or a more elaborate Lasagna of Roasted Butternut Squash (page 88). Come summertime, keep the kitchen cool by putting together a platter of Spaghettini with Uncooked Watercress (page 100).

GNOCCHI ALLA ROMANA — The word *gnocchi* means "dumplings" in Italian. Throughout Italy, various forms of this classic are prepared, generally from a dough based on potatoes in the north and on semolina flour in the south. Most of the variation comes in the sauce. Nearly every form requires rolling the dough into ropes and then cutting the ropes by hand, and sometimes even rolling the smaller pieces a second time on a butter paddle or other tool to give them a distinctive marking. Clearly, the Romans tried making these dumplings for their large feasts and ran into the same problem I have: too much work! Hence, these Roman-style gnocchi are quite different and very easy to prepare for large groups.

COOKING NOTES: You can use different cheeses for topping the gnocchi, such as crumbled blue cheese in place of the Fontina or pecorino in place of the Parmesan. In spring, I sometimes skip the substantial tomato sauce and instead arrange the gnocchi on a bed of sautéed greens.

ENTERTAINING NOTES: The sauce can be made up to 3 days ahead of serving, covered, and refrigerated. You can assemble the dishes in advance as well. The day before, spoon the sauce into the baking dishes, arrange the gnocchi on top, sprinkle the cheeses over the gnocchi, cover with plastic wrap, and refrigerate. The day of the party, pull the dishes from the refrigerator, let them sit for about a half hour to take the chill off, and then bake. Or, you can serve the gnocchi family style, with the whole batch arranged in one very large baking pan that is passed around the table.

For an hors d'oeuvre, brown the rounds of gnocchi on both sides on a hot griddle, spoon a little sauce in the middle of each one, set a small piece of Fontina cheese on the sauce, and top with a little freshly grated Parmesan. Arrange on a baking sheet and slide it under a preheated broiler until the cheese melts and the dumplings are light brown on top. Pass the hors d'oeuvres on trays.

WINE NOTES: A top-flight Chianti is the best choice here.

FOR THE SAUCE:

2 tablespoons extra-virgin olive oil

½ cup finely chopped yellow onion

1 tablespoon chopped fresh Italian (flat-leaf) parsley

1 large clove garlic, minced

3 cups fresh tomato puree (see the Pantry, page 14) or 1 can (28 ounces) whole tomatoes, pureed with their juice

1 large fresh basil sprig, with leaves removed

Finely ground sea salt, preferably gray salt

FOR THE SEMOLINA DUMPLINGS:

2 quarts (8 cups) whole milk

4 tablespoons (½ stick) unsalted butter

½ teaspoon freshly grated nutmeg

Finely ground sea salt, preferably gray salt

1 pound (3¼ cups) semolina flour

1 cup freshly grated Parmesan cheese

Extra-virgin olive oil for brushing

½ pound Fontina cheese, preferably from Valle d'Aosta, finely shredded

½ cup freshly grated Parmesan cheese

Make the sauce: In a large nonreactive saucepan, heat the olive oil over medium-low heat. Add the onion and sauté, stirring occasionally to prevent browning, until translucent, about 8 minutes. Add the parsley and garlic and cook for 10 seconds to release their fragrance. Add the tomato puree, basil, and 1 teaspoon salt, raise the heat to medium, bring to a simmer, and simmer briskly, stirring occasionally to prevent sticking, until reduced to a saucelike consistency, about 10 minutes. Note that the sauce will reduce slightly in the oven later, so you may want to leave it a little thinner than usual. The timing will depend on the ripeness and meatiness of your tomatoes and the size of your pan. If the sauce thickens too much before the flavors have developed, add a little water and continue cooking. Taste and adjust the seasoning. Remove the basil stem and discard. You should have 2 to 2 ½ cups.

Make the semolina dumplings: In a large saucepan, combine the milk, butter, nutmeg, and 1 tablespoon salt. Place over medium-high heat and heat until the milk barely simmers. Add the semolina in a steady stream, whisking vigorously. Change to a wooden spoon and stir until the mixture comes together in a thick paste, 3 to 5 minutes. Be sure to get into the corners of the pan. Reduce the heat to low and cook for 15 minutes, stirring occasionally to prevent scorching. The mixture will begin to pull away from the sides of the pan. Add the cheese, stirring again with the wooden spoon to combine thoroughly. Remove the pan from the heat.

Cut 4 pieces of aluminum foil, each about 12 by 15 inches. Brush 1 tablespoon olive oil over the bottom half of each piece of foil. Using a rubber spatula dipped in cold water, scoop up the semolina dough and divide it among the 4 sheets of foil, placing it on the oiled halves. When the semolina mixture is cool enough to handle, dampen your fingers and shape it into rough logs, each about 8 inches long and 1 ½ inches in diameter. Starting from the oiled side, gently roll the foil around each log, forming a uniform cylinder. Twist the ends of the foil in opposite directions to tighten the foil around the dough. Refrigerate the cylinders for at least 6 hours or up to overnight.

Preheat the oven to 400°F.

Lightly grease 8 to 10 individual ovenproof dishes with olive oil if serving as a first course, or 4 to 6 larger individual dishes if serving as a main course. Spoon an equal amount of the sauce on the bottom of each dish. Unwrap the dough cylinders and cut crosswise into ½-inch-thick rounds. Arrange the rounds on top of the sauce, dividing them evenly among the dishes and slightly overlapping them. Scatter the Fontina and Parmesan cheeses over the top.

Bake until golden brown on top, 20 to 25 minutes. Remove from the oven and let cool for about 5 minutes. Serve warm.

SERVES 8 TO 10 AS A FIRST COURSE, OR 4 TO 6 AS A MAIN COURSE

PARTY-METHOD FONTINA RISOTTO — Risotto is always popular at parties, but making it poses a challenge: How do you stand over the stove and stir for a half hour when you have guests to entertain? I do what I always do in restaurants: cook the risotto about halfway ahead of time, let it cool down, and then finish it quickly when I am ready to serve it.

COOKING NOTES: Making great risotto is about 50 percent technique and 50 percent flavor. You have to sweat the onions and garlic well (for the proper foundation flavor), you have to toast the rice in the oil (to maintain the individual rice shape), and you have to stir the rice almost constantly (to avoid the rice on the bottom from being cooked before the rice on the top is). And don't be afraid of the generous additions of butter and cheese at the end; they contribute big flavor. Add whatever additional flavors you like to this base method, such as pesto, roasted peppers, or sautéed mushrooms, but remember that if you add a puree or sauce, you must count it as part of the overall liquid in the recipe.

ENTERTAINING NOTES: If you plan to serve the risotto on a buffet, make it looser than you think it should be. In even a short amount of time sitting out, the rice will absorb the extra liquid. If you have leftover risotto, pour it while it is still warm into a mold or two, such as coffee mugs lined with plastic wrap. The next day, unmold the risotto, slice into disks, dust the disks with flour, and sauté them in a little butter. With poached eggs on top, these disks make a scrumptious breakfast for company—or even just for you.

WINE NOTES: Search out a good Syrah or a smooth Italian Nebbiolo.

FOR THE RICE:

4 cups chicken stock

¼ cup extra-virgin olive oil

¾ cup finely chopped yellow onion

1 tablespoon minced garlic

Finely ground sea salt, preferably gray salt

3 cups Arborio rice

¾ cup dry white wine

FOR FINISHING THE RISOTTO:

4 cups chicken stock

2 tablespoons extra-virgin olive oil

1 tablespoon minced garlic

1 teaspoon finely chopped fresh rosemary

¾ cup dry white wine

2 tablespoons unsalted butter

1 cup finely shredded Fontina cheese, preferably from Valle d'Aosta

Finely ground sea salt, preferably gray salt

Freshly ground black pepper

Partially cook the rice: In a saucepan, bring the 4 cups chicken stock to a simmer over medium-high heat. Adjust the heat to maintain a bare simmer. In a 12-inch-wide saucepan or other wide, deep pan, combine the olive oil, onion, garlic, and 1 teaspoon salt over medium heat. Cook until the onion sizzles, then reduce the heat to low. Cook the onion, stirring occasionally, until soft and translucent, about 10 minutes; do not let it color. Add the rice and cook, stirring, until the outer layer of the rice begins to crack and pop, 2 to 3 minutes. Add the wine and raise the heat to medium-high. Simmer, stirring often, until almost all the wine is absorbed. Begin adding the hot stock 1 cup at a time, stirring often and adding more liquid when the previous addition has been mostly absorbed. Adjust heat as needed to maintain a gentle simmer. Cook until the rice has the consistency of creamy oatmeal, 8 to 10 minutes after the first addition of stock.

Pour the rice onto a 13-by-18-inch rimmed baking sheet, forming a thin layer. Let cool until steam is no longer rising. Cover with plastic wrap and refrigerate until cold or up to 24 hours.

Finish the risotto: In a saucepan, bring the 4 cups chicken stock to a simmer over medium-high heat. Adjust the heat to maintain a bare simmer. Heat the olive oil over high heat in the same wide pan you used for cooking the rice. Add the garlic and rosemary and cook for about 10 seconds to release their fragrance. Using a rubber spatula, scoop up the cooled risotto and add it to the pan along with the wine. Cook, stirring often, until the mixture comes to a simmer. When almost all of the wine has been absorbed, begin adding the hot stock 1 cup at a time, stirring often and adding more liquid only when the previous addition has been mostly absorbed. When the rice is al dente, 8 to 10 minutes after the first addition of stock, remove the pan from the heat. You may not need all 4 cups stock.

Stir the butter and cheese into the risotto, mixing them in thoroughly. Season to taste with salt and pepper. Serve at once.

SERVES 6 AS A MAIN COURSE, OR 12 AS A FIRST COURSE

PAPPARDELLE WITH ASPARAGUS AND GORGONZOLA CREAM — You and your friends have been eating your chicken skinless for months, bread is a distant memory, and butter . . . well, you can forget about all that. You're all about to abandon your low-carb diets. In fact, why not host a jump-off-the-diet-wagon party? This is just the dish to satisfy your carb cravings. One night is not going to kill you, so sit back and enjoy the ride and go back to the dreaded diet mill in the morning.

COOKING NOTES: For a more substantial dish, you can mix some shredded grilled or roasted chicken into the sauce after you have added the cheese. Be sure to have plenty of bread on hand for mopping up the last bit of sauce at the bottom of the bowl. Also, be generous with cracked black pepper at the table. The sauce alone works well as a fondue, too. Use asparagus, broccoli, or torn pieces of country-style bread for dipping.

ENTERTAINING NOTES: If you are doubling this recipe for a larger party, substitute another pasta, such as rigatoni. Shorter pasta is easier to serve and eat by the spoonful, and the pasta on the bottom of the dish is not as likely to clump together under the weight of the extra pasta on top.

WINE NOTES: A rich, oaky Chardonnay is a good match for the cream sauce.

FOR THE ASPARAGUS:

2 pounds thick asparagus, tough ends removed

1 cup water

¼ cup extra-virgin olive oil

Finely ground sea salt, preferably gray salt

Freshly ground black pepper

Finely ground sea salt, preferably gray salt

1 pound dried *pappardelle* or other wide noodles

FOR THE SAUCE:

1 tablespoon unsalted butter

1 tablespoon minced garlic

1 teaspoon finely chopped fresh thyme

2 cups heavy cream

Finely ground sea salt, preferably gray salt

Freshly ground black pepper

½ pound Gorgonzola or Cambozola cheese, crumbled

2 teaspoons freshly grated lemon zest

½ cup freshly grated Parmesan cheese

Freshly ground black pepper

Cook the asparagus: In a large skillet, combine the asparagus, water, olive oil, 1 teaspoon salt, and ¼ teaspoon pepper. Cover the skillet and bring to a boil over high heat. Cook until the asparagus spears are tender but not soft, about 6 minutes. Using tongs, transfer the asparagus in a single layer to a rimmed baking sheet. Pour the liquid in the skillet over the asparagus. When the spears are cool enough to handle, cut each one crosswise into 4 equal sections and return them to the baking sheet.

Bring a large pot of salted water to a boil over high heat. Add the *pappardelle* and cook until al dente.

While the pasta water is heating, make the sauce: In a skillet, melt the butter with the garlic over medium-low heat. Cook, stirring to prevent the garlic from browning, for 2 minutes. Add the thyme and cook for about 10 seconds to release its fragrance. Add the

cream, raise the heat to medium, and season with salt and pepper. (Be careful not to add too much salt; the cheese, which is added later, will contribute a salty flavor.) Simmer until reduced by about one-fourth, 10 to 12 minutes. Add the cheese and whisk until the sauce is smooth. Taste and adjust the seasoning if necessary. You should have about 2½ cups sauce.

When the pasta is ready, drain in a colander and transfer to a warmed large serving bowl. Add the asparagus and the liquid from the baking sheet and then pour on the sauce. Add the lemon zest and mix well. Sprinkle a little of the Parmesan cheese over the top and pass the rest at the table. Finally, grind the pepper over the top. Serve at once.

SERVES 6 TO 8 AS A FIRST COURSE

PASTINA TIMBALE — I simply love the little round baby pasta called *pastina*. In my family, it is the first solid food a kid eats. Using this typical soup pasta to make this molded baked dish is a fun and innovative way to serve my favorite pasta. And the dish has huge entertainment value: remember the famous *timpano* served up by the brothers in the 1996 film *Big Night*?

COOKING NOTES: You can use other small pasta shapes, such as orzo or *riso*, or simply pulse *spaghettini* in a food processor until it breaks into tiny lengths. Over time, scientists have bred the acid out of tomatoes grown in this country, so you don't need to cook them very long to get them sweet. That means I am able to use a quick-cooked tomato sauce for this recipe, saving valuable time.

ENTERTAINING NOTES: You can make the pasta mixture the day before, put it in the molds, cover, and refrigerate. At serving time, simply reheat in a 350°F oven for 20 minutes (or until warm in the middle). Let rest for 10 minutes to firm up before attempting to turn out and serve. I like to unmold these in front of my guests, so they can be part of the suspense. If one doesn't unmold cleanly, at least my guests were entertained. With a big group, try one large (3-quart) bowl for a dramatic family-style presentation. Increase the baking time to 45 minutes and the rest time before unmolding to 15 minutes.

WINE NOTES: Pick a ripe, large, and luscious Zinfandel.

---

6 tablespoons extra-virgin olive oil, plus more for brushing

2 teaspoons minced garlic, plus 1 tablespoon thinly sliced garlic

1 cup fresh bread crumbs

½ cup coarsely chopped fresh (flat-leaf) Italian parsley

¾ cup freshly grated Parmesan cheese

1 pound spicy fresh Italian sausages

2 teaspoons thin serrano chili slices

½ cup torn fresh basil leaves

3 cups fresh tomato puree (see the Pantry, page 14) or 1 can (28 ounces) whole tomatoes, pureed with their juice

Finely ground sea salt, preferably gray salt

1 pound *pastina*

1 tablespoon unsalted butter (optional)

Freshly ground black pepper

In a skillet, heat 2 tablespoons of the olive oil and the minced garlic together over medium heat and sauté, stirring occasionally, until the garlic is light brown, about 2 minutes. Add the bread crumbs and cook, stirring occasionally, until lightly toasted, 3 to 5 minutes. Move the bread crumb mixture to a bowl and let cool. Add ¼ cup each of the parsley and Parmesan cheese and 2 more tablespoons of the oil to the bread crumb mixture and toss to mix.

Brush eight 1½-cup ramekins or small stoneware cereal bowls lightly with olive oil and line with the bread crumb mixture, using your fingers to distribute it evenly on the bottom and up the sides. Set aside.

To make the sauce, heat the remaining 2 tablespoons olive oil in a large saucepan over high heat. Add the sausages and cook, turning occasionally, until evenly browned, 10 to 12 minutes. Using tongs or a slotted spoon, transfer the sausages to paper towels to drain. Pour off all but 2 tablespoons of the fat from the saucepan. Reduce the heat to medium-low. Add the sliced garlic and chilies and cook, stirring occasionally, until the garlic begins to brown, about 1 minute. Add the basil and cook for 15 seconds. Then add the tomato puree and simmer, stirring occasionally, until reduced by one-fourth, 15 to 20 minutes.

While the sauce is simmering, bring a large pot of salted water to a boil over high heat. Add the *pastina* and cook until just shy of al dente. Drain the *pastina* in a colander.

When the sauce is ready, cut the sausages in half lengthwise, then cut crosswise ¼ inch thick, creating half-moons. Remove the saucepan with the sauce from the heat. Return the sausages to the saucepan and add the drained *pastina*. Add the remaining ¼ cup parsley, the remaining ½ cup Parmesan cheese, and the butter, if using. Season with salt and pepper and stir to combine. Taste and adjust the seasoning.

Transfer the pasta mixture to the prepared lined ramekins, spooning about 1¼ cups into each ramekin. Let cool for 10 minutes. Invert the ramekins onto warmed individual plates and serve at once.

SERVES 8 AS A FIRST COURSE OR SIDE DISH

BRODETTO OF SHRIMP-STUFFED PASTA SHELLS — Your guests will love this seafood feast for its gratifying flavors, and days later they will still remember its whimsy. Combining stuffed pasta shells and seashells on the same platter is just the kind of playfulness that takes a good meal from eating to entertainment.

COOKING NOTES: In Italy, the word *brodetto* is commonly used for a seafood stew, although it can refer to meat-based dishes as well. When I am cooking the garlic in this recipe, I tilt the pan so it fries in a little pool of oil collected on one side. By doing this, I am concentrating the cooking in a smaller surface area, which prevents overbrowning. If garlic gets too dark, it becomes bitter. If you cannot find rock shrimp, use 2¼ pounds medium-sized regular shrimp, peeled, deveined, and halved lengthwise.

ENTERTAINING NOTES: You can boil the pasta shells, stuff them with the shrimp mixture, and then cover and refrigerate them for up to 24 hours before finishing the dish. They will need to remain in the oven a little longer than 15 minutes to heat the filling. The broth can also be made the day before. When it is time to eat, bake the pasta in the oven, cook the clams and mussels in the broth, and that's it!

WINE NOTES: Serve with a dry Chardonnay that has strong citrus notes.

Finely ground sea salt, preferably gray salt	Pinch of saffron threads (about ¼ teaspoon)
24 jumbo pasta shells *(conchiglie)* (about one 12-ounce box)	2 pounds mussels, scrubbed and debearded
½ cup plus 3 tablespoons extra-virgin olive oil	2 pounds clams, scrubbed
2 pounds rock shrimp	¼ cup finely chopped fresh Italian (flat-leaf) parsley
Freshly ground black pepper	2 tablespoons finely chopped fresh basil
3 tablespoons thinly sliced garlic	2 teaspoons finely chopped fresh tarragon
2 teaspoons fennel seeds	¼ cup fine dried bread crumbs
¼ cup Pernod or brandy (optional)	2 tablespoons freshly grated Parmesan cheese
2 cups dry white wine	4 tablespoons (½ stick) unsalted butter (optional)
3 cups fresh tomato puree (see the Pantry, page 14) or 1 can (28 ounces) whole tomatoes, pureed with their juice	

Bring a large pot of salted water to a boil over high heat. Add the pasta shells and cook until three-fourths done, about 10 minutes. Drain in a colander and immediately rinse under running cold water to stop the cooking. Drain thoroughly, transfer to a wide, shallow bowl, and toss with 1 tablespoon of the olive oil, coating the shells evenly.

Preheat the oven to 375°F.

Spread the shrimp on a rimmed baking sheet covered with plastic wrap and liberally season them with salt and pepper. In a large skillet, heat ¼ cup of the olive oil over high heat. When the oil just begins to smoke, add the shrimp, spreading them out in a single layer. Do not stir them. Cook the shrimp for 1 minute, turn them over, and cook the second side halfway, about 1 minute longer. Throw away the plastic wrap the shrimp were on, and transfer the shrimp to the baking sheet. Let cool.

Return the skillet to high heat and add 2 tablespoons of the olive oil. When the oil is hot but not smoking, add the garlic. Tilt the pan to collect the oil and garlic on one side. When the garlic begins to brown, after about 30 seconds, set the pan flat on the burner and, standing back a little in case the Pernod should flame, add the fennel seeds and Pernod, if using. Wait until any flames subside, then add the wine and scrape up any browned bits from the pan bottom. Add the tomato puree and saffron and cook, uncovered, over medium-high heat until the liquid is reduced by half, 20 to 25 minutes. Season to taste with salt and pepper.

Add the mussels and clams (discarding any that do not close to the touch), cover, reduce the heat to medium, and cook for 3 to 4 minutes. Uncover the skillet and remove any opened clams and mussels to a platter (the mussels will probably open first). Re-cover the skillet and continue to cook for 8 to 10 minutes longer, checking every now and again and removing the remaining mussels and clams as they open (discard any unopened mussels or clams).

Return the shrimp to the skillet and cook for 15 seconds. Remove the pan from the heat and, using a slotted spoon, transfer the shrimp to a food processor. Process the shrimp for 15 seconds.

Add 6 tablespoons of the tomato broth to the shrimp. Combine the parsley, basil, and tarragon in a small bowl; add half of the herb mixture to the shrimp and half to the broth remaining in the pan. Add the bread crumbs and cheese to the shrimp; pulse to combine the ingredients. You should have about 4 cups shrimp mixture.

Using a large spoon, fill the pasta shells with the shrimp mixture and place them, shell opening facing up, in an oiled 9-by-13-inch baking dish. Drizzle the remaining $\frac{1}{4}$ cup olive oil over the top of the shells. Cover the dish with aluminum foil. Bake the shells until the filling is warm throughout, about 15 minutes.

Meanwhile, place the skillet with the tomato broth over high heat, add the butter (if using), and allow to melt. Add the reserved mussels and clams with any accumulated juices. Cook, stirring occasionally, until the broth and the mollusks are warm, 2 to 3 minutes.

Arrange the baked pasta shells on a warmed large, deep platter. Using a slotted spoon, remove the mussels and clams from the broth and arrange on the platter with the shells. Pour the tomato broth over the pasta shells and shellfish. Serve at once.

SERVES 8 AS A MAIN COURSE

think outside the box

Here a glass fishbowl doubles as a serving bowl for a Brodetto of seafood.

LASAGNA OF ROASTED BUTTERNUT SQUASH

— Who says lasagna has to be made with layers of pasta? Why not roll pasta sheets around a savory filling and cover the rolls with sauce? Not only do the rolls look fantastic, but they are also easier to serve.

COOKING NOTES: Cutting the squash into small chunks means you can cover more surface area with the herbs and spices. Also, when you roast the chunks, you get better caramelization and more flavor.

ENTERTAINING NOTES: The morning before your party, fill the pasta sheets with the squash and cheese, arrange the rolls in baking dishes, pour the sauce over the top, cover with plastic wrap, and refrigerate. Then, 1 ½ to 2 hours before serving, slip the lasagna, uncovered, into the oven and bake until golden brown.

WINE NOTES: A nice, big Pinot Noir is great with this dish.

FOR THE SQUASH:

1 large or 2 small butternut squashes, about 3 pounds total weight

2 tablespoons extra-virgin olive oil

1 ½ tablespoons finely chopped fresh sage

Finely ground sea salt, preferably gray salt

1 tablespoon Toasted Spice Rub (page 16)

2 cups whole-milk ricotta cheese (one 15-ounce container)

1 cup freshly grated Parmesan cheese

2 large eggs

1 teaspoon freshly grated nutmeg

Freshly ground black pepper

Finely ground sea salt, preferably gray salt

1 pound dried lasagna sheets (24 sheets), each 6 ½ by 3 inches

Extra-virgin olive oil for tossing

FOR THE SAUCE:

2 quarts (8 cups) whole milk

6 tablespoons (¾ stick) unsalted butter

2 tablespoons minced fresh sage

2 teaspoons minced garlic

6 tablespoons all-purpose flour

Finely ground sea salt, preferably gray salt

1 teaspoon freshly grated nutmeg

1 pound mozzarella cheese, finely shredded

1 cup freshly grated Parmesan cheese

1 ½ teaspoons Toasted Spice Rub (page 16)

Roast the squashes: Preheat the oven to 400°F. Cut the squash(es) in half crosswise. Trim about ½ inch off the rounded end of each half so you can stand it upright on a cutting board. Working with one half at a time and using a sharp knife, cut downward to remove the hard shell. Remove the seeds and coarsely chop the squash into ½-inch chunks.

Line a baking sheet with aluminum foil. In a bowl, toss the squash with the olive oil, sage, 1 teaspoon salt, and the spice mixture. Spread the squash in a single layer on the baking sheet. Roast the squash, stirring once or twice, until very soft and beginning to brown, 40 to 50 minutes.

Remove the squash from the oven and transfer to a food processor. Process until smooth. You should have 2 to 2½ cups puree. In a large bowl, combine the squash puree, ricotta and Parmesan cheeses, eggs, nutmeg, 1 teaspoon salt, and ½ teaspoon pepper. Stir until well mixed. Cover and refrigerate until needed.

Bring a large pot of salted water to a boil over high heat. Add the lasagna sheets and cook until al dente. Drain the sheets in a colander, toss with a little olive oil to coat lightly, and spread them on a rimmed baking sheet. Set aside.

Make the sauce: In a large saucepan, bring the milk to a slow simmer over medium heat. Adjust the heat so the milk stays hot but is not simmering. In a large pot, melt the butter over medium-low heat. Add the sage and garlic and cook, stirring occasionally, until fragrant and the garlic begins to soften, about 30 seconds. Add the flour and stir for 2 to 3 minutes to combine well with the butter. Do not allow the mixture to color. Add the milk all at once, whisking vigorously to prevent lumps. Add 2 teaspoons salt and the nutmeg and adjust the heat to maintain a slow simmer. Cook, whisking frequently, until the sauce coats the back of a spoon, about 8 minutes. Remove from the heat. You should have about 8 cups sauce.

Preheat the oven to 375°F. Butter two 9-by-13-inch baking dishes.

Spread each lasagna sheet flat on a work surface. Spread about 3 tablespoons of the squash mixture evenly over each sheet, leaving about ½ inch of the sheet uncovered at one of the shorter ends. Sprinkle about 2 tablespoons mozzarella cheese on top of each sheet. Working with 1 sheet at a time, and starting at the shorter end where the squash mixture covers completely to the edge, loosely roll the sheet into a cylinder. As the cylinders are formed, layer them in a single layer in the 2 prepared baking dishes. Using half of the sauce for each pan, pour it evenly over the rolls. Dust the tops evenly first with the Parmesan cheese and then the spice mixture.

Bake the rolls until golden brown and bubbling, 1 to 1¼ hours. Remove from the oven and let rest for 5 minutes before serving.

SERVES 8 TO 10 AS A MAIN COURSE

2 days before	1 day before	morning of	1 hour before	service
shop	prepare squash puree, prepare sauce, grate cheese	assemble lasagna rolls, set table	heat sauce to finish lasagna and bake, open wine	serve and enjoy

PAELLA, ITALIAN STYLE — Paella for a large group is one of my all-time favorite ways to entertain. I once helped a friend of mine, famous chef Julian Serrano, make enough paella for two thousand people. We cooked and served it in giant paella pans the size of a person. Incredible! Taking the flavor of my cooking and applying it to a traditional paella results in a Spanish-Italian sensation. One of the best things about dishes like this one is you get the protein, vegetable, and starch all in one big treat.

COOKING NOTES: You need to overseason when you sauté because a lot of seasoning gets lost in the pan. By being generous, there is plenty of seasoning for the rice, too. The paprika has to be the real deal, so look for Spanish *pimentón de La Vera*. Ramos brand has a good smoky flavor, a signature of this Iberian product. For the spicy sausage, seek out a Calabrian salami or *soppressata* or dried Spanish chorizo. The addition of *pepperoncini*, small, pickled lime-green hot peppers packed in jars, is a southern Italian touch that my family always favors. They are widely carried in supermarkets. Bruno's is my favorite brand.

ENTERTAINING NOTES: It's a good idea to buy one large or a few smaller paella pans if you intend to make this recipe. Look for them at better cookware stores or at online sources.

WINE NOTES: Make a batch of my Blood Orange White Sangria (page 194) and watch the party take on its own life! Or, pour a more reserved Spanish claret.

---

4 boneless, skinless chicken breast halves, about 2 pounds total weight

Finely ground sea salt, preferably gray salt

Freshly ground black pepper

1 pound large shrimp, peeled and deveined

⅓ cup extra-virgin olive oil

6 ounces spicy dried Italian sausage, cut crosswise into ¼-inch-thick slices, and slices quartered if large

3½ teaspoons Spanish paprika

2 tablespoons fresh oregano leaves

1 cup finely chopped yellow onion

½ cup finely chopped celery

½ cup finely chopped carrot

3 cups Arborio rice

6 cups chicken stock

1 teaspoon saffron threads

1 can (14½ ounces) crushed tomatoes or 1 pound fresh tomatoes, peeled, seeded, and quartered through the stem end

1 small jar *pepperoncini*

Remove the tenderloins (small muscle on the underside) from the chicken breasts and reserve for another use. Cut the chicken breasts in half lengthwise, then cut crosswise into 1½-inch pieces. Season with 1½ teaspoons salt and ½ teaspoon pepper and set aside. Season the shrimp with ½ teaspoon salt and ¼ teaspoon pepper and set aside.

Select a large ovenproof pan. A sauté pan or skillet 12 inches wide and 3 to 4 inches deep is a good choice, or a paella pan if you have one. Place the pan over high heat and add the olive oil. When the oil is almost smoking, add the chicken. Cook, turning once, until well browned on both sides, 6 to 7 minutes total. Add the sausage to the pan and cook for 10 seconds. Add the shrimp to the pan, stir once, and then cook for 2 to 3 minutes until it begins to turn pink. Add 1½ teaspoons of the paprika and the oregano and stir once. Pour the mixture onto a baking sheet to cool.

Return the pan to high heat. Add the onion, celery, and carrot and then pour in the juices from the baking sheet. When the vegetables sizzle, reduce the heat to medium-low and cook, stirring occasionally, until the vegetables are soft but not brown, about 10 minutes.

Meanwhile, preheat the oven to 350°F.

Raise the heat to high. Add 1 teaspoon salt, ½ teaspoon pepper, and the remaining 2 teaspoons paprika. Cook for 2 minutes, stirring occasionally. Add the rice. Stir to coat the kernels evenly with the oil and seasonings and then cook for 1 minute. Add the stock and bring to a simmer. Add the saffron, then taste and adjust the seasoning if needed. Cook until the liquid returns to a simmer, then add the tomatoes and stir to incorporate.

Cover the pan (if you don't have a lid, use aluminum foil), place in the oven, and cook for 15 minutes. Liquid will no longer be visible on the surface. Remove the pan from the oven and return the chicken, sausage, and shrimp to it, distributing them evenly. Re-cover the pan and return it to the oven. Cook until everything is heated through and the rice is tender, 10 to 15 minutes longer.

Open the jar of *pepperoncini* and empty them and their vinegary brine into a small bowl. Spoon the paella onto warmed plates, or set the pan on the table and let your guests help themselves. Pass the *pepperoncini* at the table. Invite guests to add a couple *pepperoncini* and a drizzle of the brine to their servings.

SERVES 8 TO 10 AS A MAIN COURSE

2 days before	1 day before	morning of	1 hour before	service
rest	shop, prepare vegetables	set table	saute meat, fish and vegetables, start rice	finish paella in the oven

PEA-AND-POTATO RAVIOLONI WITH SAGE BROWN BUTTER — Tender peas are typically the first spring

vegetable to appear in Northern California. As much as we locals would like winter to be over, when peas arrive, we are still in a shoulder season between winter and spring. By pairing a winter-satisfying potato with the first kiss of spring, you and your guests will be able to celebrate both.

COOKING NOTES: The term *ravioloni* indicates that these will be big stuffed pastas (the term *raviolini*, in contrast, is used for particularly small *ravioli*). The size will save you time in the kitchen and the presentation will be more dramatic.

ENTERTAINING NOTES: For a larger group, you can partially cook the *ravioloni* up to one hour in advance. Parboil them for 3 to 4 minutes in boiling salted water, then, using a slotted spoon, transfer them in a single layer to 1 or 2 rimmed baking sheets, depending on size. Add a little of the pasta water to the baking sheet(s), and cover the stuffed pastas with a large cloth napkin that has been dipped in the pasta water. Keep at room temperature. When ready to serve, heat the napkin-covered *ravioloni* in a 350°F oven for 5 to 7 minutes.

FOR THE DOUGH:

4 extra-large eggs, at room temperature

1 tablespoon extra-virgin olive oil

¼ teaspoon finely ground sea salt, preferably gray salt

2 cups all-purpose flour, plus more for dusting work surface

1 cup semolina flour, plus more for dusting dough

FOR THE FILLING:

1½ pounds russet potatoes, peeled and cut into 1½- to 2-inch chunks

Finely ground sea salt, preferably gray salt

2 tablespoons unsalted butter

½ teaspoon minced garlic

1 teaspoon finely chopped fresh thyme

1 cup heavy cream

1 teaspoon grated lemon zest

3 cups shelled English peas (from 3 pounds unshelled)

½ cup freshly grated Parmesan cheese

Freshly ground black pepper

1 egg beaten with 2 teaspoons water for egg wash

Finely ground sea salt, preferably gray salt

FOR THE SAGE BROWN BUTTER:

¾ cup (1½ sticks) unsalted butter

24 fresh sage leaves, torn in half

Finely ground sea salt, preferably gray salt

Freshly ground black pepper

Make the dough: Put the eggs, olive oil, and salt in the bowl of a stand mixer fitted with the paddle attachment or in a food processor. If using a stand mixer, mix on low until well blended. Add the all-purpose and semolina flours and continue to mix on low speed just until mixed. If using a food processor, pulse the wet ingredients to blend, then pulse in the dry ingredients just until distributed, but not so much that the mixture forms a ball. Mixing too much will make the dough tough.

Using your hands, gather the dough into a ball. On a lightly floured work surface, knead the dough gently with your palms,

repeatedly folding the dough over onto itself until it forms a smooth mass. Divide the mass into 2 equal portions. Pat each portion into a ball, flatten slightly, wrap in plastic wrap, and refrigerate for 20 minutes or up to overnight. (The dough may also be frozen at this point for about 1 month. Thaw in the refrigerator.)

Make the filling: In a saucepan, combine the potatoes with water to cover by 1 inch. Add 1 tablespoon salt and bring to a simmer over high heat. Reduce the heat to maintain a simmer and cook until very tender, about 20 minutes. Drain the potatoes in a colander, then transfer them to a large bowl. While they are still warm, mash them with a fork or potato masher until fairly smooth.

In a saucepan, melt the butter over medium-high heat. Add the garlic and cook, stirring occasionally, until beginning to soften, about 30 seconds. Add the thyme and cook for 10 seconds to release its fragrance. Add the cream and lemon zest and bring to a boil. Add the peas, reduce the heat to medium, and simmer until the peas are barely tender, 2 to 3 minutes. Remove from the heat, pour into the food processor, let cool slightly, and then process to form a smooth puree, 45 to 60 seconds. Immediately add the pea puree to the mashed potatoes. Then add the Parmesan and, using a rubber spatula, mix until well blended. Season to taste with salt and pepper. Set aside.

Working on a lightly floured work surface, roll out half of the dough as thinly as possible (less than 1/16 inch thick). Try also to roll it into as much of a rectangle as possible to facilitate cutting. Repeat with the second dough portion. Dust the pasta sheets well with semolina flour. Using a sharp knife, cut the sheets into 4-inch squares. You will need at least 36 squares to make 18 *ravioloni*.

To fill the *ravioloni*, center 1½ teaspoons or so of filling on half the pasta squares, brush all around the filling with the egg wash, and then top with the remaining pasta squares. Using your finger-tips, seal each filled pasta closed, starting from the filling and pressing gently out to the edges to force out all the air. Lay the *ravioloni* on a baking sheet lined with a flour-dusted tea towel. Lightly dust the tops with semolina flour. Use immediately or cover with a tea towel and leave at room temperature for several hours.

When ready to cook, bring a large pot of salted water to a boil. While the water is heating, make the brown butter: Put the butter in a cold skillet and place it over medium heat. Cook, stirring occasionally to prevent it from burning in spots but without moving the pan, until it stops foaming and browns evenly, 3 to 4 minutes. Add the sage leaves and cook briefly until they crisp in the hot butter. Season with salt and pepper. Remove from the heat and keep warm.

Reduce the heat under the boiling water so that the water simmers. Add half the *ravioloni* and cook until they float to the surface and feel tender on the edges, 6 to 8 minutes. Using a slotted spoon, lift out the *ravioloni* and keep them warm in a shallow layer of water on a large rimmed baking sheet.

When all of the *ravioloni* are done, transfer them to a warmed platter or individual plates and drizzle the brown butter sauce over them. Serve at once.

SERVES 6 AS A MAIN COURSE

2 days before	1 day before	morning of	1 hour before	service
shop, borrow pasta machine (if you don't have one)	make dough, prepare vegetables	roll and fill ravioli, cover and refrigerate; set table	boil water, open wine	cook ravioli, make sauce

out, out damn spot

A combo of meat tenderizer (plain) and cold water will remove
meat juice or milk stains, or any stain made from protein.

OPPOSITE: PEA-AND-POTATO RAVIOLONI WITH SAGE BROWN BUTTER, PAGE 92

too little time, so many recipes

Not a problem, if you get creative with your presentation you can serve the
same recipe three ways to triple your repertoire. Here I take one risotto and
serve it in a Chinese spoon for an hors d'oeuvre, inside a squash for an individual
serving, and finally in a multipurpose serving bowl for family style or a buffet.

PUMPKIN RISOTTO — When the air turns cool and the grape harvest is finally over in the Napa Valley, I crave autumnal flavors. Nothing evokes the season better than risotto laced with pumpkin. The colder it gets, the deeper I roast the pumpkin. A dish like this one is rich enough so that you can skip meat at the meal altogether.

COOKING NOTES: A good eating pumpkin, such as the Sugar Pie, is what you need for this dish, rather than a field pumpkin, which is better left for making a jack-o'-lantern. The wine used in the second round "freshens" the flavor of the risotto. Its acidity balances with the natural sweetness of the pumpkin.

ENTERTAINING NOTES: At the table, first drizzle truffle oil over each serving of risotto, followed by a shower of black truffle shavings. You'll see your guests' jaws drop and their mouths begin to water as the powerful scents fill the air, creating incredible anticipation for the first bite. Make sure you have paid the rent before you decide to do this, however, as the double dose of truffles will set you back at least fifty dollars.

WINE NOTES: The great thing about roasted pumpkin is that it allows you to enjoy a big Napa Zinfandel.

FOR THE PUMPKIN:

1 pumpkin, 3 to 4 pounds

2 tablespoons extra-virgin olive oil

1 tablespoon finely chopped fresh rosemary

Finely ground sea salt, preferably gray salt

Freshly ground black pepper

FOR THE RICE:

4 cups chicken stock

¼ cup extra-virgin olive oil

¾ cup finely chopped yellow onion

1 tablespoon minced garlic

Finely ground sea salt, preferably gray salt

3 cups Arborio rice

¾ cup dry white wine

FOR FINISHING THE RISOTTO:

3 cups chicken stock

2 tablespoons extra-virgin olive oil

2 tablespoons finely chopped shallot or yellow onion

¾ cup dry white wine

2 tablespoons unsalted butter

½ cup finely shredded Fontina cheese, preferably from Valle d'Aosta

½ cup freshly grated Parmesan cheese

1 teaspoon finely chopped fresh rosemary

Finely ground sea salt, preferably gray salt

Freshly ground black pepper

Balsamic vinegar for serving

Roast the pumpkin: Preheat the oven to 400°F. Cut the pumpkin in half crosswise. Trim about ½ inch off the rounded end of each half so you can stand it upright on a cutting board. Working with one half at a time and using a sharp knife, cut downward to remove the hard shell. Remove the seeds and coarsely chop the pumpkin into ½-inch chunks.

Line a 13-by-18-inch rimmed baking sheet (or 2 smaller sheets) with aluminum foil. In a bowl, toss the pumpkin with the olive oil,

rosemary, 1 teaspoon salt, and ¼ teaspoon pepper. Spread the pumpkin in a single layer on the baking sheet. Roast the pumpkin, stirring once or twice, until very soft and beginning to brown, 40 to 50 minutes. Remove the pumpkin from the oven and transfer to a food processor. Process until smooth. You should have about 2 cups puree.

Partially cook the rice: In a saucepan, bring the 4 cups chicken stock to a simmer over medium-high heat. Adjust the heat to maintain a bare simmer. In a 12-inch-wide saucepan or other wide, deep pan, combine the olive oil, onion, garlic, and 2 teaspoons salt over medium heat. Cook until the onion sizzles, then reduce the heat to low. Cook the onion, stirring occasionally, until soft and translucent, about 10 minutes; do not let it color. Add the rice and cook, stirring, until the outer layer of the rice begins to crack and pop, 2 to 3 minutes. Add the wine and raise the heat to medium-high. Simmer, stirring often, until almost all the wine is absorbed. Begin adding the hot stock 1 cup at a time, stirring often and adding more liquid only when the previous addition has been mostly absorbed. Adjust the heat as needed to maintain a steady, gentle simmer. Cook until the rice has the consistency of creamy oatmeal, 8 to 10 minutes after the first addition of stock. Stir in the pumpkin puree.

Pour the rice onto the now-rinsed baking sheet(s), forming a thin layer. Let cool until steam is no longer rising. Cover with plastic wrap and refrigerate until cold or up to 24 hours.

Finish the risotto: In a saucepan, bring the 3 cups chicken stock to a simmer over medium-high heat. Adjust the heat to maintain a bare simmer. Heat the olive oil over high heat in the same wide pan you used for cooking the rice. Add the shallot and sauté until soft, about 3 minutes; do not let it color. Using a rubber spatula, scoop up the cooled risotto and add it to the pan along with the wine. Cook, stirring often, until the mixture comes to a simmer. When almost all of the wine has been absorbed, begin adding the hot stock 1 cup at a time, stirring often and adding more liquid only when the previous addition has been mostly absorbed. When the rice is al dente, 8 to 10 minutes after the first addition of stock, remove the pan from the heat. You may not need all 3 cups stock.

Stir the butter, Fontina and Parmesan cheeses, and rosemary into the risotto, mixing them in thoroughly. Season to taste with salt and pepper. Serve at once. Pass the balsamic vinegar at the table for drizzling over the top.

SERVES 6 AS A MAIN COURSE, OR 12 AS A FIRST COURSE

2 days before	1 day before	morning of	1 hour before	service
shop	prepare pumpkin, prepare vegetables and herbs, grate cheese	make risotto to first phase, set table	finish risotto to second phase, open wine	serve and enjoy

SPAGHETTINI WITH UNCOOKED WATERCRESS — A project arrives on your desk during the last hour of the workday, and it needs to be done in time for a morning meeting. You know it will take at least two hours to complete, but it is also your turn to host your friends for dinner. Ever happen to you? It happens to me all the time and I am the boss. To the rescue comes my remake of an Italian classic, *pasta aglio e olio*, reborn with plenty of greens to make a complete meal in one dish in only the time it takes for the pasta to cook.

COOKING NOTES: Be sure to start the oil and garlic together in a cold pan to create a deeply flavored oil before the garlic gets brown. For an additional layer of flavor, stir 3 anchovy fillets in with the garlic. You will have most of the ingredients for this recipe around the house. If watercress is not handy, use young, tender arugula or baby spinach. The greens are mostly there for color. This dish is full of garlic, but not too pungent.

ENTERTAINING NOTES: Simple pastas like this one are superb served with nothing more than a platter of different cheeses and salamis and a hot loaf of crunchy artisanal bread.

WINE NOTES: Pour a nice red from Sicily or Sardinia, or both.

Finely ground sea salt, preferably gray salt

1 pound *spaghettini*

FOR THE SAUCE:

6 tablespoons extra-virgin olive oil

3 tablespoons thinly sliced garlic

½ teaspoon red pepper flakes

Finely ground sea salt, preferably gray salt

6 cups small watercress leaves

¼ cup chopped fresh Italian (flat-leaf) parsley

2 tablespoons Prosciutto Bits (page 19)

½ cup freshly grated pecorino cheese

Bring a large pot of salted water to a boil over high heat. Add the pasta and cook until al dente.

While the pasta is cooking, make the sauce: In a 12-inch skillet, combine 4 tablespoons of the olive oil and the garlic over medium heat. Cook, stirring occasionally, until the garlic begins to brown, about 2 minutes. Add the red pepper flakes and a pinch of salt and cook for 10 seconds. Scoop out ½ cup of the water from the pasta pot, add to the skillet, and remove the skillet from the heat.

When the pasta is almost cooked, return the skillet to medium heat. Remove another ½ cup of the pasta water from the pot and reserve it to the side. When the pasta is ready, drain it in a colander.

Add the pasta to the skillet and toss it with the hot oil. Add the remaining 2 tablespoons olive oil and enough of the reserved pasta water to coat the pasta lightly. Cook, stirring and tossing, for 2 to 3 minutes. Remove the skillet from the heat and add the watercress, parsley, and Prosciutto Bits and stir to wilt the leaves in the hot pasta.

Serve the pasta in warmed individual bowls or family style on a warmed large platter. Sprinkle the pecorino cheese over the top.

MAKES 6 TO 8 SERVINGS AS A MAIN COURSE,

OR 10 TO 12 SERVINGS AS A FIRST COURSE

backyard lobster bake

fish & shellfish

Large groups and fish generally don't go well together. Fish tends to be difficult to time for perfect doneness. I decided not to fight that kitchen battle, and instead created some fish recipes that love a crowd. Whole roasted Prime Rib of Swordfish (page 113) will impress the hard to impress. Ask your friends to "chip in" and bring some fish along for the "real San Francisco treat," Cioppino (page 108). Or, pull out all the stops for a Backyard Lobster Bake (page 104). Take the gloves off; you've won the fight.

Remember to preorder your fish from a local fishmonger to ensure freshness. And always follow my motto, No Fish Parties on Sunday. Most fish wholesalers are open only Monday through Friday, so the fish you buy on Saturday for a Sunday feast was probably caught no later than Thursday.

BACKYARD LOBSTER BAKE—Not everyone is lucky enough to live near the beach, but don't let that stop you from bringing the feeling of the seaside to your own backyard with a lobster bake. Start with the freshest seafood and, for an added taste of summer, prepare homemade Limoncello (page 195) for an aperitif and sangria (page 194) for guests to enjoy with the feast. You might instead hold your lobster bake at a nearby campsite. Most come with a prebuilt fire pit, which allows you to focus more on the cooking and the eating and less on the cleanup. Wherever you stage this party, you will need a large galvanized washtub, a big piece of burlap, and plenty of fuel.

COOKING NOTES: If you are tempted to buy lobsters larger than the ones I am suggesting here, never get talked into ones that weigh over 5 pounds. Larger lobsters tend to have stringy meat. Look for flexibility in the tail and a healthy sheen when selecting the crustacean. Ask your fishmonger for the seaweed, reserving it in advance. Linguica is a slender, cured Portuguese pork sausage highly flavored with garlic and paprika. It is sold in delicatessens and many supermarkets. Grilling it adds a nice smokiness and caramelized flavor to the dish. You can make this recipe on the stove top, too, using the same method. Be sure the pot overlaps a couple of burners to get the heat you will need.

ENTERTAINING NOTES: This is a casual affair. Spread newspapers out on the table and outfit guests with lobster crackers and lobster picks and with the spice mixtures, gray salt, and melted butter. Provide plenty of napkins, too.

WINE NOTES: As already noted, sangria is a natural choice. If you prefer wine, Chardonnay is a good counterpoint to the richness of the lobster.

---

4 pounds linguica sausages

15 pounds seaweed

16 live lobsters, each 1½ pounds

5 pounds small red potatoes, parboiled for 15 minutes in salted water and drained

16 ears corn, shucked

10 pounds large clams, scrubbed

2 quarts (8 cups) water

2 quarts (8 cups) dry white wine

Melted unsalted butter, Toasted Spice Rub (page 16), Roasted-Garlic Spice (page 20), and coarse sea salt (preferably gray salt) for serving

---

Purchase a no. 3 galvanized washtub at your local hardware store. Dig a fire pit in your backyard large enough to accommodate the tub. Build a fire with charcoal, mesquite chips or kindling, and wood fireplace logs in the pit. It will take 2 hours for you to get the fire and coals very hot. The fire needs to burn for at least 3 hours, so have plenty of wood on hand for continuous stoking. The coals are ready for cooking when they are covered with white ash. If you need to build a safety ring of rocks around the fire, make sure you use mountain rocks and not river rocks. River rocks are known to explode. Set a grill rack over the coals and grill the sausages, turning as needed, until well browned, 5 to 7 minutes. Remove the sausages and set aside.

Layer the bottom of the tub with a thick layer of seaweed to protect the lobsters from burning. Place the lobsters on top of the seaweed. Cover with more seaweed. Place the potatoes and corn in a ring around the edge of the tub. Place the clams (discard any that do not close to the touch) inside the ring of potatoes and corn. Pour about 1 quart (4 cups) of the water into the tub.

Place the tub on top of the fire. As it starts to steam, after 8 to 10 minutes, dampen a 2-yard-long piece of burlap and use it to cover the top of the tub. Every 15 minutes, remove the burlap and add more liquid, alternating between the wine and the water. After 1 hour, add the sausage and cook for an additional 10 to 15 minutes. At this point, the lobsters and vegetables will be fully cooked and the sausages will be heated through.

Strew the lobsters, clams (discard any unopened clams), sausages, potatoes, and corn on a newspaper-covered table. Accompany with melted butter, the spice mixtures, and piles of coarse sea salt for guests to use for dipping.

SERVES 8 TO 10

HALIBUT T-BONE STEAKS WITH HERB BUTTER — When my favorite fish, halibut, is in season, I tell the cook in me to stand back and let the fish take center stage. This classic technique is perfect on a warm summer day, is as easy to eat as it is to prepare, and definitely lets the fish be the star.

COOKING NOTES: To be sure you can get halibut steaks, rather than fillets, call your fishmonger a few days in advance to preorder them. When chopping the fresh basil, cut into a chiffonade first (stack the leaves, roll lengthwise, and cut the roll crosswise), and then go back with just a few chops. This will keep the basil from turning black.

ENTERTAINING NOTES: The butter can be made and refrigerated up to 1 week in advance or frozen up to 1 month in advance. Sear the halibut steaks an hour before your guests arrive and then finish them in a preheated 425°F oven. (You need a slightly higher temperature because the fish will no longer be warm.) For a special occasion, break out the fine caviar and put a spoonful on top of each steak. Yow! Serve the halibut with Garlicky Vegetables Primavera (page 167) and with steamed tiny Yukon Gold potatoes for soaking up the butter.

WINE NOTES: A good Napa Valley Chardonnay will add some complexity to this simple meal and has enough brightness to pair nicely with the compound butter.

FOR THE BUTTER:

1 cup (2 sticks) unsalted butter, at room temperature

2 tablespoons finely chopped fresh basil

2 tablespoons finely chopped fresh Italian (flat-leaf) parsley

1 tablespoon finely chopped fresh oregano

1 tablespoon finely chopped fresh thyme

1 teaspoon grated lemon zest

Finely ground sea salt, preferably gray salt

Freshly ground black pepper

½ cup all-purpose flour

8 halibut steaks, each 8 to 10 ounces and about 1 inch thick

Finely ground sea salt, preferably gray salt

Freshly ground black pepper

½ cup extra-virgin olive oil

2 lemons, thinly sliced crosswise

⅓ cup fresh Italian (flat-leaf) parsley leaves

Make the butter: In a bowl, combine all the ingredients, including 1 teaspoon salt and ¼ teaspoon pepper, and mash them together with a fork until evenly mixed. Cover and refrigerate until firm enough to shape into a log, about 30 minutes.

Put a 12-inch sheet of aluminum foil on a work surface. Spoon the butter down the center of the foil, forming a strip about 1½ inches in diameter. Enclose the butter in the foil and twist the ends to form an even log. Refrigerate for at least 30 minutes.

Preheat the oven to 400°F.

Spread the flour on a dinner plate. Season the halibut steaks on both sides with salt and pepper. In a sauté pan large enough to hold 2 halibut steaks at a time, heat ¼ cup of the olive oil over high heat. When the oil begins to smoke, dredge 2 halibut steaks on both sides in the flour, shaking off the excess, and place in the hot oil. Sear until golden brown on the first side, 4 to 5 minutes. Turn the halibut steaks over and sear on the second side for 30 sec-

onds. Move the steaks to a large rimmed baking sheet. Repeat with the remaining 6 steaks, dredging and cooking in batches of 2 steaks each time and arranging the steaks in a single layer on the baking sheet. After cooking 4 steaks, discard the oil in the sauté pan and add the remaining ¼ cup olive oil, heating it until it begins to smoke before continuing.

With the butter log still wrapped in the foil, cut the butter log crosswise into 16 equal slices. Unwrap each slice and let it sit at room temperature for 5 to 10 minutes.

Bake the fish steaks until the flesh barely begins to pull away from the bone, about 7 minutes.

Arrange the fish steaks on warmed individual plates or a platter and pour the juices from the baking sheet over them. Set 2 slices of butter on each steak. Garnish with the lemon slices and parsley. Serve at once.

SERVES 8

CEDAR-PLANKED SIDE OF SALMON WITH CHIVE OIL — Every chef I know would rather cook large pieces of fish than small fillets, because the larger the piece, the more it retains flavor and moisture during cooking. When the fish is cooked on a piece of cedar, the situation gets even better. Imagine walking into a house and smelling the aroma of toasting cedar wafting from the kitchen. That starts the party!

COOKING NOTES: This longtime Northwest Native American technique can be used for meats as well, and don't forget to try vegetables on a cedar plank. You will be surprised by how good they taste. Search for untreated cedar planks at your local hardware store, cookware store, or online. Be sure the plank is untreated; the presence of any chemicals can taint the salmon. You can wash and reuse the plank twice before cutting it into kindling. If you can't purchase a whole side of salmon, you can use fillets.

ENTERTAINING NOTES: The cedar plank provides three things: a cooking vessel, an element of flavor and aroma, and a presentation piece. Scoring the salmon ahead of time and dividing the portions with lemon slices and rosemary sprigs means you know exactly how many servings you have. Set the roasted salmon out on a buffet table with a little clear glass cruet of the chive oil for a wonderful presentation. The fish is delicious warm or at room temperature.

WINE NOTES: Pour a full-bodied, crisp Chardonnay. Stay away from a heavily oaked wine.

1 skin-on whole side of salmon, 2½ to 3 pounds and about ¾ inch thick,
    pin bones removed
1 lemon
¼ cup small fresh rosemary sprigs

FOR THE SEASONING MIX:
1 lemon
1 tablespoon fresh rosemary leaves
Finely ground sea salt, preferably gray salt

1 untreated cedar plank, about 18 by 7 inches,
    submerged in water for 1 hour
Extra-virgin olive oil for brushing and drizzling

FOR THE CHIVE OIL:
1 cup finely chopped fresh chives
1 cup olive oil
⅛ teaspoon powdered ascorbic acid (Vitamin C) (optional)

Preheat the oven to 400°F.

Starting at the head end, cut the salmon in half lengthwise through the flesh but not through the skin, stopping about 4 inches from the tip of the tail end. Again starting at the head end and cutting through the flesh but not through the skin, cut the salmon crosswise in sections about 2 inches apart to create individual portions.

Cut the lemon crosswise into thin slices. Remove the seeds from the slices, and then cut each slice in half, creating half-moons. Insert a piece of lemon and a rosemary sprig into each crosswise cut in the salmon to mark the individual portions.

Make the seasoning mix: Using a vegetable peeler, remove the zest from the lemon (reserve the lemon for another use). On a cutting board, finely chop together the lemon zest and rosemary and place in a small bowl or cup. Add 1 tablespoon salt and mix well. Sprinkle the seasoning mix over the top of the salmon, spreading more on the thicker head end than the tail end.

Place the cedar plank in the oven and leave it until it begins to turn dark brown, 15 to 30 minutes. Remove the plank from the oven and lightly brush it on one side with olive oil. Carefully place the salmon, skin side down, on the oiled side of the plank and drizzle a little more oil over the salmon. Return the plank to the oven and roast the salmon until medium-rare when tested with the tip of a knife, 25 to 30 minutes.

Meanwhile, make the chive oil: In a blender, combine all the ingredients and puree until very smooth. Strain the mixture through a fine-mesh sieve placed over a bowl. Discard the solids. You should have about ⅔ cup chive oil.

Remove the salmon from the oven and serve warm or at room temperature with the chive oil. The platter is the plank!

SERVES 8 TO 10

lettuce wrap; ancient Chinese secret

If you have leftover salmon, try flaking it into a salad, or serve on crostini flavored with brown butter and toasted spice rub (page 16), and top with a little mayonnaise flavored with minced fresh tarragon and lemon juice.

CIOPPINO— This dish originated on the San Francisco docks in the late 1800s. As the story goes, the word *cioppino* is Italian-Portuguese slang for "chip in." One fisherman would make a large pot of broth and ask all the others to "chip in," contributing a little of their daily catch. After a hard day's work on the boats, everyone would enjoy a bowl of hearty fish soup and argue over the best spots to fish the next morning. I love to make this dish for large groups and tell them the story ahead of time. That way, they are not shocked when I ask them to "chip in" and bring a pound of this or that.

COOKING NOTES: Call your fishmonger a few days ahead and request that he or she save any white-fish bones for you for making the fumet, which is a concentrated stock or essence. The fumet recipe yields more than you need for the soup, but you can freeze it for up to 3 months, and you will be glad you have it on hand the next time you need some for this soup or another recipe. Also, ask your fishmonger to crack the crab, devein the shrimp, remove the side muscle from the scallops, and, if you are really pressed for time, dice the fish fillets. Good fishmongers are fast and efficient, and most will be happy to do it for you. I have suggested serving a red wine with the soup, but if you instead opt for a white, switch to a dry white wine for adding to the soup, too.

ENTERTAINING NOTES: I know this recipe looks like a killer, but it's really quite simple and the entire thing can be made up to 4 hours in advance. Then all you need to do is drop in the precooked seafood at the last moment. If you cook the seafood more than 1 hour in advance, be sure to refrigerate it until it is needed. When close friends are your guests, you can skip transferring the soup to a tureen or ladling it into individual bowls in the kitchen and instead serve it directly from the pot at the table. The beauty of this dish is that you need only crusty garlic bread and a simple salad served along with it, and everyone leaves fully satisfied.

WINE NOTES: Chianti is perfect for this southern Italian–tasting dish.

FOR THE FISH FUMET:

5½ pounds bones and trimmings from white fish

2½ quarts (10 cups) water

6 ounces fresh mushrooms, sliced

1 small yellow onion, thinly sliced

2 tablespoons fresh lemon juice

2 cups dry white wine

10 fresh Italian (flat-leaf) parsley sprigs

1 small fresh thyme sprig

2 teaspoons black peppercorns

1 teaspoon fennel seed

1 bay leaf

Pinch of saffron threads (about ¼ teaspoon)

1 pound skinless red snapper or halibut fillets, cut into 1½-inch pieces

Finely ground sea salt, preferably gray salt

Freshly ground black pepper

½ to ¾ cup extra-virgin olive oil

¾ pound sea scallops, side muscle removed

1½ tablespoons minced garlic

2 cups finely chopped yellow onion

1 cup thinly sliced fennel (about 1 bulb)

1 tablespoon fennel seeds

2 tablespoons tomato paste

½ cup Pernod or brandy

1½ cups dry red wine

1 can (28 ounces) plum tomatoes, drained, squeezed of excess juice, and chopped

1 bay leaf

1 teaspoon dried oregano

1 jalapeño chili, seeded and diced

½ cup (1 stick) unsalted butter, at room temperature

1½ to 2 pounds littleneck clams

¼ cup chopped fresh Italian (flat-leaf) parsley

3 tablespoons chopped fresh basil

2 tablespoons chopped fresh tarragon

1 pound cooked crab legs, cracked into 2- to 3-inch pieces

1 pound large shrimp, deveined but not peeled

Make the fumet: Rinse the fish bones in cold water to remove any traces of blood. In a stockpot, combine all the ingredients and bring to a simmer over high heat. Reduce the heat as needed to maintain a gentle simmer and simmer for 30 minutes. Remove from the heat and strain through a fine-mesh sieve lined with cheesecloth into a clean container. Discard the solids. Measure out 2 cups to use for the soup and place in a small saucepan. Let the remaining fumet cool (you should have about 2 quarts/8 cups), transfer to a tightly covered container, and freeze for other uses.

Bring the 2 cups fumet to a simmer, add the saffron, and then remove from the heat and set aside.

Season the fish with salt and pepper. In a large (8-quart) stockpot, heat ¼ cup of the olive oil over medium-high heat. When the oil begins to smoke, add the seasoned fish, spreading it out on the bottom of the pot in a single layer. Cook, without stirring, until light brown, 1 to 2 minutes. Then turn and cook for 30 seconds longer. The fish will be slightly underdone. Using a slotted spoon, remove from the pot and set aside. Add another ¼ cup olive oil to the pot and repeat with the scallops. Remove from the pot with the slotted spoon and set aside.

You will need ¼ cup olive oil in the pot. Add as much of the remaining ¼ cup oil as needed to arrive at that amount and place the pot over medium heat. Add the garlic, onion, sliced fennel, and fennel seeds. Stir and cook for 2 minutes. Add the tomato paste and cook for 3 to 4 minutes. Add the Pernod and stir well. Add the wine, tomatoes, bay leaf, oregano, and chili. Season with 1 ½ teaspoons salt and ½ teaspoon pepper. Cook this tomato broth over medium-low heat until the liquid has reduced by one-fourth, about 15 minutes.

Add the butter, clams (discard any that do not close to the touch), parsley, basil, and tarragon to the tomato broth. Simmer until the clams open, about 3 minutes (discard any unopened clams). Add the crab pieces and heat through. Using a slotted spoon, transfer the crab and clams to a large serving bowl. Add the sautéed fish and scallops to the tomato broth and heat through. Using the slotted spoon, transfer the fish and scallops to the serving bowl. Place the shrimp in the tomato broth and cook until just done, then transfer them to the bowl.

Taste the broth and adjust the seasoning. Ladle the broth over the fish and seafood, then serve in warmed individual bowls.

SERVES 8 TO 10

2 days before	1 day before	morning of	1 hour before	service
rest	shop for non-seafood ingredients and fish bones only, prepare vegetables, make fumet	shop for fish, set table	assemble cioppino, open wine	finish and serve

goes great with . . .

The richness of the beans, contrasted with sharp greens, fills your mouth with flavor.

OLIVE OIL–BRAISED SNAPPER WITH FENNEL AND ORANGE — Olive oil poaching is a wonderful way to capture all the delicate flavors of fish. In this recipe, the olive oil takes on the character of the fennel and citrus, ingredients that are then used to dress the fish when serving.

COOKING NOTES: This same technique also works beautifully for salmon or tuna.

ENTERTAINING NOTES: You may cook the seafood halfway 30 minutes before serving, and then simply immerse it in the broth for a couple of minutes before your guests sit down for dinner. I have prepared this dish quite easily for twenty people, since all of the steps can be done in advance.

WINE NOTES: Sauvignon Blanc and citrus are a great combination.

2 fennel bulbs	4 snapper fillets, each about 6 ounces and 1 inch thick
3 navel oranges	Juice of l lemon
¾ cup extra-virgin olive oil	Freshly ground black pepper
Finely ground sea salt, preferably gray salt	½ cup thinly sliced red onion
1 bay leaf	1 cup fresh Italian (flat-leaf) parsley leaves

Cut off the stalks and feathery leaves from the fennel bulbs (if still attached), remove any bruised outer leaves, and then cut each bulb in half lengthwise so some core is still attached to each half. Cut each half lengthwise into 4 equal wedges, making sure a little of the core is attached to each wedge.

Using a vegetable peeler, remove the zest from 1 orange in strips. Squeeze the juice of that orange into a bowl. To peel the remaining 2 oranges, place 1 orange on a cutting board and, using a sharp knife, cut a slice off the stem and blossom end, revealing the flesh. Place the orange upright and cut off the peel and pith, following the contour of the fruit. Repeat with the remaining orange. Cut the oranges crosswise into ¼-inch-thick slices, and remove any seeds. You need 16 slices in all.

In a skillet, heat the olive oil over medium heat. Meanwhile, season the fennel wedges with salt to taste. When the oil begins to simmer, add the fennel, orange zest, and bay leaf. Cook the fennel, stirring occasionally, until tender, about 15 minutes. Using a slotted spoon, transfer the fennel to a plate and cover to keep warm. Set aside.

While the fennel is cooking, cut a piece of parchment paper into a round the same diameter as the skillet. Generously season the snapper fillets on both sides with salt. Once the fennel has been removed from the pan, using a slotted spatula, carefully lower the fillets, one at a time, into the hot oil. Reduce the heat to maintain a slow simmer (145°F), cover the fillets with the parchment round, and cook until the fillets are opaque throughout, about 20 minutes, occasionally tilting the pan to coat the fish with the oil. Using the slotted spatula, remove the fillets from the oil to a warmed plate and reserve them, covered with the parchment. Pour the liquid from the skillet through a fine-mesh sieve placed over a heatproof measuring pitcher.

Add the lemon juice to the bowl holding the orange juice. Then add ¾ cup of the strained liquid from the skillet and whisk to emulsify, forming a vinaigrette. Whisk in salt and pepper to taste.

To serve, alternate 4 fennel wedges and 4 orange slices on each plate. Place 1 snapper fillet in the center of each plate. In a small bowl, toss the red onion and parsley with 2 tablespoons of the vinaigrette, and place a small mound of this mixture on the top of each snapper fillet. Spoon the remaining vinaigrette over and around the fish. Serve at once.

SERVES 4

PRIME RIB OF SWORDFISH — One of my newest ideas, this recipe is having its debut in this cookbook. I created it to answer my own question of, "What if we roasted a whole swordfish loin just like a prime rib and carved it right at the table?" Even though I have a pretty creative imagination, the results surprised even me.

COOKING NOTES: Ask your fishmonger to cut out as much of the bloodline as possible from the swordfish loin. That might create a flap, which you should tie. Swordfish is best carved with an electric knife or a very sharp serrated knife.

ENTERTAINING NOTES: When planning for any party, whether a simple dinner for eight or cocktails for thirty, always work backward from the serving time to determine how much time you'll need. The swordfish in this recipe takes 15 minutes to sear, 1 ¼ hours to roast, and 10 to 15 minutes to rest. That means you need to start cooking it 1 ¾ hours before serving time. I especially enjoy this dish with Lemon Oil Smashed Potatoes (page 155) and "Quintesssential" Roasted Vegetable Platter (page 163). Spoon a little basil pesto, homemade (page 21) or purchased, over the top of the vegetables and enjoy.

WINE NOTES: If you can find a good Chardonnay with a couple of years of cellar time, it will go wonderfully with the swordfish. Failing that, look for an oaky Chardonnay.

---

3 pounds boneless, skinless center-cut swordfish loin

Finely ground sea salt, preferably gray salt

2 tablespoons Fennel Spice Rub (page 16)

¼ cup extra-virgin olive oil

Preheat the oven to 350°F. Set a rack inside a rimmed baking sheet.

Using kitchen string, tie the swordfish crosswise at 3 evenly spaced places. (This step is not imperative, but the fish will hold together a little better.) Season with 1 tablespoon salt and the fennel mixture, pressing the spices evenly into the flesh.

In a 12-inch skillet, heat the olive oil over medium heat. When the oil is hot, add the swordfish and, turning occasionally, brown on all sides, including the top and bottom, about 15 minutes total.

Transfer the swordfish to the rack inside the baking sheet and roast until the internal temperature reaches 120°F, or about 1 ¼ hours. Remove from the oven and allow to rest for 10 minutes before carving.

Transfer the swordfish to a warmed platter. Snip the strings, if used, and carve the fish crosswise into ½-inch-thick slices. Serve at once.

SERVES 6 TO 8

it's finally here ... summer

I come from a long line of ranchers and butchers. We love to cook the less-commercial cuts and save the steaks for the customers. With that in mind, try my gaucho-style skirt steak (page 126), spiced with *chimichurri* sauce, hot off the grill. The finer cuts are not ignored here, of course. Sit back and relax with a seven-hour Forever-Roasted Lamb with Herbes de Provence (page 125)—the longer you nap, the better it tastes. Or, go vertical for the perfect roasted chicken (page 116). And if you have friends who are committed carnivores, don't miss the chance to serve them my mixed grill (page 142), which includes something to satisfy everyone.

meat & poultry

Remember, when we buy natural meat and poultry, we are not only treating ourselves better and getting real flavor, but we are also caring for the planet and our children and grandchildren at the same time. Do the right thing and go natural. We can't afford not to respect our environment.

VERTICAL ROASTED CHICKEN COCORICO — *Cocorico* is French for cockle-doodle-do, which is the noise I make while eating this chicken. It is also the brand name of a vertical chicken roaster currently on the market (see Equipment, page 226). Even I doubted that such an average-sounding recipe for roasted chicken would end up tasting so extraordinary. Once you experience the lightly crispy skin and the evenly caramelized meat that result from vertical roasting, you'll have renewed interest in America's most-consumed protein.

COOKING NOTES: There are a number of vertical roasters on the market today, some wire and some clay. My preference is for the clay type. When you roast a chicken vertically, the entire bird gets brown, and because the legs are at the top, they cook in the same amount of time as the breast. By cooking from the inside and outside at the same time, you are reducing your cooking time by 33 percent and all the juices stay inside the bird. A convection oven gives the chicken a crispier skin, which adds to the flavor, so I have provided directions. I have included spring onions among the vegetables. These are young onions that look similar to green onions, except that the white bulb base is round (about 1 ½ inches in diameter), rather than straight. Vary the spices each time you make this dish to keep the idea fresh. The Toasted Spice Rub (page 16) and the Fennel Spice Rub (page 16) are especially good on chicken.

ENTERTAINING NOTES: If you are using a clay roaster, it can go from the oven to the table. Your guests can watch while you carve the bird and dish out the roasted vegetables that have been basted in the chicken juices, making for a little extra entertainment.

WINE NOTES: Ask your wine merchant for a light and bright Rhône red.

¾ pound Yukon Gold potatoes, halved

Finely ground sea salt, preferably gray salt

1 whole chicken, 3½ to 4 pounds, wing tips removed

¼ cup extra-virgin olive oil

¼ cup Citrus Salt (page 15)

3 fresh rosemary sprigs

1 lemon, quartered

½ pound yellow or red bell peppers

½ pound green bell peppers

½ pound spring onions (6 to 8 onions)

Preheat the oven to 450°F or to 425°F on the convection setting.

In a saucepan, combine the potatoes with water to cover by 2 inches. Add 1 tablespoon sea salt and bring to a boil over high heat. Cook the potatoes for 3 to 4 minutes, then drain and set aside.

Rinse the chicken under cold running water and pat thoroughly dry. Coat the outside with 2 tablespoons of the olive oil. Season the chicken on the inside and outside with 3 tablespoons of the Citrus Salt. Place the rosemary sprigs and lemon quarters inside the cavity. Carefully place the chicken, legs facing up, onto the vertical roaster. Push down on the chicken as needed to make sure it is far enough down on the roaster's cone to be steady.

Put the vertical roaster in the center of the oven and roast the chicken for 15 minutes. During this time, halve and seed the bell peppers and cut them lengthwise into 1-inch-wide strips. Cut off the green tops and root ends of the onions and discard, then cut the bulbs in half lengthwise. In a bowl, toss together the bell peppers, onions, and potatoes with the remaining 2 tablespoons olive oil and 1 tablespoon Citrus Salt.

After the chicken has roasted for 15 minutes, place the seasoned vegetables on the tray at the base of the roaster cone. Reduce the oven temperature to 375°F and continue roasting until the juices run clear when the thigh is pierced with a skewer, 45 to 60 minutes longer. While the chicken roasts, rotate the roaster at least a quarter turn every 15 minutes or so.

Remove the roaster from the oven and let the chicken rest, still on the roaster, for 15 minutes. Carefully remove the chicken from the roaster and carve into serving portions. Transfer to a warmed platter. Serve at once with the roasted vegetables.

SERVES 6

BUTTERFLIED CHICKEN DIABLO AL MATTONE— Two chickens, four bricks *(mattone)*, and lots of flavor—that's what we call killing two birds with four stones! This dish is based on a traditional Italian technique, which basically squishes the living hell out of the chicken but seals in all the flavor and juices. It's often served during Lent, as it is believed to scare away the evil spirits. Outside of Bologna, I attended a Lenten festival where kids with plastic bats wandered the streets and tried to beat the evil spirits out of you, literally. Afterward, this dish was served. Maybe I will skip the beating next time and head right to the feast!

COOKING NOTES: Making an incision between each drumstick and thigh allows the heat to reach the bone quickly, so the dark meat will be done at the same time as the white breast meat. You wouldn't think the chicken would get crispy, but it really does. And it cooks faster under bricks, which means it ends up being juicier. Also, the flavor of the chili paste gets right down to the bone. If you don't have Calabrian Chili Paste, a substitute recipe can be found on page 15.

ENTERTAINING NOTES: You can start marinating the chickens up to 24 hours in advance of cooking. I like to serve the chickens right on the bricks I used for cooking them. I simply cover the bricks with a piece of parchment paper first.

WINE NOTES: For spicy dishes like this one, I like Riesling or Gewürztraminer.

2 whole chickens, each about 4 pounds	Extra-virgin olive oil for brushing
¼ cup Calabrian Chili Paste (page 15)	4 lemons, halved crosswise
Finely ground sea salt, preferably gray salt	2 tablespoons finely chopped fresh oregano

Rinse the chickens under cold running water and pat dry thoroughly. Place the chickens, breast side down, on a work surface, with the cavity end facing you. Working with 1 chicken at a time, and using a sharp knife or kitchen scissors, cut along one side of the backbone down its entire length. Then cut along the other side of the backbone and discard the backbone. Make an incision at the joint between each drumstick and thigh. Turn the chicken over, skin side down, and spread it out like an open book. Repeat with the remaining chicken.

Again working with 1 chicken at a time, gently work your fingers under the skin over the breast and legs to loosen the skin. Using a small spoon, scoop up about one-fourth of the chili paste and push it between the loosened skin and meat. Using your fingertips, spread the paste evenly under the skin. Repeat with the second chicken. Turn the chickens over and lightly coat their underside with the remaining chili paste. Season the chickens all over with 2 teaspoons salt. Cover with plastic wrap and refrigerate for 2 to 3 hours. Remove the chickens from the refrigerator 20 to 30 minutes before you are ready to cook them.

Ready a charcoal or gas grill for indirect heat grilling over a medium-hot fire, or preheat the oven to 425°F and put a large rimmed baking sheet on 2 stove-top burners turned on to medium. Wrap 4 bricks in aluminum foil.

Lightly brush the chickens all over with olive oil. Place the chickens, skin side down, on the grill rack or on the preheated baking sheet. Place a large rimmed baking sheet on top of the chickens, and balance 4 bricks in a single layer on the baking sheet. Cover the grill. Or, place the double-pan arrangement in the oven. Cook the chickens until the skins are well browned and crispy, 40 to 50 minutes. Using thick oven mitts, remove the hot bricks and the baking sheet. Carefully turn the chickens over and continue to cook, on the grill or in the oven, until the meat is no longer pink at the bone, 10 to 15 minutes longer.

Using a wide spatula, carefully move the chickens from the grill to a cutting board, or remove the baking sheet from the oven and then transfer the chickens to the board. Allow the chickens to rest for 3 to 5 minutes.

Meanwhile, lightly brush the cut sides of the lemon halves with olive oil. Place the lemons, cut side down, on the grill over the hottest part of the fire. If using the oven, turn on the broiler, place the lemon halves, cut side up (cut a thin slice off the opposite end if necessary to keep the lemon halves upright), on a small baking sheet, and slip under the broiler close to the heat source. Grill or broil until well browned and caramelized, about 3 minutes. Remove the lemons from the grill or broiler.

Cut the chickens into serving pieces. Serve warm with the oregano sprinkled over the top and the grilled lemons on the side. SERVES 8

easy as 1...2...3...

Three steps to a dramatic, succulent roasted chicken.

CRESPELLI "SHORT STACKS" WITH SHREDDED CHICKEN AND BALSAMIC BBQ SAUCE—

When I was a young cook, I was blessed with the opportunity to *stagier* (work for free to gain experience) in a number of kitchens around the country and in Europe. I spent a special week in the kitchen of An American Place, superchef Larry Forgione's groundbreaking restaurant in New York City. This dish was inspired by one of his dishes. Like most chefs, I am a collection of my experiences. Once you make this, you will be thanking Larry as well . . . it's delicious.

COOKING NOTES: For a true culinary adventure, substitute duck or rabbit for the chicken. You can also use any of your favorite sauces for chicken in place of the BBQ sauce.

ENTERTAINING NOTES: You can make the sauce up to 1 week in advance, let it cool, cover, and refrigerate. You can make the crepe batter 1 day in advance and cook the crepes the following day. Or, you can cook the chicken, cook the crepes, and assemble the *crespelli* stacks the day before serving. To store overnight, assemble the stacks between layers of parchment paper and refrigerate. Bring the stacks back to room temperature before placing them in the pie pans and then in the oven. This is a great first course or light lunch. I love to serve dishes like this one on a pedestal plate to give them the showcase they deserve.

WINE NOTES: Pour a ripe, intense California Zinfandel.

FOR THE SAUCE:

1 tablespoon extra-virgin olive oil

1 tablespoon minced garlic

¾ cup ketchup

6 tablespoons balsamic vinegar

⅓ cup honey

3 tablespoons soy sauce

3 tablespoons brewed espresso

Grated zest of 1 orange

FOR THE CREPES:

1 cup all-purpose flour

Finely ground sea salt, preferably gray salt

Freshly ground black pepper

2 large eggs

1 cup whole milk

2 tablespoons unsalted butter

4 green onions, including all but 2 inches of green tops, finely chopped

FOR THE CHICKEN:

9 bone-in, skin-on chicken thighs, about 4 pounds total weight

Finely ground sea salt, preferably gray salt

Freshly ground black pepper

¼ cup extra-virgin olive oil

Olive oil cooking spray for preparing pans

FOR THE SLAW:

1 Granny Smith apple

1 teaspoon fresh lemon juice

6 cups very thinly sliced Napa cabbage

4 green onions, including all but 2 inches of green tops, finely chopped

Finely ground sea salt, preferably gray salt

Freshly ground black pepper

Make the sauce: In a saucepan, heat the olive oil over medium-low heat. Add the garlic and sauté until golden, 1 to 2 minutes. Remove from the heat and let the garlic cool in the oil. Whisk in the ketchup, vinegar, honey, soy sauce, and espresso, return to medium-low heat, and simmer gently for 15 minutes to blend the flavors. Remove from the heat and let cool. Reserve the orange zest for adding to the sauce later. You should have about 1⅔ cups.

Make the crepe batter: In a bowl, stir together the flour, ½ teaspoon salt, and a pinch of pepper. In a small bowl, whisk together the eggs and milk until well combined. Add the milk mixture to the flour mixture, whisking to prevent lumps. Do not overbeat the batter. Put the butter in a cold skillet and place over medium heat. Cook, stirring occasionally to prevent it from burning in spots but without moving the pan, until it browns evenly, about 2 minutes.

Add the green onions, mix well, and cook for 15 seconds. Add the green onion mixture to the batter and whisk to combine. The batter should just coat the back of a spoon. If it seems too thick, whisk in a little milk or water. You should have about 2 cups batter. Cover and refrigerate the batter until you are ready to cook the crepes or up to 24 hours.

Preheat the oven to 350°F.

Cook the chicken: Generously season the chicken thighs on both sides with salt and pepper. In a 12-inch skillet, heat the olive oil over medium-high heat. When the oil just begins to smoke, add the chicken thighs, skin side down, and cook until nicely caramelized on the first side, 10 to 12 minutes. Carefully pour off all but 2 tablespoons of the fat. Turn the thighs over and cook until the second side is lightly caramelized, 2 to 3 minutes longer.

Pour off all the remaining chicken fat and carefully add the sauce to the skillet. When the sauce begins to simmer, move the skillet to the oven and cook until the thighs are tender and the meat easily pulls away from the bones, 30 to 40 minutes. Remove the skillet from the oven, add the reserved orange zest, and allow the chicken to cool in the sauce.

Heat a 10-inch nonstick skillet over medium heat. Add ¼ cup of the crepe batter to the hot skillet. Remove the skillet from the heat and tilt it to coat the bottom evenly with the batter. Return the skillet to medium-high heat and cook until the underside is lightly browned, 50 to 60 seconds. Using your fingertips, carefully turn the crepe over and cook on the second side for 10 to 15 seconds. Set the cooked crepe aside on a baking sheet. Repeat with the remaining batter to make 8 crepes total.

Remove the chicken from the sauce. Pull the meat and skin from the bones, discard the skin and bones, and tear the meat into ¼-inch-wide strips. Remove ¾ cup of the sauce and set aside. Return the chicken strips to the remaining sauce.

Lightly spray the bottom of two 10-inch pie pans or plates with olive oil cooking spray. Stack 2 crepes in the bottom of each pan. Spread a single layer of chicken over each stack of crepes, and set 1 more crepe over each layer of chicken. Spread another layer of chicken on top. Finish each stack with 1 more crepe. Cover each pan with aluminum foil.

Bake the crepe stacks until hot throughout, 30 to 40 minutes.

Meanwhile, make the slaw: Quarter and core the apple. Using a mandoline or a sharp knife, slice the apple as thinly as possible into julienne and place in a large bowl. Add the lemon juice and mix well. Add the cabbage, green onions, ½ teaspoon salt, and ¼ teaspoon pepper and mix well. You should have about 8 cups.

When the stacks are ready, remove from the oven, remove the foil, and carefully invert each pie pan onto a cutting board. Lift off the pans. Cut each stack into quarters. Place a wedge on each serving plate. Arrange a bundle of the slaw beside each wedge, and drizzle some of the reserved sauce over each plate. Serve at once.

SERVES 8

2 days before	1 day before	morning of	1 hour before	service
shop	make sauce, prepare crepes	cook chicken, assemble short stacks, set table	heat stacks in oven, make slaw, open wine	cut and serve

practice makes perfect

Crepes are really quite easy to make. After your first try you'll

be tempted to move to Brittany and open a crêperie.

CRESPELLI "SHORT STACKS" WITH SHREDDED CHICKEN AND BALSAMIC BBQ SAUCE, PAGE 120

DOUBLE-CUT BISTECCA ALLA FIORENTINA WITH EXTRA-VIRGIN OLIVE OIL AND LIME—

I know that many believe that the classic steak house is an American invention, but did you know that some of the oldest steak houses in the world are Italian? Without a doubt, my favorite way to enjoy beef is in typical Florentine fashion—wonderful meat, grilled to perfection, served with simple *condimenti* such as grilled lemon or twenty-year-old balsamic vinegar.

COOKING NOTES: A porterhouse steak is a cut of meat that has both the New York and the filet mignon in one piece. The term *double-cut* refers to the thickness of the steak. I ask the butcher to cut these for me and watch his eyes open wide when I show him how thick I want them. Preorder them from your butcher to be sure you get the thickness and cut you want. The temperature of the meat before it goes on the grill is hypercritical to the success of the dish. Due to the density of cold meat, if you cook a from-the-refrigerator steak, half of the steak will be well done and the other half will be very rare. If you wait for the meat to reach room temperature, the fibers open up, allowing the heat to penetrate evenly throughout. The results are a perfect medium-rare, end to end. Once cooked, a steak must rest for 10 minutes before cutting or carving. True of all meats, this allows the steak to retain its juices and settle at its new temperature without the shock of immediate carving.

ENTERTAINING NOTES: The reason for the supersized steaks is not to serve one per person, but rather to create an awesome spectacle as you carve these monsters tableside. I love to pull out my favorite carving board and knives and tell the story of my first Italian steak house experience. Paired with Potato "Torta" Stuffed with Pancetta and Caramelized Onions (page 156) and Salt-Roasted Onions (page 162), you'll have a deceptively simple meal fit for Renaissance royalty.

WINE NOTES: Cabernet Sauvignon is the king of red-meat wines, but I have poured Petite Sirah, a high-intensity wine with good depth of character, for this meal, and it has stood up well.

---

2 porterhouse steaks, each about 2½ pounds and 1¾ inches thick

Extra-virgin olive oil for coating

Finely ground sea salt, preferably gray salt

Freshly ground coarse black pepper

3 limes, halved crosswise

Allow the steaks to sit at room temperature for 30 to 60 minutes. Then lightly coat the steaks on both sides with olive oil and season them on both sides with 1 tablespoon salt and 1½ teaspoons pepper, pressing the spices into the meat.

Ready a charcoal or gas grill for both direct and indirect heat grilling over a hot fire.

Grill the steak over direct heat for 4 minutes. Rotate the steak 90 degrees and continue to grill over direct heat until seared on the first side, 3 to 4 minutes longer. Turn the steaks over and repeat the same timing and rotating on the second side.

Meanwhile, grill the limes cut side down over direct heat until well browned and caramelized, about 3 minutes. Remove the limes from the grill.

After the steaks have been seared on both sides, move them and the limes (cut side facing up) over indirect heat. Grill the steaks until cooked to your preference, about 5 minutes longer for rare or 7 to 10 minutes longer for medium-rare. To be sure they are done to your liking, test with an instant-read thermometer, which should register 120°F for rare or 130°F for medium-rare. Remove the steaks and limes from the grill. Allow the steaks to rest at room temperature for about 10 minutes.

Using a sharp knife, cut along the bone of each steak to remove the large pieces of meat.

Cut the meat into ½-inch-thick slices and arrange on either warmed individual plates or a platter. Drizzle a little olive oil over the slices and season with salt. Serve warm with the lime halves.

SERVES 6

FOREVER-ROASTED LAMB WITH HERBES DE PROVENCE—Anyone who has cooked with me knows my mantra: when it comes to cooking meats, it is either low and slow (heat and time) or high and fast. No good comes from the middle ground of temperatures. For years, I have been "forever" roasting meats, very slowly at low temperatures, and am a huge fan of the outcome. If you have ever been to a lamb or pig roast, you know that it takes hours to cook the animal, but, boy, it's worth the wait! I guarantee that your guests will never have tasted lamb this good.

COOKING NOTES: You will be tempted to raise the temperature in hopes of cutting down the cooking time, but the lamb will be ruined. This low-and-slow technique keeps the meat melt-in-your-mouth tender. It pays to know your butcher. He or she will bone out the leg of lamb properly. I don't care for the netted boneless roasts; they are uneven and not as fresh. And trust me, there is no need for a thermometer to test when the lamb is ready. It is well done, period.

ENTERTAINING NOTES: Once you season and shape the leg, you can refrigerate it overnight before continuing, but bring it to room temperature (about 1 ½ hours) before slipping it in the oven. When the lamb is cooked, you can bring it to the table on a large serving platter, and let your guests pull off their own serving of meat to get the full effect of how tender it is. If I am plating the servings, I will often pull off a larger piece of lamb with my tongs and serve it on risotto or polenta. If the lamb is done before your guests arrive, simply reduce the oven temperature to 200°F and it will hold for another hour. Serve the lamb with Potato "Torta" Stuffed with Pancetta and Caramelized Onions (page 156) and Sautéed Greens, Calabria Style (page 153) for a wonderfully simple meal.

WINE NOTES: Pinot Noir is a match made in heaven for lamb.

---

1 bone-in leg of lamb, 8 to 10 pounds, boned (6 to 8 pounds after boning)
Extra-virgin olive oil for rubbing
2 tablespoons *herbes de Provence*

Finely ground sea salt, preferably gray salt
Freshly ground black pepper

If you have brought the lamb leg home with the bone intact, the first thing you need to do is bone it: Slip a boning knife between the bone and flesh and, keeping the knife blade as close to the bone as possible, cut down along the bone to free it from the flesh. Discard the bone or save it to make lamb stock.

Preheat the oven to 275°F. Line a roasting pan or heavy rimmed baking sheet with heavy-duty aluminum foil, to catch the drippings and for easier cleanup. Set a wire rack inside the roasting pan.

Rub the lamb all over with olive oil. Season with the herbs, 2 tablespoons salt, and 1 teaspoon pepper, pressing the herbs and spices into the meat. Reshape the lamb so that it resembles a leg,

and then tie it lightly with kitchen string so it will hold its shape. Place the lamb in the center of the rack.

Roast the lamb until it is fork-tender, 8 to 10 hours. Remove from the oven and let rest for at least 15 minutes before removing the string.

Transfer the lamb to a cutting board and, using 2 forks, pull the meat apart into fist-sized pieces. Arrange on a warmed platter. You can use some wine or water to deglaze the pan on the stove top and pour the jus over each plate. Serve warm.

SERVES 8 TO 10

GRILLED GAUCHO STEAK WITH BLUE CHEESE AND PITA — On a long trip to South America, I fell in love with the Argentinean way of cooking and eating beef. On the pampas, the steak was skewered on a metal rod and placed in the ground right in the fire. When it was ready, it was sliced and served on bread with the amazing *chimichurri* sauce. We duplicate this at home by using a hearth grill (slipped right into the living-room fireplace for cooking) and setting up the entire dinner on the coffee table in front of the roaring fire.

COOKING NOTES: A skirt steak is a relatively tough cut from the underbelly of the animal. It is usually about ½ inch thick and is popularly used for making fajitas. You will have *chimichurri* sauce left over. Cover and refrigerate for up to 1 month. Use it as a marinade and/or sauce for other grilled meats, such as pork or lamb.

ENTERTAINING NOTES: This is a perfect dish for serving on a buffet. Simply plate each component and let your guests serve themselves. Find some Argentinean music to play in the background for the full effect.

WINE NOTES: Ask your local wine shop for a good, affordable Chilean or Argentinean red.

FOR THE *CHIMICHURRI* SAUCE:

1 bunch fresh Italian (flat-leaf) parsley, finely chopped

2 bay leaves, broken into small pieces

6 cloves garlic, minced

1½ teaspoons Spanish paprika

1 tablespoon finely chopped fresh oregano leaves

½ cup red wine vinegar

1¼ cups extra-virgin olive oil

Finely ground sea salt, preferably gray salt

Freshly ground black pepper

FOR THE CHILI WATER:

1 tablespoon Spanish paprika

Finely ground sea salt, preferably gray salt

1 cup warm water

2 red onions, sliced crosswise ½ inch thick

Extra-virgin olive oil for brushing

Finely ground sea salt, preferably gray salt

Freshly ground black pepper

2½ pounds skirt steak, about ½ inch thick

8 pita breads

½ pound blue cheese, crumbled

4 ripe tomatoes, cored, cut crosswise into ¼-inch-thick slices, and slices halved

---

Make the *chimichurri* sauce: In a food processor, combine the parsley, bay leaves, garlic, paprika, oregano, vinegar, olive oil, ½ teaspoon salt, and ¼ teaspoon pepper. Pulse until well mixed. Transfer the sauce to a glass or plastic container; you should have about 2½ cups. Measure out about ¾ cup for this recipe. Cover and refrigerate the remainder for other uses.

Ready a charcoal grill or gas grill for direct heat grilling over a hot fire. Preheat the oven to 225°F.

Make the chili water: In a small bowl, combine the paprika, 2 tablespoons salt, and the water and stir until the salt dissolves.

Lightly brush the onion slices on both sides with olive oil and season with salt and pepper. Place on the grill and cook, turning once, until well caramelized and softened, 3 to 4 minutes on each side.

At the same time, season the steaks with salt and brush on some of the chili water. Place the steaks on the grill and cook, basting 2 or 3 more times with the chili water and turning once, until cooked to desired doneness, 4 to 6 minutes total for medium-rare. Transfer to a cutting board and let rest for 4 minutes.

Lightly brush the pita breads with olive oil and set on the grill, turning once, to heat for 1 minute. Remove from the grill.

Cut the top 20 percent off each pita bread (save the trimmings for another use). Divide the blue cheese evenly among the pita breads, stuffing it into the pockets. Lay the pita breads in a single layer on 2 rimmed baking sheets and place in the oven to keep warm.

Cut the skirt steaks across the grain into ½-inch-thick slices and place in a bowl. Add ½ cup of the *chimichurri* sauce and toss well.

Remove the pita breads from the oven and place on warmed individual plates. Divide the meat and tomato slices among the pita breads, slipping them into the pockets. Pull the onion slices apart into rings and slip the onion rings into the pockets as well. Spoon 1½ teaspoons *chimichurri* sauce over each stuffed pita bread and serve at once.

SERVES 8

don't get chapped . . .

about entertaining. A recipe like my Grilled Gaucho Steak with Blue Cheese and Pita will adapt for any course to satisfy any carnivore.

GIANT BEAN CASSOULET WITH FENNEL-SPICED CHICKEN AND ROASTED VEGETABLES—

This recipe's origin dates to a rainy November night several years ago when Burgess Smith, the general manager at Tra Vigne, and I got together after a successful pheasant hunt. I had some cooked beans. We cooked the pheasant and beans just like this in the fireplace and poured a Petite Sirah from Stags' Leap.

COOKING NOTES: The caramelization of the vegetables and the roasted chicken flavors are what make this dish special. Season the chicken pieces well, because in turn they will season the beans. Cut the vegetables obliquely into wedges. It makes for interesting shapes, much better than the frozen-vegetable look. The dish is flexible. It works great with lamb, or it works great with just vegetables and beans. Or, try adding some tomatoes for depth and color. I have called for dried giant white beans here. Corona beans, which are grown primarily in Italy and California, are my favorite, but you can use other large white beans. If you're short on time, you can even use canned large white beans. Some of them are pretty darned good. Just throw out the liquid in the can and use a good-quality chicken stock for the liquid in the recipe. Add the canned beans when you are combining everything in the ovenproof pot, and use 4 cups stock and no water.

ENTERTAINING NOTES: This cassoulet is perfect for times when you want to do virtually all the cooking and cleaning ahead of time. You can cook the beans up to 2 days in advance, cover, and refrigerate. You can assemble the dish fully up to 1 day in advance. Then, as the guests come through the door, simply slip the cassoulet into the oven and, in a half hour, you will be serving a one-pot meal with minimal cleanup at the end of the evening. This is also the time to pull out that large copper pan you have had for years but never knew when to use.

WINE NOTES: Open a Petite Sirah, a big, fleshy red with enough body to stand up to huge flavors.

FOR THE BEANS:

1 pound dried giant white beans such as Corona

1 yellow onion, quartered lengthwise

1 celery stalk, quartered crosswise

1 carrot, peeled and quartered crosswise

2 large cloves garlic, lightly crushed

1 bay leaf

4 cups chicken stock

Finely ground sea salt, preferably gray salt

12 Brussels sprouts

Finely ground sea salt, preferably gray salt

1 red onion, peeled

3 carrots

1 parsnip

½ cup extra-virgin olive oil

¼ cup Fennel Spice Rub (page 16)

1 whole chicken, about 4 pounds, plus 2 bone-in,
   skin-on chicken breast halves

6 cloves garlic

¼ pound pancetta, cut into strips about ½ inch thick,
   ½ inch wide, and 1 inch long (optional)

Cook the beans: Pick over the beans and discard any misshapen beans or grit. Rinse the beans, place in a saucepan, and add cold water to cover by 2 inches. Bring to a boil, cover, and remove from the heat. Let stand for 1 hour, then drain.

Return the beans to the saucepan and add the onion, celery, carrot, garlic, and bay leaf. Pour in the chicken stock and then water as needed to cover the beans by ¾ inch. Slowly bring to a simmer over medium-low heat. (If you heat them too fast, the skins may break.) Adjust the heat to maintain a bare simmer and cook, uncovered, until the beans are almost tender, 30 to 45 minutes or so, depending on the age of the beans. Add salt to taste, remove from the heat, and let cool in the liquid.

While the beans are cooking, remove the tough outer leaves and the stems from the Brussels sprouts. Bring a saucepan of salted water to a boil, add the Brussels sprouts, and boil for 30 seconds. Drain the Brussels sprouts and quickly cool them in a bowl of ice water. Cut each one in half through the stem end. Cut the onion through the stem end into 6 equal wedges. Peel the carrots and parsnip and cut obliquely into $3/4$-inch pieces.

Place a deep ovenproof pot about 12 inches in diameter over high heat and add $1/4$ cup of the olive oil. When the oil is hot but not smoking, add the onion, carrots, and parsnip and cook, turning as needed, until lightly browned on all sides, 1 to 2 minutes. Add the Brussels sprouts to the pot and season with salt. Continue to cook, turning as needed, until all the vegetables are well browned, about 10 minutes. Season the vegetables with 1 tablespoon of the spice mixture and continue to cook for 30 to 60 seconds. Remove the vegetables from the pot, and remove the pot from the heat and reserve it.

Preheat the oven to 425°F.

Rinse the whole chicken and chicken breasts under cold running water and pat dry. Cut the whole chicken into 8 pieces: 2 breasts, 2 thighs, 2 drumsticks, and 2 wings. (Reserve the back and neck for making stock.) Cut the breasts from the whole chicken and the 2 additional half breasts in half crosswise.

Put the remaining $1/4$ cup olive oil into the pot used for the vegetables and heat the oil over high heat. Season the chicken pieces with the remaining 3 tablespoons spice mixture. When the oil is hot but not smoking, add the chicken pieces skin side down, working in batches if necessary to avoid crowding. Cook, turning as needed, until the chicken is dark brown on all sides, about 12 minutes. Remove the chicken from the pot. Tilt the pot and pour off all but 2 tablespoons of the fat. Reduce the heat to medium, add the garlic and the pancetta, if using, and cook, turning occasionally, until browned, 1 to 2 minutes.

Discard the vegetables and bay leaf from the beans and add the beans and their liquid to the garlic and pancetta. Bring to a simmer over medium heat and cook to reduce the liquid until a layer of beans shows above the surface of the liquid. Add the caramelized vegetables and the chicken, skin side up.

Put the pot in the oven and roast, uncovered, until the chicken is fully cooked and the surface is nicely caramelized, 25 to 30 minutes. Remove from the oven and let rest at room temperature for 10 to 15 minutes, then serve warm.

SERVES 6 TO 8

2 days before	1 day before	morning of	1 hour before	service
shop, prepare beans	prepare vegetables	set table	cook chicken, add vegetables and bake	serve and enjoy

GRILLED AND BRAISED SHORT RIBS, BRASCIOLE STYLE — Long-braised meats are among my favorite

main courses, especially in fall and winter. The low and slow method of cooking (see Forever-Roasted Lamb, page 125) is ideal for encouraging the tenderness out of typically tough cuts, from oxtails to shanks to short ribs. While at Tra Vigne, I created a slew of short rib recipes that soared in popularity with each passing year. The flavor of the ribs, properly cooked, is nothing short of spectacular. Here, the brining both seasons the meat throughout and helps the meat adhere to the bone.

COOKING NOTES: Be sure to ask your butcher for Chinese-style cross-cut ribs. Otherwise you may get a long-bone English cut, which is not nearly as meaty. If you braise on the stove top, keep the heat as low as possible. I like the oven because you don't have to watch the heat. Put the ribs on to braise and let them go for hours.

ENTERTAINING NOTES: When the ribs are ready, you can remove them from the oven, allow them to cool, and then cover and refrigerate overnight. The next day, remove from the refrigerator and spoon off all the fat that has solidified on top. Place the pan over medium heat until the sauce is at a slow simmer, then cover the pan with aluminum foil and place in a preheated 300°F oven. The ribs will be hot throughout in about 30 minutes; then plate and garnish them as directed. Serve with crusty bread to soak up all the juices, or with golden squares of polenta (see Polenta Crostini, page 44; cut the polenta into large squares and omit the cheese and herb topping).

WINE NOTES: A fruity Petite Sirah is a good partner for the earthy flavors of this dish.

FOR THE BRINE:

2 quarts (8 cups) water

2 cups firmly packed brown sugar

2 cups kosher salt

2 tablespoons juniper berries

3 bay leaves

8 cross-cut short ribs, about 1 pound each

¼ cup extra-virgin olive oil

2 tablespoons thinly sliced garlic

2 teaspoons fennel seeds

½ teaspoon red pepper flakes

4 cups Marinara Sauce (page 18) or good-quality jarred sauce

4 cups chicken stock

⅓ cup drained capers

2 bay leaves

3 tablespoons finely chopped fresh Italian (flat-leaf) parsley

1 tablespoon grated lemon zest

Make the brine: In a large saucepan, combine all the ingredients over high heat and bring to a boil, stirring to dissolve the sugar. Remove from the heat and let cool completely.

Arrange the ribs, bone side up, in a single layer in two 9-by-13-inch baking dishes. Pour the brine over the ribs. Cover with plastic and refrigerate for 3 hours.

Ready a charcoal or gas grill for direct heat grilling over a hot fire.

Remove the ribs from the brine and discard the brine. Place the ribs, fat side down first, on the grill and cook, turning occasionally, until seared on all sides, 8 to 10 minutes.

Preheat the oven to 300°F.

In a large 12-by-15-inch roasting pan, heat the olive oil over medium-high heat. Add the garlic and tilt the pan to collect the oil and garlic in one corner. When the garlic begins to brown, after about 30 seconds, lay the pan flat on the burners and add the fennel and red

pepper flakes. Cook the spices in the oil for 10 seconds to release their fragrance. Add the Marinara Sauce, chicken stock, capers, and bay leaves and stir to mix well. Arrange the ribs in a single layer in the pan. Bring the liquid to a simmer.

Cover the pan, move it to the oven, and cook the ribs for 3 to 4 hours. They are ready when the meat pulls away from the bones easily. Remove the pan from the oven and transfer the ribs to a platter, leaving the sauce behind in the pan; cover to keep warm. Using a large spoon, skim as much of the fat as possible off the top of the sauce. If the sauce has cooled, reheat it on the stove top.

Divide the short ribs among warmed individual plates and spoon the hot sauce over them. In a small bowl, mix together the parsley and lemon zest. Sprinkle a little of the mixture over each serving and serve immediately.

SERVES 8

low and slow

*Never ever braise over 300°F or shoe
leather is what you'll end up with.*

also good as . . .

*A wonderful pappardelle, short rib and
English pea pasta the next day or day after.*

PAN-ROASTED PORK TENDERLOIN WITH FENNEL AND PANCETTA-MOLASSES DRESSING—

When I was twenty-two, I opened a restaurant called Toby's Bar and Grill in Miami. The food was progressive new American. Even though my style of cooking has changed considerably over the years, some of my first-time-chef creations have stood the test of time and still impress. This is one of those dishes. The dressing is a version of *agrodolce*, or "sweet and sour," a popular pairing in southern Italy.

COOKING NOTES: Be sure to season the pork liberally. Cooks tend to underseason meats, forgetting that half of the seasoning comes off in the pan and on the cutting board. I like sliced garlic and shallots in the dressing. That way, they are more like vegetables.

ENTERTAINING NOTES: To cook this dish for a larger group, double the recipe, then sear the tenderloins in batches and make the dressing ahead of time. Closer to the time of service, roast the tenderloins all at once on a baking sheet. Serve with grapes, apples, or persimmons.

WINE NOTES: Serve with a Petite Sirah, Dolcetto, or Zinfandel.

FOR THE DRESSING:

1 pound pancetta, sliced ¼ inch thick

2 shallots, thinly sliced

2 tablespoons thinly sliced garlic

1 tablespoon finely chopped fresh sage

¼ cup light molasses

¼ cup balsamic vinegar

3 pork tenderloins, 1 to 1¼ pounds each

¼ cup Fennel Spice Rub (page 16)

2 tablespoons extra-virgin olive oil

¾ pound baby spinach or baby Swiss chard

Finely ground sea salt, preferably gray salt

Freshly ground black pepper

Make the dressing: To make cutting the pancetta easier, roll up the slices into a log, wrap it in plastic wrap, and put it in the freezer for about 1 hour. Remove the pancetta from the freezer and cut the log into julienne strips ¾ inch long and ¼ inch wide and thick.

In a large skillet, cook the pancetta over medium heat, stirring occasionally, until it is almost crisp, about 5 minutes. Raise the heat to medium-high. Add the shallots and cook for 1 minute, stirring occasionally. Add the garlic and cook, stirring occasionally, until it turns golden brown, about 3 minutes. Add the sage and cook for 10 seconds to release its fragrance. Stir in the molasses and vinegar. Cook until half the liquid has evaporated, about 3 minutes. Remove from the heat.

Preheat the oven to 425°F.

Trim any excess fat and sinew from the pork tenderloins. Evenly coat the tenderloins with the fennel mixture. In a 12-inch ovenproof skillet, heat the olive oil over high heat. When the oil is hot but not smoking, sear the tenderloins on all sides, about 5 minutes total. Move the skillet to the oven and cook the tenderloins until an instant-read thermometer registers 155°F for medium, 6 to 8 minutes.

Remove the pan from the oven and transfer the tenderloins to a cutting board to rest for 3 to 5 minutes. Meanwhile, pour off all but 1 tablespoon of the oil from the skillet. Place the skillet over high heat. When it is hot, add the spinach and cook just until it is barely wilted, about 20 seconds. Season to taste with salt and pepper. Immediately remove the spinach from the pan to halt the cooking, and divide it among warmed individual plates.

Slice the pork tenderloins across the grain on the diagonal. Arrange the slices on the plates alongside the spinach. Whisk the dressing briefly and spoon it over the top of the pork. Serve the pork warm or at room temperature.

SERVES 8

"CHEAP AND TASTY" PORK AND ORANGE STEW — After so many years of cooking à la carte meals in restaurants, I crave long-cooked, all-in-one dishes like this stew. They are always a triple play for me: they offer intense and rich flavors from the long cooking, they can be prepared far in advance of my guests' arrival, and they are nice and easy on the entertaining budget.

COOKING NOTES: Simmer the stew slowly to coax the tenderness out of this pork cut, which is not naturally tender.

ENTERTAINING NOTES: This stew is wonderful served atop Party-Method Fontina Risotto (page 82) or soft cooked polenta (see Polenta Bites with Caramelized Mushrooms, page 38; make only the polenta, omitting the mushrooms).

WINE NOTES: The softness of a good Merlot marries well with the pork.

1½ pounds boneless pork shoulder, cut into bite-sized chunks

Finely ground sea salt, preferably gray salt, or Citrus Salt (page 15)

6 tablespoons extra-virgin olive oil, or more if needed

2 teaspoons Fennel Spice Rub (page 16) or toasted fennel seeds

2 tablespoons Cointreau

1 cup dry red wine

1 cup fresh orange juice

6 cups chicken stock

1 bay leaf

1½ tablespoons unsalted butter

¾ pound yellow-fleshed potatoes, peeled and cut into ½-inch cubes

12 pearl onions, peeled

2 cups stemmed fresh shiitake mushrooms, quartered

12 baby carrots, peeled

1 tablespoon minced garlic

1 tablespoon finely chopped fresh rosemary

Freshly ground black pepper

1 tablespoon grated orange zest

2 tablespoons finely chopped fresh Italian (flat-leaf) parsley

---

Season the pork well with 2 teaspoons salt. In a large sauté pan, heat ¼ cup of the olive oil over medium-high heat until it begins to smoke. (The generous amount of oil allows the meat to brown well. The excess will be drained off.) Working in batches if necessary to avoid crowding the pan, add the pork and let brown on the first side before turning, then sauté until well browned all over, about 10 minutes total. Pour the contents of the pan into a sieve to drain the excess fat.

Return the pan to high heat and return the meat to the pan. Add the fennel mixture, Cointreau, wine, and orange juice. Stir and scrape the bottom and sides of the pan to loosen all the browned bits. Bring the mixture to a boil, then reduce the heat slightly and simmer until reduced by half, about 5 minutes. Add the stock and bay leaf, reduce the heat to low, cover, and simmer slowly until the meat is very tender, about 45 minutes.

About 15 minutes before the meat is ready, in a large sauté pan, heat the remaining 2 tablespoons olive oil with the butter over medium-high heat. Add the potatoes, onions, mushrooms, and carrots and sauté until all the vegetables are well browned, about 15 minutes. Adjust the heat so the vegetables brown but do not burn, adding additional oil if necessary. Add the garlic and rosemary and sauté briefly just to brown the garlic. Season to taste with salt and pepper.

Scrape the contents of the sauté pan into the stew. Cook the stew until the vegetables are tender and the flavors have blended, about 15 minutes. Just before serving, stir the orange zest and parsley into the stew. Taste and adjust the seasoning, then serve.
SERVES 6

ROASTED WHOLE RACK OF PORK WITH DRIED-CHERRY STUFFING

ROASTED WHOLE RACK OF PORK WITH DRIED-CHERRY STUFFING—Over the years, we have evolved from roasting whole cuts of meat and poultry to little tiny pieces of meat, hoping it would be quicker. What we have given up is the scrumptious, satisfying quality of meat cooked on the bone. The saying "The closer to the bone the sweeter the meat" is true.

COOKING NOTES: Be sure to ask for a center-cut loin. To save you time, ask the butcher to trim any excess fat, remove the chine bone, and to french the ribs (trim away the meat and fat, exposing the ends of the bones), so that about 2 inches of each bone are exposed. If you have some Toasted Spice Rub (page 16) on hand, rub 2 tablespoons on the pork before roasting it. The cinnamon in the spice mix is perfect with the pork.

ENTERTAINING NOTES: When serving a whole rack of meat, remember to present the entire rack to your guests for the ooh and aah factor before you carve it. I will often show it off, then return to the kitchen to carve it. Serve with Honey-Roasted Applesauce (page 153).

WINE NOTES: A fruity Merlot or Syrah complements the fruit in this dish.

FOR THE STUFFING:

2 tablespoons unsalted butter

1 bay leaf

1½ tablespoons finely minced fresh rosemary or sage

1 cup finely chopped yellow onion

¼ cup firmly packed light brown sugar

1 tablespoon brandy

1 tablespoon fresh lemon juice

½ cup fresh orange juice

1 cup dried sour cherries, soaked in 1 cup water to plump for 5 minutes, then drained and water reserved

Finely ground sea salt, preferably gray salt

1 loaf country-style bread, about 1 pound, or 1 large loaf Aunt Mary's Panettone Cake (page 177)

1 bone-in center-cut pork loin roast, 6 to 7 pounds (8 bones), chine bone removed and rib bones frenched

Finely ground sea salt, preferably gray salt

Freshly ground black pepper

¼ cup extra-virgin olive oil

1 cup dry white wine

2 cups chicken stock

1 bay leaf

Preheat the oven to 350°F.

Make the stuffing: In a 10-inch skillet, melt the butter over high heat and cook, without stirring, until it browns, 3 to 4 minutes. Add the bay leaf and rosemary and stand back (they might pop). Reduce the heat to medium, add the onion, and sauté until soft, about 5 minutes. Stir in the sugar. When the sugar has melted, add the brandy and stand back (it might flame). Add the lemon juice. Cook for 15 seconds, then add the orange juice, the water from the cherries, and ¼ teaspoon salt. Stir and cook until the liquid has

reduced by half and has a syrupy consistency, about 3 minutes. You should have about ½ cup. Add the drained cherries. Remove and discard the bay leaf.

Using a serrated knife, shave off the thicker parts of the crust from the bread loaf. Cut the bread into ½-inch cubes. You should have about 8 cups. Place the bread in a large bowl, add ¼ cup of the brown butter syrup, and toss to coat evenly. Spread the bread cubes in a single layer on a rimmed baking sheet. Bake the bread cubes, turning occasionally for even coloring, until golden and crispy on the outside and still chewy inside, 15 to 20 minutes. Remove from the oven and set aside.

Remove the pork roast from the refrigerator 20 to 30 minutes before cooking to allow it to come to room temperature. Season the trimmed pork roast generously with salt and pepper. In a roasting pan, heat the olive oil over high heat. When the oil begins to smoke, add the pork roast, bone side down. Cook, turning as needed, until well browned on all sides, including the ends, about 15 minutes total. Remove the pork and set a roasting rack inside the pan. Set the pork, bone side up, on the rack. (If you do not have a rack, simply leave in the pan, but bone side down.)

Place the roast in the oven and cook to medium, or until an instant-read thermometer inserted in the thickest part of the roast not touching bone registers 155°F, about 1 hour. Remove from the oven, cover lightly with aluminum foil, and let rest for 15 to 20 minutes. Leave the oven on.

Pour the fat out of the roasting pan. Place the pan on the stove top over high heat. Add the wine, bring to a boil, and scrape the browned bits off the pan bottom. Cook until the wine is reduced to about ¼ cup, about 2 minutes. Add the stock, the bay leaf, and the remaining ¼ cup brown butter syrup, and cook until about 1 cup of the liquid remains, about 5 to 7 minutes.

Put the croutons in a 9-by-13-inch baking pan, pour ½ cup of the liquid from the roasting pan evenly over the croutons, and mix well. Cover the pan with aluminum foil and put in the oven to heat through, about 15 minutes. Remove the foil and bake for an additional 10 minutes.

Slice the pork roast between the bones to separate the 8 chops. Remove the stuffing from the oven and spoon it in the middle of a large platter. Arrange the pork chops around the stuffing, leaning them on their sides against the stuffing so the bones are sticking up in the air and the meat overlaps slightly. The bones should look like points. Drizzle the remaining ½ cup liquid from the roasting pan evenly over the chops. Serve at once.

SERVES 8

2 days before	1 day before	morning of	1 hour before	service
rest	shop, prepare vegetables	prepare croutons, set table	make stuffing, remove pork from refrigerator 20 minutes before roasting, roast pork for 2 hours, open wine	slice and enjoy

MINESTRA RISOTTO WITH LONG-COOKED CHICKEN — Growing up, I noticed that each of my aunts made the dishes of their childhood differently. My dear aunt Rose inspired this version of risotto, which is really more of a *minestra,* or "soup," with the chicken served on the side, than a creamy risotto. With her nine children, I imagine she stretched out the normal recipe for risotto for four with enough liquid to feed the army of hungry mouths.

COOKING NOTES: For this recipe, I like to use free-range whole chickens and cut them up, rather than buy individual pieces, which are usually lesser quality. I sometimes substitute different meats, such as pork shoulder, veal necks, or whatever the butcher has that's inexpensive. You will end with about 4 quarts of the soupy risotto, more than you need for this meal. Freeze the remainder and serve it a week or so later when you need something on the table fast.

ENTERTAINING NOTES: Serve this dish right from the kitchen stove, as hungry stomachs gather around. To match the casual occasion, serve the risotto in soup plates with just-warmed crusty bread and jelly jars or tumblers for wineglasses. Pass the chicken as a second course.

WINE NOTES: I generally do not drink wine with soupy dishes, but Sauvignon Blanc would be a simple choice for a white and Zinfandel for a red.

⅓ cup extra-virgin olive oil	1 cup dry, fruity red wine such as Petite Sirah or Zinfandel
2 cups diced yellow onion	3 cans (28 ounces each) whole tomatoes, pureed with their juice
1 cup diced carrot	Freshly ground black pepper
1 cup diced celery	2 cups water
2 tablespoons minced garlic	1½ cups Arborio rice
2 bay leaves	½ cup minced fresh basil
Finely ground sea salt, preferably gray salt	¼ cup minced fresh Italian (flat-leaf) parsley
2 chickens, each about 4 pounds	½ cup freshly grated Parmesan cheese

Preheat the oven to 325°F.

In a large ovenproof pot, heat the olive oil over high heat. When it is hot but not smoking, add the onion, carrot, celery, garlic, bay leaves, and 1 teaspoon salt. Cook, stirring occasionally, for about 3 minutes, then reduce the heat to medium and cook, stirring occasionally, until the vegetables are lightly browned, 15 to 20 minutes.

Meanwhile, rinse the chickens under cold running water and pat thoroughly dry. Cut each chicken into 8 pieces: 2 breasts, 2 thighs, 2 drumsticks, and 2 wings. (Reserve the backs and necks for making stock.) Cut each breast in half crosswise.

When the vegetables are ready, add the wine to the pot, raise the heat to medium-high, and scrape the bottom with a wooden spoon to loosen any flavorful bits. Add the tomatoes, 1 tablespoon salt, and ½ teaspoon pepper. Taste and add more salt if needed. It is important to add enough salt so that the chicken seasons as it cooks. Submerge the chicken pieces in the sauce, with the legs and thighs on the bottom, and bring the sauce to a simmer.

Move the pot to the oven. Cook, uncovered, until the chicken is very tender, 1½ to 2 hours. Remove the pot from the oven and allow the contents to cool for 30 minutes.

Using a slotted spoon, remove the chicken pieces and set them aside on a warmed platter; cover to keep warm. Add the water to the contents of the pot and put the pot on the stove top over high heat. Add the rice and bring the mixture to a boil. Reduce the heat to a simmer and cook for 15 minutes. Mix in the basil and parsley. Continue to cook until the rice is al dente, about 5 minutes longer.

Remove the pot from the heat. Spoon the risotto into warmed soup plates (you won't need all of it) and sprinkle 1 tablespoon of the cheese on top of each serving. Follow the risotto with the chicken, passed on the platter.

SERVES 8

THIRTY-MINUTE PRIME RIB—There is nothing better than a prime rib roast. But to have the best, you need to find a butcher that carries the USDA "prime" grade. Most of the beef sold in markets today is "select" or "choice" grade. If you find the best, you have made a substantial financial investment, so then you are faced with the fear that you may undercook it. This recipe is my answer to that anxiety. You get all the benefits of the roast with none of the worry.

COOKING NOTES: Remember to preorder your meat if you want USDA prime beef. Then, focus on the two most important rules whenever you cook meat: let it come up to room temperature before cooking, and give the cooked roast plenty of time to rest before you carve it.

ENTERTAINING NOTES: Since the meat is such a luxurious treat, keep the accompaniments simple. Serve with Lemon Oil Smashed Potatoes (page 155) and Sautéed Greens, Calabria Style (page 153).

WINE NOTES: This is the time to pull out one of your fine old bottles of Cabernet Sauvignon. If you don't have one, visit your wine shop and buy the best.

---

3 prime-grade rib-eye steaks, each 2 to 2½ pounds and
  1¾ to 2 inches thick
Finely ground sea salt, preferably gray salt
Freshly ground black pepper

1 cup whole garlic cloves, unpeeled (about 2 heads)
6 tablespoons extra-virgin olive oil
2 tablespoons minced fresh rosemary
2 lemons, cut into wedges

Remove the steaks from the refrigerator 2 hours before cooking, and season them generously on both sides with salt and pepper.

Preheat the oven to 450°F.

Trim the stem ends off the garlic cloves and peel away any loose skin. Lightly crush the cloves and place them in a small skillet with 4 tablespoons of the oil. Set the skillet over medium heat, bring the oil to a simmer, reduce the heat to low, and cook the garlic cloves, tossing them occasionally with tongs, until golden brown, about 10 minutes. Add the rosemary and remove the skillet from the heat. Allow the garlic to cool in the oil.

When the garlic is cool enough to handle, using a slotted spoon, remove the garlic cloves from the oil, reserving the oil. Remove the skins from the cloves and discard. In a mortar using a pestle, or on a cutting board using a chef's knife, mash the garlic to a paste. Mix the mashed garlic with the reserved oil and rosemary in the mortar or a bowl. You should have about ½ cup paste.

Line a 13-by-18-inch rimmed baking sheet with aluminum foil. Set a rack a little smaller than the baking sheet on top of the foil.

In a large skillet, heat the remaining 2 tablespoons olive oil over high heat. When the oil is hot but not smoking, add the steaks in batches (do not crowd the pan) and sear, turning once, until well browned on both sides, about 5 minutes on the first side and 3 minutes on the second side.

Smear 2 generous tablespoons of the paste over the first seared side of each steak. Place the steaks, paste side facing up, on the rack. Finish cooking the steaks in the oven until done to your preference, 10 to 12 minutes for rare or slightly longer for medium-rare. To be sure they are done to your liking, test with an instant-read thermometer, which should register 120°F for rare or 130°F for medium-rare. Remove the pan from the oven and allow the steaks to rest on the rack for about 10 minutes.

Transfer the steaks to a cutting board. Cut between the bone and meat of each steak. Cut each steak across the grain into 1-inch-thick slices. Serve on warmed individual plates with the lemon wedges.

SERVES 8 TO 10

goes great with . . .

perfectly grilled radicchio and
honey-roasted applesauce

OPPOSITE: SPICED AND HONEY-GLAZED HAM, PAGE 143; ABOVE: "MEAT COUNTER" MIXED GRILL, PAGE 142

"MEAT COUNTER" MIXED GRILL—Cooking for a group made up of folks with different likes and dislikes can be nerve-racking for any cook. Believe me, special requests used to fly around the restaurant every night, and they were no fun! When entertaining at home, put together a platter of three or four meats and everyone is thrilled. If you live on the West Coast, don't forget a couple of grilled vegetables for your vegetarian friends.

COOKING NOTES: Blanching the sausages makes them a little juicier and keeps the grilling time to a minimum. If you don't want to french the lamb racks yourself (trim away the meat and fat, exposing the ends of the bones), ask your butcher to do it for you.

ENTERTAINING NOTES: You can partially cook all the meats about an hour ahead of time. To do so, arrange them on baking sheets and flash them in a preheated 400°F oven for 8 to 10 minutes. Serve your mixed grill the ultrasimple Tuscan way: pass lemon wedges, sea salt, and really great olive oil, and that's it!

WINE NOTES: A *collezione* of meats calls for a quartet of red wines. Open a Cabernet Sauvignon, Zinfandel, Syrah, and Petite Sirah.

Finely ground sea salt, preferably gray salt

6 spicy fresh Italian sausages, about 1½ pounds total weight

FOR THE CHICKEN:

4 bone-in, skin-on whole chicken breasts, each about ¾ pound, trimmed
    of excess fat

¼ cup extra-virgin olive oil

1 lemon, halved

4 teaspoons finely chopped fresh thyme

Freshly ground black pepper

FOR THE LAMB:

2 racks of lamb, each about 2 pounds, frenched and trimmed of excess fat

2 tablespoons balsamic vinegar

¼ cup extra-virgin olive oil

2 tablespoons finely chopped fresh rosemary

1 tablespoon minced garlic

1 teaspoon freshly ground black pepper

FOR THE PORK TENDERLOIN:

2 pork tenderloins, each ¾ to 1 pound, excess fat and sinew removed

2 tablespoons extra-virgin olive oil

4 teaspoons Toasted Spice Rub (page 16)

Extra-virgin olive oil

Finely ground sea salt, preferably gray salt

4 lemons, halved crosswise

Freshly ground black pepper

Bring a large saucepan of salted water to a gentle boil. Add the sausages and boil for 3 minutes. Drain them in a colander, let cool, and then cover and refrigerate.

Marinate the chicken: Arrange the chicken breasts in a single layer in a nonreactive baking pan. Drizzle the olive oil evenly over the top, then squeeze the juice from the lemon halves evenly over the top. Sprinkle evenly with the thyme and ¾ teaspoon pepper. Turn the chicken breasts several times to coat them thoroughly. Lay a piece of parchment paper over the chicken and refrigerate for 8 hours or up to overnight.

Marinate the lamb: Arrange the lamb racks in a single layer in a nonreactive baking pan. Drizzle the vinegar over the top and rub it all over the meat. Add the olive oil, rosemary, garlic, and 1 teaspoon pepper. Turn the lamb racks several times to coat them thoroughly. Lay a piece of parchment paper over the lamb and refrigerate for 8 hours or up to overnight.

Marinate the pork: Arrange the pork tenderloins in a single layer in a baking pan. Drizzle the olive oil evenly over the top, then sprinkle the spice mixture evenly over the top. Turn the tenderloins several times to coat them thoroughly. Lay a piece of parchment paper over the pork and refrigerate for 8 hours or up to overnight.

Bring the meats to room temperature before grilling, 20 to 30 minutes. Ready a charcoal grill or gas grill for both direct and indirect heat grilling over a medium fire.

Lightly coat the sausages with olive oil. Season the chicken on all sides with 2 teaspoons salt, pressing it into the meat. Season the lamb racks on all sides with 2 teaspoons salt, pressing it into the meat. Season the pork tenderloins on all sides with 2 teaspoons salt, pressing it into the meat. Lightly coat the cut side of the lemons with olive oil and season with ½ teaspoon salt and ¼ teaspoon pepper.

Grill the chicken and lamb racks over direct heat, turning occasionally, until well browned on all sides, 6 to 8 minutes. Move the chicken and lamb to indirect heat and continue to cook, turning once, for 10 minutes longer. Leave the chicken and lamb racks to continue cooking over indirect heat, and grill the sausages and pork tenderloins over direct heat, turning occasionally, until the sausages are fully cooked and the pork tenderloin is cooked to medium, 12 to 15 minutes. At this point the chicken should be opaque throughout and the lamb racks should be tender. During the last few minutes of grilling, grill the lemons cut side down over direct heat until well browned and caramelized, about 2 minutes.

Remove everything from the grill and let the meats rest for 5 to 10 minutes. Cut the meats into serving-sized pieces. Arrange on a large platter and garnish with the lemons. Encourage guests to squeeze the lemons over their servings.

SERVES 8 TO 10

SPICED AND HONEY-GLAZED HAM — It seems like everyone loves honey-baked hams. The salty cure of the ham against the sweet crystallized sugar crust is simply irresistible. I have invented a spicy home-baked alternative to the usual store-bought ham. It's so good, you will anticipate the leftovers as much as the original dinner.

COOKING NOTES: There are many types of hams on the market. For this dish, I like to use a high-quality fully cooked ham.

ENTERTAINING NOTES: The ham can be glazed in advance and kept wrapped in the refrigerator for the next day or two. Simply let it come to room temperature before baking. Serve with Savory Bread Pudding (page 166, preferably using the fall ingredients suggestions in the Cooking Notes).

WINE NOTES: Open a cool, fruity Petite Sirah.

½ cup mild honey such as clover or orange blossom
1½ tablespoons Toasted Spice Rub (page 16)
1 apple wood–smoked or honey-cured, boneless,
    fully cooked ham, about 4 pounds

Preheat the oven to 325°F.

In a small bowl, stir together the honey and the spice mixture. With a sharp knife, make a series of cuts, ½ inch deep and ½ inch apart, the entire length of the ham. Rotate the ham 90 degrees and make a second series of cuts, the same depth and the same distance apart, across the width of the ham.

Line a rimmed baking sheet with aluminum foil and place the ham on the pan. Bake, basting every 15 minutes with the honey mixture, until an instant-read thermometer inserted into the thickest part registers 150°F, 1 to 1¼ hours. Remove the ham from the oven and let rest for 10 minutes.

Carve the ham across the grain into slices of desired thickness. Arrange on a platter and drizzle with any remaining honey mixture.

SERVES 8 TO 10

POTATO CAKES WITH QUICK BOLOGNESE SAUCE — As a child, potato cakes were one of my favorite Friday night suppers, which were always meatless for us Italian Catholics. We used to eat them with a spicy tomato sauce. I have never forgotten how good they tasted, and so they became a foundation for building more sophisticated dishes like this one.

COOKING NOTES: If you make the sauce ahead of time, you may need to add a little stock or water to loosen it up when you reheat it.

ENTERTAINING NOTES: To give yourself a head start, make the sauce and the cakes ahead of time. The sauce can be prepared and stored in the refrigerator for up to 4 days or in the freezer for up to 2 months. The cakes can be made and stored in the refrigerator for up to 1 day in advance. When it's time to serve, dust the cakes with flour and sauté them until crispy on the outside, then place them on a baking sheet and warm them through to the center in a preheated 375°F oven for 10 minutes. Meanwhile, reheat the sauce. Serve it up, pat yourself on the back, and go enjoy dinner. These cakes are also fantastic done as appetizers: form the potato mixture into 1-inch cakes, brown them, and top the cakes with mozzarella and basil pesto (homemade, page 21, or purchased).

WINE NOTES: A good Chianti or Zinfandel would pair perfectly. Foods like this like to have a red wine with a little acid left in it to pair with the acid in the sauce.

FOR THE SAUCE:

½ ounce (½ cup) dried porcini mushrooms

1 cup hot water

3 tablespoons extra-virgin olive oil

1 pound ground veal

½ pound ground pork

1 cup chopped yellow onion

2 tablespoons minced garlic

2 teaspoons minced fresh rosemary

Finely ground sea salt, preferably gray salt

Freshly ground black pepper

⅔ cup dry white wine

1½ cups veal stock or chicken stock

½ cup water

2 tablespoons finely chopped fresh Italian (flat-leaf) parsley

1½ cups fresh tomato puree (see the Pantry, page 14) or 1 can
    (14½ ounces) whole tomatoes, pureed with their juice

FOR THE POTATO CAKES:

3 pounds large russet potatoes

Finely ground sea salt, preferably gray salt

Freshly ground black pepper

¼ pound fresh mozzarella cheese

¼ cup all-purpose flour

6 tablespoons extra-virgin olive oil, or as needed

¼ pound Parmesan cheese

Make the sauce: In a small bowl, combine the porcini with the hot water and let soak for 30 minutes. Using a slotted spoon, lift out the porcini, squeeze out the excess moisture, and chop finely. Line a sieve with a double thickness of damp paper towels and strain the liquid through the sieve into a small bowl. Reserve the porcini and liquid separately.

Meanwhile, in a large skillet, heat 2 tablespoons of the olive oil over medium heat. Add the veal and pork and cook, breaking the meats up with a wooden spoon, until they release their moisture and brown, 10 to 12 minutes. Using a slotted spoon, transfer the meats to a bowl.

Add the remaining 1 tablespoon olive oil to the skillet over medium-high heat. Add the onion and sauté until softened, about 5 minutes. Do not allow the onion to color. Add the garlic and rosemary and sauté for 10 seconds to release their fragrance. Season to taste with salt and pepper. Add the porcini and return the meats to the skillet. Cook until any moisture evaporates and the meats begin to sizzle. Add the wine and ¼ cup of the reserved porcini liquid, and cook for a minute or two to evaporate the liquid. Add the stock, water, and parsley. Simmer briskly for 2 minutes. Add the tomato puree, reduce the heat to a gentle simmer, and cook for 12 to 15 minutes to blend the flavors. You should have 4 to 5 cups sauce. Set aside.

Make the potato cakes: Preheat the oven to 450°F. Prick each potato once or twice with a fork, place directly on the oven rack, and bake until a thin knife blade easily slides into them, 1 to 1¼ hours. Remove from the oven and, when cool enough to handle, cut in half and scoop out the flesh. Reserve the potato skins, if desired, for another use.

Pass the potatoes through a potato ricer or grate them on the large holes of a box grater-shredder. You should have about 6 cups. Season the potatoes with 1 teaspoon salt and ½ teaspoon pepper, and then divide into 16 equal balls. Press each ball into a patty about 4 inches in diameter and ⅓ inch thick. Cut the mozzarella cheese into 8 slices, each ¼ inch thick. Center a slice on top of half of the patties. Cover with the remaining patties. Shape the patties into smooth disks.

Spread the flour on a dinner plate. Lightly dust the patties on both sides with the flour.

Put two 12-inch skillets over medium-high heat. Add 3 tablespoons of the oil to each skillet. When the oil is hot but not quite smoking, place 4 patties in each skillet. When you hear the patties sizzle, reduce the heat to medium. Cook, turning once, until browned and crispy on both sides, 10 to 12 minutes total. If the potatoes absorb all the oil, add another tablespoon oil to each skillet.

To serve, reheat the sauce until hot. Spoon ½ cup of the sauce into each of 8 individual shallow bowls. Using a spatula, arrange 2 patties in each bowl. Serve immediately. Pass the Parmesan cheese and a hand grater around the table.

SERVES 8

2 days before	1 day before	morning of	1 hour before	service
shop	prepare vegetables	prepare potato cakes, set table	prepare sauce, open wine	cook potato cakes, heat sauce and serve

TURKEY OSSO BUCO — In the mid-1980s, I made my first variation on traditional osso buco, substituting lamb shanks for veal shanks. Since then, I have worked my way through every other drumstick in the world, including turkey. I have also turned the traditional *gremolata* mixture of lemon zest, parsley, and garlic into a more elaborate topping.

COOKING NOTES: The proteins in meat coagulate when the braising liquid is slightly under 200°F. The better you maintain that temperature, the more tender your results will be, particularly for the leaner, tougher cuts of meat and poultry. You need good-sized drumsticks for this dish, from at least 14-pound birds. Ask your butcher to cut about 1 inch from the top and bottom of each drumstick, and then to cut each drumstick in half crosswise. Each of the 6 pieces of turkey should be 1 ½ to 2 inches long and 2 to 2 ½ inches in diameter.

ENTERTAINING NOTES: Braised foods should be cooked ahead of time. The flavors improve as the meat cools in the sauce and sits overnight. This dish can be made 2 days in advance and refrigerated. When it's time to eat, bring the dish to room temperature, then reheat in the oven and make the *gremolata*. The osso buco is wonderful with Party-Method Fontina Risotto (page 82). You can also create osso buco sandwiches by pulling the turkey meat off the bone, layering it with fresh basil leaves on a slice of *ciabatta*, and topping it with a spoonful of the sauce.

WINE NOTES: Pour a full-flavored Pinot Noir.

½ ounce (½ cup) dried porcini mushrooms

6 drumsticks from large turkeys, ends trimmed and then drumsticks halved crosswise

Finely ground sea salt, preferably gray salt

Freshly ground black pepper

¼ cup all-purpose flour

¼ cup extra-virgin olive oil, or more if needed

2 cups coarsely diced yellow onion

1 cup coarsely diced carrot

1 cup coarsely diced celery

6 large cloves garlic, peeled but left whole

1 tablespoon fresh rosemary leaves

1 bay leaf

2 tablespoons finely chopped fresh Italian (flat-leaf) parsley

¾ cup dry white wine

2 lemon zest strips, each about 2 inches long and ½ inch wide

1 cup fresh tomato puree (see the Pantry, page 14) or canned whole tomatoes, pureed with their juice

2 cups chicken stock

FOR THE *GREMOLATA*:

2 tablespoons unsalted butter

1 tablespoon minced garlic

1 teaspoon minced fresh rosemary

1 ¼ cups fresh bread crumbs

Finely ground sea salt, preferably gray salt

Freshly ground black pepper

1 tablespoon finely chopped fresh Italian (flat-leaf) parsley

1 teaspoon grated lemon zest

In a small bowl, combine the mushrooms with hot water to cover and set aside to soak.

Season the turkey pieces on all sides with salt and pepper. Spread the flour on a dinner plate and lightly dredge each piece of turkey in the flour, shaking off the excess (you will not need all the flour).

Preheat the oven to 350°F.

In a 12-inch sauté pan, heat the olive oil over high heat until it begins to smoke. Working in batches if necessary to avoid crowding the pan, add the turkey pieces in a single layer and cook, turning only occasionally, until the turkey is deep brown on all sides, 12 to 15 minutes. Using tongs or a slotted spoon, transfer the turkey pieces in a single layer to a 9-by-13-inch baking dish.

If there is no oil left in the skillet, add 2 tablespoons more olive oil and then the onion, carrot, celery, and garlic. Reduce the heat to medium. After 2 to 3 minutes, when the vegetables have released some of their liquid, use a wooden spoon to scrape the browned bits off the pan bottom. Add the rosemary and bay leaf and continue to cook until the vegetables are well browned, 2 to 3 minutes longer. Add the parsley. Drain the porcini mushrooms, discarding the liquid, and add them to the skillet. Add the wine and then scrape the bottom of the skillet again. Cook until almost all of the liquid has evaporated, 3 to 5 minutes. Add the lemon zest strips, tomato puree, and chicken stock and season to taste with salt and pepper. Bring to a simmer and pour over the turkey in the baking dish.

Cover the baking dish with aluminum foil and place in the oven. Braise the turkey until the meat is very tender and separates easily from the bone, 1 1/2 to 1 3/4 hours. Remove the baking dish from the oven and let the turkey cool in the braising liquid.

Remove the turkey pieces from the braising liquid and place them on a platter. Using needle-nose pliers or tweezers, remove the off-white tendons sticking out of the meat near the bones. Remove the bay leaf from the braising liquid. In a food processor, puree the braising liquid to make a smooth sauce (you should have about 6 cups). Taste and adjust the seasoning. If the sauce seems too thick, stir in a little water. Pour the sauce back over the turkey pieces.

Make the *gremolata:* If you have turned the oven off while the turkey cooled, preheat it again to 350°F. In a 10-inch ovenproof skillet, melt the butter over medium-high heat. Add the garlic and cook, stirring occasionally, until it begins to brown, about 30 seconds. Add the rosemary and cook for 10 seconds to release its fragrance, and then add the bread crumbs and season to taste with salt and pepper. Mix well.

Place the skillet in the oven and toast the bread crumbs, stirring once or twice, until golden brown and crispy, 12 to 15 minutes. Remove the skillet from the oven. Add the parsley and lemon zest and mix well. Leave the oven on.

Cover the baking dish holding the turkey with aluminum foil. Place the dish in the oven for 15 to 30 minutes to reheat. Remove from the oven and transfer the turkey pieces to a warmed platter. Taste the sauce and adjust the seasoning, then pour the sauce over the meat. Sprinkle the *gremolata* over the top and serve.

SERVES 6

2 days before	1 day before	morning of	1 hour before	service
shop	*prepare vegetables, make* gremolata	*braise the turkey, set table*	*gently reheat turkey, add* gremolata; *open wine*	*serve and enjoy*

sides that go together

Most chefs spend the lion's share of their creative time on fancy meat and seafood dishes. I, on the other hand, am most impressed with someone who can apply their creativity to side dishes without losing the integrity of the produce. Growing up Italian, everyone in my family worshipped the garden gods and celebrated the arrival of every season. What could be better than Lemon Oil Smashed Potatoes (page 155) with Double-Cut Bistecca alla Fiorentina (page 124), Honey-Roasted Applesauce (page 153) underneath a just-carved rack of pork (page 136), or a platter heaped with "Meat Counter" Mixed Grill (page 142) and Garlicky Vegetables Primavera (page 167)?

side dishes

Do your cooking—and your guests—a favor and use produce that is in season and at the peak of freshness. We all know that fish is like house-guests: the longer it stays around, the more it smells. Produce has about the same shelf life as seafood, so buy just what you need, on the day you need it if possible. And remember, no matter what else you do, leave the tomatoes in the market come winter. The grocers will get the hint and fill that area with produce that is in season once that's all shoppers are buying.

Wines are generally chosen to complement the main course, so there are no wine suggestions in this chapter. Ask yourself if the flavors of the side dish you are choosing match the flavors of your main course. If they do, the wine you have chosen for the main course will be a good match for your side dish, too.

TWICE-BAKED STUFFED PEA POTATOES — One of the tricks professional chefs use to create memorable food experiences is to take retro classics, like twice-baked potatoes, and reinvent them with modern ingredients and popular flavors. Serve these potatoes alongside grilled lamb chops, and you're sure to hear someone at the table relate a twice-baked memory from childhood.

COOKING NOTES: As an alternative to all butter in the stuffing, substitute equal amounts butter and extra-virgin olive oil.

ENTERTAINING NOTES: These stuffed potatoes can easily be made the day before and heated through when needed. The potatoes will be colder to start, so you will need to increase the reheating time by 5 to 10 minutes. When you want to go more "high-cotton," the pea puree is an ideal bright-green foundation on which to float sautéed scallops or halibut.

5 large russet potatoes, unpeeled	1 ½ cups heavy cream
10 tablespoons unsalted butter	1 teaspoon grated lemon zest
1 cup chopped leeks, white part only	2 cups shelled English peas (about 2 pounds unshelled)
2 tablespoons thinly sliced garlic	Extra-virgin olive oil for oiling potato skins
Finely ground sea salt, preferably gray salt	¾ cup freshly grated Parmesan cheese
1 teaspoon finely chopped fresh thyme	¼ cup Prosciutto Bits (page 19)

Preheat the oven to 450°F.

Prick each potato once or twice with a fork, place directly on the oven rack, and bake until a thin knife blade easily slides into them, 1 to 1 ¼ hours. Remove from the oven and let sit until cool enough to handle. Reduce the oven temperature to 400°F.

While the potatoes are cooling, begin to make the stuffing. In a saucepan, melt 2 tablespoons of the butter over high heat. Add the leeks, garlic, and a pinch of salt, reduce the heat to medium-low and cook, stirring occasionally, until the leeks are very soft, 8 to 10 minutes. Add the thyme and cook for 10 seconds to release its fragrance. Add the cream and lemon zest and bring to a boil. Add the peas and simmer until the peas are half-cooked, about 2 minutes. Pour the mixture into a food processor and let cool slightly. Process until the peas form a smooth puree, 45 to 60 seconds. Set aside.

When the potatoes are cool enough to handle, cut each one in half lengthwise and scoop the flesh out into a bowl, being careful not to break the potato skins. Stir the potato with a wooden spoon to break apart any big pieces. Lightly oil the potato skins inside and outside and set aside.

In a large skillet, melt 3 tablespoons of the butter over medium heat. Add the potatoes and cook for 2 minutes, stirring occasionally. Add the pea puree and stir until well combined. Add the remaining 5 tablespoons butter and stir well. Then add ½ cup of the cheese and stir again until the butter has melted and the cheese is fully incorporated. Taste and add salt if needed, then pour the stuffing onto a rimmed baking sheet and spread it out to cool. You should have about 8 cups.

To serve, spoon the cooled puree into the potato shells and place the shells on a clean rimmed baking sheet. Scatter the remaining ¼ cup cheese and the Prosciutto Bits on top. Bake until heated through, about 30 minutes. Remove from the oven and serve at once.

SERVES 10

PARMESAN FRENCH FRIES—At the Ajax Tavern, my one-time restaurant in Aspen, I served these French fries with shaved black truffles and truffle oil. I called them twenty-five-dollar fries and charged that much, too. They sold like mad. Imagine coming off the slopes and sitting down at the end of the day with a glass of Champagne and a basket of those fries.

COOKING NOTES: Rinsing the potatoes in water leaches out most of the starch, which allows them to crisp nicely in the oil. Soaking them overnight is perfectly okay. Fry them in smaller batches so the temperature of the oil doesn't drop dramatically when you add the potatoes. And it is critical that you fry them twice, not just one long time: once makes them soggy; twice makes them crispy.

ENTERTAINING NOTES: Try serving these French fries in paper cones or widemouthed glasses. I sometimes create an assortment of differently flavored fries for an interesting presentation. For a more gourmet taste, in addition to the cheese, parsley, and zest, toss the fries with 1 tablespoon truffle oil. Or, for a more casual barbecue version, omit the Parmesan cheese and lemon zest and toss the fries with 2 tablespoons Spanish paprika; 2 ounces pecorino cheese, shaved with a vegetable peeler; and the 2 teaspoons finely chopped fresh Italian (flat-leaf) parsley. I sometimes line an antique sugar mold with paper cones, fill them with the assortment of fries, and let guests take their pick. You might pour some Champagne, too.

Peanut oil for deep-frying

3 pounds russet potatoes, peeled

Finely ground sea salt, preferably gray salt

Freshly ground black pepper

2 ounces Parmesan cheese, cut into shavings with a vegetable peeler

2 teaspoons finely chopped fresh Italian (flat-leaf) parsley

1 teaspoon grated lemon zest

Pour the peanut oil to a depth of at least 4 inches into a deep fryer or a heavy, 8-inch-deep stockpot and heat to 325°F. Make sure the pot is at least 8 inches deep to allow room for the oil to foam up without risk.

Meanwhile, cut the potatoes lengthwise into ¼-inch-thick slices. Then stack the slices and cut the stacks into ¼-inch-wide strips. Rinse the potato strips in a bowl of cold water, changing the water until it runs clear. Dry thoroughly with paper towels.

Working in 2 batches, fry the potatoes for 2 minutes to cook them partially. Using a slotted spoon, transfer the potatoes to paper towels to drain.

Reheat the oil to 375°F. Again working in 2 batches, fry the potatoes until golden brown and crispy, about 5 minutes. Using the slotted spoon, transfer to paper towels to drain briefly, then put the French fries in a large bowl and season to taste with salt and pepper. Add the Parmesan cheese, parsley, and lemon zest and toss to coat the fries evenly. Serve at once.

MAKES 6 TO 8 SERVINGS

PERFECTLY GRILLED RADICCHIO—Throughout Italy, you'll find bitter greens are appreciated by nearly everyone, with the chicory family enjoyed year-round. The greens are frequently grilled alongside meats, and old-world Italians like to dress them simply, with just olive oil and red wine vinegar, to savor their smoky, round bitterness. Over the years, however, chefs have moved radicchio to center stage and it is now often given a more elaborate treatment. This recipe celebrates this contemporary status.

COOKING NOTES: To remove bitterness, I used to blanch radicchio in vinegar water, but I found that it lost too much flavor. The method I use here, immersing it in ice water, solves that problem. Before the party, have the radicchio drained and in the vinaigrette in the refrigerator. Grill just until the outside is crispy and caramelized, yet still a little cool in the center. Drizzle any leftover dressing over the top of the grilled radicchio.

ENTERTAINING NOTES: It's a grilled salad, it's an antipasto, it's a side dish, and it can even be a main course. I often set the radicchio alongside a leg of lamb or grilled steak, but on a summer's eve, I sometimes stuff it with provolone cheese and serve it as the menu's main attraction.

1 large, round head radicchio, about ¾ pound

8 olive oil–packed anchovy fillets

6 cloves garlic

2 teaspoons fresh thyme leaves

½ teaspoon red pepper flakes

½ cup extra-virgin olive oil

4 teaspoons balsamic vinegar

Finely ground salt, preferably gray salt

Freshly ground black pepper

Discard any bruised outer leaves of the radicchio, then cut lengthwise into quarters, being sure to keep some of the stem attached to each quarter. Trim off any dark bits of stem. Submerge the radicchio quarters in ice water for 1 hour to remove some bitterness. Put a plate on top of the radicchio quarters to keep them submerged.

Meanwhile, on a cutting board and using a chef's knife, mince and mash together the anchovies, garlic, thyme, and red pepper flakes. In a bowl, combine the anchovy mixture, olive oil, and balsamic vinegar and mix well. You should have about ¾ cup.

Ready a charcoal or gas grill for direct heat grilling over a medium fire, or preheat a grill pan over medium heat.

Shake the water off the radicchio. Gently open up the leaves and spoon some of the anchovy mixture between them. Spoon the remaining anchovy mixture over the outside of each radicchio quarter. Season the quarters generously with salt and pepper.

Grill the radicchio, turning occasionally, until browned on the outside but still raw in the center, 3 to 5 minutes. Be careful, as the oil mixture may cause flare-ups. Serve warm.

SERVES 4

SAUTÉED GREENS, CALABRIA STYLE—

When I was a child, greens prepared by this method were on the table at least once a week. During the wild mustard season, we would go out and forage for bucketfuls of the wonderful greens. The combination of perfectly sautéed bitter greens and a hint of vinegar always tasted fantastic. The cooked greens would sit around our kitchen for days, and we would eat them at room temperature or chop them up and toss them with hot pasta and some olive oil. As I always say, if you start with great ingredients, your cooking can get simple and quick, allowing you more time to enjoy family and friends around the table.

COOKING NOTES: You can use a variety of greens in this recipe, such as kale, broccoli rabe, chard, bok choy, turnip greens, big spinach leaves, and arugula. Just remember to trim away any tough stems.

ENTERTAINING NOTES: Like many of my favorite vegetable side dishes, or *contorni*, one of the best things about these greens is that they are actually better served at room temperature. That's a big bonus when entertaining, because you eliminate the worry about getting all the dishes piping hot on the table at the same time. These greens are a particularly good sidekick to a grilled rib-eye steak or whole roasted chicken. They also stand out on a buffet.

¼ cup extra-virgin olive oil

2 tablespoons thinly sliced garlic

6 quarts (24 cups) lightly packed trimmed greens, any combination of
  3 types (see Cooking Notes)

Finely ground sea salt, preferably gray salt

Freshly ground black pepper

2 to 4 tablespoons red wine vinegar

In a large skillet, heat the olive oil over high heat. Add the garlic and tilt the pan to collect the oil and garlic on one side. When the garlic begins to brown, after about 30 seconds, set the pan flat on the burner and add the firmest of the 3 types of greens. Using tongs to stir and toss the greens, cook the greens until they wilt and barely cover the bottom of the skillet. Add the second firmest greens to the skillet and cook until they are wilted, stirring often. Add the last type of greens and cook until all of the greens are tender, stirring often. The timing will depend on the type of greens you are using. If at any time the skillet is dry, add a couple tablespoons water.

Season the greens to taste with salt and pepper, then spread them on a rimmed baking sheet and allow them to cool. Add the vinegar to taste and toss well. Serve at room temperature.

SERVES 6

HONEY-ROASTED APPLESAUCE—

When I was young, I used to go to visit relatives who were ranchers in the Mount Shasta area of Northern California, and there were always great mountain-grown apples to eat. We sometimes roasted them in the wood-burning stove—a true fall treat. Applesauce is so simple to make that it seems silly to even think of buying it. And the great thing about making your own is that you can flavor it in interesting ways.

COOKING NOTES: Most applesauce recipes call for cooking the apples on the stove top from start to finish. But I prefer to start them on the stove top and then finish them in a hot oven. The oven heat concentrates their flavors by drying and caramelizing them slightly. Although I have suggested a couple of apple varieties, you can use what good cooking apples are available in your area.

ENTERTAINING NOTES: The applesauce can be made up to 3 days in advance, covered and refrigerated. I love to serve applesauce not only with pork, its best-known partner, but also with roasted chicken, beef, or even framing a single oversized pumpkin ravioli.

12 apples such as Gravenstein or McIntosh, 4 to 5 pounds total weight

3 tablespoons fresh lemon juice

4 tablespoons (½ stick) unsalted butter

Finely ground sea salt, preferably gray salt

⅓ cup honey

Preheat the oven to 425°F.

Quarter and core the apples, then peel and cut into 1-inch chunks. As each apple is ready, place it in a large bowl and toss with the lemon juice.

In a large ovenproof sauté pan, melt the butter over medium-high heat. When the butter begins to brown, add the apples and ½ teaspoon salt and sauté until the edges just begin to color, 3 to 4 minutes. Add the honey, stir to mix well, and move the pan to the oven. Bake the apples until they are soft and lightly caramelized, about 20 to 30 minutes.

Remove from the oven. Mash the apples with a fork for a chunky version or process in a food processor for a smoother sauce. Serve warm, at room temperature, or cold.

SERVES 8

texture's a flavor

*By fork mashing, not machine mashing,
you gain lots of flavor from the texture*

LEMON OIL SMASHED POTATOES—Few things are easier than cooking up some tasty potatoes, casually mashing them with a fork, folding in heaps of flavor, and then taking your bow and accepting the applause. I predict that this dish will quickly find its way onto your entertaining A-list.

COOKING NOTES: Select medium-sized potatoes and cook them whole so they don't get waterlogged and dilute the final dish. Once you perfect this version, try it with basil oil (page 20), chili oil, or an exceptional-quality green (early press) Tuscan olive oil. You'll find many flavored oils at your specialty grocer, but because this recipe relies entirely on that flavor, invest in the best. Adjust the herbs in the potatoes to marry with the oil flavor you choose.

ENTERTAINING NOTES: This potato mixture also makes wonderful panfried cakes. Use the method from Potato Cakes with Quick Bolognese Sauce (page 144) and serve as a side dish.

3 pounds Yukon Gold potatoes, unpeeled

Finely ground sea salt, preferably gray salt

Grated zest of 4 lemons

¼ cup minced fresh chives

2 tablespoons finely chopped fresh thyme

1 tablespoon finely chopped fresh tarragon

Freshly ground black pepper

2 cups lemon extra-virgin olive oil or 2 cups extra-virgin olive oil
   and the grated zest of 4 more lemons

In a large saucepan, combine the potatoes with water to cover by 1 inch. Add 2 tablespoons salt and bring to a boil over high heat. Reduce the heat to medium and simmer until the potatoes are tender, 15 to 20 minutes. Drain the potatoes in a colander and place in a bowl.

Mash the potatoes with a fork until broken up but not smooth. Add the lemon zest, chives, thyme, tarragon, 2 teaspoons salt, and ½ teaspoon pepper and mix well with the fork. Add the lemon olive oil, ½ cup at a time, mixing well after each addition. You may find you do not need all the oil. The potatoes are ready when they are still chunky and begin to glisten with oil.

Taste and adjust the seasoning. Serve at once.

SERVES 8

POTATO "TORTA" STUFFED WITH PANCETTA AND CARAMELIZED ONIONS — While living in Miami, I had the opportunity to frequent the famous Joe Crab House many times. The waiters would literally run through the dining room with huge trays of stone crabs and plate after plate of skillet potato cake. The potatoes, which were baked first and then turned into a cake, were amazing. This is my version, and I guarantee you will love it.

COOKING NOTES: Be sure to let the baked potatoes cool to ensure a less starchy texture in the finished dish. Shred each potato on the large holes of a box grater-shredder, running the potato in a single direction with the holes to yield long strands, not beat-up pieces. Turn the potato as needed so the surface area is no wider than the grater.

ENTERTAINING NOTES: These can easily be made hours before and reheated in a 375°F oven for 15 minutes.

3 pounds large russet potatoes, unpeeled

½ pound pancetta, sliced ¼ inch thick

¾ cup plus 2 tablespoons extra-virgin olive oil

3 yellow onions, about 1½ pounds total

Finely ground sea salt, preferably gray salt

Freshly ground black pepper

4 teaspoons finely chopped fresh thyme

3 tablespoons balsamic vinegar

Preheat the oven to 375°F.

Prick each potato once or twice with a fork, place directly on the oven rack, and bake until a thin knife blade easily slides into them, 1 to 1¼ hours. Remove from the oven and let cool for 30 minutes.

Meanwhile, to make cutting the pancetta easier, roll up the slices into a log, wrap it in plastic wrap, and put it in the freezer for about 1 hour. Remove the pancetta from the freezer and cut the log into julienne strips 1 inch long and ¼ inch wide and thick.

In a 12-inch nonstick ovenproof skillet, combine 2 tablespoons of the olive oil and the pancetta over low heat. Cook the pancetta, stirring occasionally, just until it begins to crisp and the fat is rendered, about 20 minutes. Using a slotted spoon, transfer the pancetta to paper towels to drain. Remove the skillet from the heat, add 2 tablespoons more olive oil to the skillet, and set aside.

While the pancetta is cooking, peel the onions, trim off the root and stem ends, and then cut in half lengthwise through the stem end. Cut each half lengthwise into ¼-inch-thick slices.

Add the onions to the reserved skillet and season with ½ teaspoon salt and ¼ teaspoon pepper. Set the skillet over medium heat and cook the onions, stirring occasionally, until golden brown and tender, about 20 minutes. Add 1 teaspoon of the thyme and cook, stirring once or twice, for 15 seconds to release its flavor. Add the vinegar and cook for 2 minutes, stirring occasionally to loosen browned bits on the pan bottom. Return the pancetta to the skillet, stir briefly, and then remove from the heat.

Using a paring knife, peel the potatoes. You want to keep the potatoes whole, so peel gently. Grate the potatoes on the largest holes of a box grater-shredder onto a large plate, always moving the potato in a single direction. You will give up the last ½ inch or so of each potato (or your knuckles). Transfer the grated potatoes to a bowl. Add ¼ cup of the olive oil, ½ teaspoon salt, and ¼ teaspoon pepper and mix well.

In a 12-inch nonstick skillet, heat ¼ cup of the olive oil over high heat. When the oil begins to smoke, spread half of the potatoes across the bottom of the skillet. Cook for 2 minutes to release some moisture from the potatoes. Sprinkle the remaining 3 teaspoons thyme evenly over the layer of potatoes in the pan. Spread the onion mixture on top in an even layer. Place the remaining potatoes on top of the onions, pressing them down very lightly. Drizzle the remaining 2 tablespoons olive oil around the outer edge of the skillet.

Place the skillet in the oven and cook until the potatoes are golden brown on top, about 45 minutes. Remove from the oven and let cool for 10 minutes. Run a spatula along the outer edge of the torta to release any potatoes stuck to the pan sides. Invert a round rimmed platter larger than the skillet on top of the skillet. Then, holding the plate and the skillet, invert them together. The torta should release onto the plate. Lift off the pan, then pour off any extra oil from the platter. Alternatively, use 2 large spatulas to carefully slide the torta out of the pan onto the platter. Let cool for 10 to 15 minutes longer. Cut into wedges and serve warm.

SERVES 8 TO 10

ROASTED EGGPLANT AND TOMATO STACKS—During the summer months, when the days are hot and long, I prefer dishes that can be made well ahead and served at room temperature. They both fit the weather and fit my family's active summer lifestyle. The caramelization of the eggplant and tomatoes will fill your mouth with flavor and texture, allowing you to eat less and stay light for summer activities.

COOKING NOTES: Serving something warm and cooked (eggplant and tomato) against something cool and uncooked (mozzarella) is a simple trick for building layers of flavor. Look for ways to contrast textures, temperatures, and flavors in your cooking. In the winter, instead of raw tomato, use Marinara Sauce (page 18) and roast the stacks until the cheese melts.

ENTERTAINING NOTES: You can put one of these stacks on each dinner plate alongside a simple grilled meat, or if you are serving a lavish mixed grill (page 142), put all the stacks on a platter and pass the platter at the table. If you want to serve the stacks as a light main course, use fresh goat, Teleme, or blue cheese to boost the flavors up to the level a centerpiece requires.

3 large globe eggplants, each about 1 pound, cut crosswise into ½-inch-
    thick slices (16 slices)
½ cup kosher salt
¼ cup extra-virgin olive oil, plus more for coating and drizzling
2 tablespoons balsamic vinegar
16 large tomato slices, each ¼ inch thick

1½ teaspoons minced garlic
Finely ground sea salt, preferably gray salt
Freshly ground black pepper
½ pound fresh mozzarella cheese,
    cut into ¼-inch-thick slices (16 slices)

In a large bowl, toss the eggplant slices with the kosher salt. Using your fingertips, evenly distribute the salt on both sides of each slice. Place the eggplant slices in a large colander and set aside for 2 hours.

Preheat the oven to 450°F.

Rinse the eggplants under cold running water and dry thoroughly with paper towels. In a large bowl, toss the eggplant slices with the olive oil and vinegar, coating evenly.

Line 2 large rimmed baking sheets with heavy-duty aluminum foil. Grease the foil with a thin coating of olive oil. Arrange the eggplant slices in a single layer on 1 baking sheet. Arrange the tomato slices in a single layer on the second baking sheet. Sprinkle the garlic, ½ teaspoon salt, and ⅛ teaspoon pepper over the tomato slices.

Roast the tomato slices, without turning, until they are very soft and just beginning to brown, 10 to 15 minutes. Roast the eggplant slices, without turning, until they are tender and well browned, 20 to 30 minutes. (You may need to rotate the baking sheets 180 degrees to ensure even cooking.) Remove from the oven and let the tomato and eggplant slices cool just until you can handle them with your fingers.

For each stack, start with an eggplant slice and top it with a tomato slice. Top with 2 slices of the mozzarella, and then another eggplant slice, followed by a tomato slice. Drizzle with olive oil and serve warm.

SERVES 8

SALT-ROASTED ONIONS— Many cooks seem to have forgotten the simple beauty and flavor of salt-roasted vegetables. The old-world technique of roasting on a bed of salt encourages the heat to surround the onions and roast them to sweet perfection.

COOKING NOTES: Try using different varieties of traditional and heirloom onions. If you are looking for a more caramelized flavor, score an X in the stem end of each onion, making it about ½ inch deep, and the onion will open up and color beautifully.

ENTERTAINING NOTES: You can hold the whole cooked onions in a 200°F oven for up to 45 minutes before serving. Leftover onions are a welcome treat in pastas or salads, or even with your sausage and eggs the next morning.

6 yellow onions, unpeeled

Kosher salt

½ cup balsamic vinegar

Finely ground sea salt, preferably gray salt

Freshly ground black pepper

Preheat the oven to 350°F.

Cut a thin slice off the stem end and root end of each onion but do not peel. Spread a ¼-inch-thick layer of salt on the bottom of a baking dish large enough to hold 6 whole onions with about ½ inch between them. Arrange the onions, stem end up, on top of the salt. Roast the onions until they are dark brown in spots and quite soft when pierced with a knife, 1½ to 1¾ hours.

Meanwhile, in a saucepan, cook the vinegar over low heat until reduced by half to form a syrup, 20 to 25 minutes. Remove the pan from the heat.

Remove the dish from the oven, and then remove the onions from the dish. While the onions are still warm, pick them up one at a time in a kitchen towel and remove a layer or two of the papery skin, but leave a little skin attached. Carefully cut each onion in half through the stem end, capturing any hot juices the onions release in a small bowl.

Arrange the split onions, cut side up, on a platter. Drizzle the balsamic syrup and the onion juices over the top and season with salt and pepper. Serve warm.

SERVES 6 TO 8

"QUINTESSENTIAL" ROASTED VEGETABLE PLATTER—I like nothing better than a platter laden with perfectly roasted vegetables. When the roasting technique is done right, all the vegetables' natural sugars deliver a wonderful caramelized flavor. This is my go-to vegetable dish, one that has probably adorned half of my party tables.

COOKING NOTES: Buy carrots with their tops still attached. They always taste sweeter and better than "horse" carrots. Cipollini onions, which are small, yellow sweet onions with flattened tops, are hard to peel raw. Trim off any roots but do not cut into the root end. On the stem end, trim off a thin piece to make peeling easier. Then, cut the onions in half as directed and peel them.

ENTERTAINING NOTES: The vegetables can be roasted in advance and left at room temperature for 1 to 2 hours. Then, just before serving, simply reheat them for 10 to 12 minutes in an oven set at the same temperature.

4 quarts water

Finely ground sea salt, preferably gray salt

1 pound small Yukon Gold potatoes

6 to 8 medium carrots, peeled and trimmed

1 pound jumbo asparagus, tough ends removed

1 pound cipollini onions, about 1½ inches in diameter, cut in half through the stem end and then peeled

½ cup extra-virgin olive oil

¾ pound fresh shiitake mushrooms, stems removed and caps cut into quarters

¼ cup thinly sliced garlic

Freshly ground black pepper

1 tablespoon finely chopped fresh thyme

1 tablespoon fennel seeds

Preheat the oven to 400°F.

In a stockpot, bring the water to a boil over high heat and add 2 tablespoons salt. Add the potatoes, reduce the heat to medium-high, and simmer briskly for 6 minutes. Then add the carrots and continue to simmer for 2 minutes. Finally, add the asparagus and onions and simmer for 2 minutes longer. Drain all the vegetables in a colander, then quickly spread them out on a baking sheet and place in the refrigerator for 15 minutes to cool quickly.

While the water for parboiling the vegetables is heating, place a large ovenproof skillet over medium-high heat and add ¼ cup of the olive oil. When the oil is hot but not smoking, add the mushrooms in a single layer and cook, without stirring, until well caramelized on the first side, about 4 minutes. Turn the mushrooms once, add the garlic, and continue to cook until the garlic is lightly browned and any mushroom juices that were released have evaporated, about 2 minutes. Season with ½ teaspoon salt and ¼ teaspoon pepper, then, using a slotted spoon, transfer the mushrooms and garlic to a plate and set aside. Pour off any oil remaining in the skillet, then wipe out the skillet with paper towels.

Remove the vegetables from the refrigerator. Quarter the potatoes and cut the carrots and the asparagus on the diagonal into 1½-inch pieces. Return the skillet to medium-high heat and add the remaining ¼ cup olive oil. When the oil is hot but not smoking, add the potatoes in a single layer and cook, turning once, until they just begin to brown, about 6 minutes. Add the carrots and onions and continue to cook until all the vegetables are lightly browned, about 5 minutes longer. Season to taste with salt and pepper.

Move the pan to the oven and roast the vegetables until they are medium brown, about 20 minutes. Add the reserved mushrooms and asparagus, the thyme, and the fennel seeds, toss well, and return to the oven for 5 minutes to continue browning and to heat through the asparagus and mushrooms.

Remove the vegetables from the oven and taste and adjust the seasoning. Serve warm.

SERVES 8 TO 10

pre-roast for success

An age old restaurant trick will gain you more time at the table.

SAVORY BREAD PUDDING — Being a chef and being Italian, I have a certain addiction that I cannot contain: I love good bread. My mother, the wise and wisecracking member of our household, always wanted to know why Americans buttered their bread. She thought, well, they should just make better bread. I must say she had a point. So when I started a bakery in San Francisco, my obsession reached a new level. I figured out that one way to make great bread even better is to add great cheese. Combine these two in a whimsical twist on a typical sweet favorite and you have a recipe for success.

COOKING NOTES: Once you have mastered this bread pudding technique, you can change the bread and add a seasonal ingredient to suit your taste. For example, in fall, you might combine walnut bread and roasted pumpkin cubes; in spring, brioche and cooked asparagus (in 1-inch lengths); and in summer, sourdough bread and stemmed cherry tomatoes, halved. Use about 2 cups of the vegetables and add them to the toasted bread just before you add the milk mixture.

ENTERTAINING NOTES: Serve this savory pudding with grilled meats, roasted chicken—or turkey during the holidays—or as a light supper with an arugula salad on the side. If oven space is tight, make the pudding earlier in the day and reheat for just 15 minutes in a 300°F oven.

1 loaf country-style bread, 1 pound	¾ cup plus 2 tablespoons freshly grated Parmesan cheese
5 tablespoons unsalted butter, cut into tablespoon-sized pieces	3 cups whole milk
1 cup finely chopped yellow onion	6 large eggs
Fincly ground sea salt, preferably gray salt	½ teaspoon freshly grated nutmeg
1 tablespoon finely chopped fresh thyme	¼ pound blue cheese, crumbled

Preheat the oven to 425°F.

Using a serrated knife, shave off the thicker parts of the crust from the bread loaf. Cut the bread into 1-inch cubes and place in a large bowl.

In a skillet, melt 4 tablespoons of the butter over high heat and cook, without stirring, until it turns nut brown, about 5 minutes. Reduce the heat to medium, add the onion and a pinch of salt, and cook, stirring occasionally, until the onion begins to brown, about 5 minutes. Add the thyme and cook for 10 seconds to release its fragrance. Pour the onion mixture over the bread. Add ¾ cup of the Parmesan cheese and toss well.

Spread the bread mixture in a single layer on a 13-by-18-inch rimmed baking sheet. Bake until lightly toasted, about 8 minutes.

Remove from the oven and return the bread to the large bowl. Leave the oven on.

In a medium bowl, whisk together the milk, eggs, and nutmeg. Pour the milk mixture over the bread and toss well.

Butter a 9-by-13-inch baking dish with the remaining 1 tablespoon butter. Arrange the toasted bread evenly in the baking dish. Pour the custard evenly over the bread. Scatter the blue cheese and the remaining 2 tablespoons Parmesan cheese over the top. Bake until the bread is golden brown and crispy on top and a thin knife blade inserted into the custard comes out almost clean, about 30 minutes.

Remove the dish from the oven and let cool for 15 minutes. Cut into individual servings and serve warm.

SERVES 10 TO 12

GARLICKY VEGETABLES PRIMAVERA — When spring comes to our house, we simplify our cooking and rely on fresh ingredients to celebrate the sweet, subtle tastes of the season's produce. Having waited ten months between asparagus seasons, we embrace them with open arms when they first arrive at our local farmers' market, cooking them once every week for eight weeks. Then, as quickly as they came, they disappear and we must wait until the next year.

COOKING NOTES: In summer, I use this same technique, substituting zucchini and halved cherry tomatoes for the asparagus and peas.

ENTERTAINING NOTES: In the Napa Valley, the weather is still cool when the first asparagus come to market. Therefore, with this dish, I create a bridge: a little taste of winter with a kiss of spring. Try veal or lamb osso buco with these vegetables for the perfect welcome to the new season.

12 small cloves garlic, peeled but left whole

¼ cup extra-virgin olive oil

1 pound asparagus, tough ends removed and cut on the diagonal into
    ½-inch pieces

5 carrots, peeled and cut on the diagonal into ½-inch pieces

2 very thin lemon zest strips, each about 1½ inches long and ¾ inch
    wide

½ cup water

1 cup shelled English peas (about 1 pound unshelled)

½ cup torn fresh basil leaves

Finely ground sea salt, preferably gray salt

Freshly ground black pepper

In a skillet, combine the garlic and olive oil and place over high heat. When the oil is hot but not smoking, tilt the pan to collect the oil and garlic on one side. When the garlic begins to brown, after 3 to 4 minutes, set the skillet flat on the heat and add the asparagus, carrots, lemon zest strips, and water. Simmer until the vegetables are tender, 5 to 7 minutes.

Add the peas and basil and sauté until the peas are just tender, about 2 minutes. Season to taste with salt and pepper and stir to mix well. Serve warm.

SERVES 6

artisanal wine and cheese party

Nothing says home cooking better than freshly baked bread. Indeed, I am happiest when my host has baked a special bread or uses bread imaginatively in a menu. Cheese is an equally important part of the entertaining arsenal, with the added advantage that, unlike bread, someone else makes it and hosts get to share its great flavors in interesting ways.

bread & cheese

Most cookbooks include a few recipes featuring bread and cheese. But more and more often these days, such dishes have been stricken in favor of recipes based on boneless, skinless chicken breasts. I'm a holdout for moderation, and I love both bread and cheese, so I have included a chapter devoted to this indispensable pair. In other words, I am a loyal partisan and you're going to have to pry my cold dead fingers off a wedge of Sweet Focaccia with Golden Raisins and Rosemary (page 188) topped with Point Reyes blue cheese or a Scharffen Berger Chocolate Panini (page 172).

I have seven words for anyone who disagrees with me on the merits of these two great foods: Long live the spirit of Julia Child.

"SQUEEZED" TOMATO BRUSCHETTA—Nothing is more perfect in flavor, texture, seasonality, and ease than this simple bruschetta. Be sure to wait until the tomato season is in full glory and you will be rewarded with a flavor that defines what Italian cooking is all about.

COOKING TIPS: I like to brush the bread with the olive oil after it is toasted, rather than before, because I can better taste the fruitiness and character of the oil. This is a great place to use your best deep green Tuscan olive oil.

ENTERTAINING TIPS: Serve the bruschetta alongside a tableful of assorted antipasti, or pair with an arugula salad for lunch in midsummer.

WINE NOTES: Make Fresh Tomato Bloody Marys (page 202) with fresh tomato juice to continue the tomato celebration.

1 loaf country-style bread, 1 pound

¼ cup extra-virgin olive oil

3 super-ripe vine-ripened tomatoes, halved crosswise

Finely ground sea salt, preferably gray salt

Freshly ground black pepper

Ready a charcoal or gas grill for direct heat grilling over a hot fire, preheat a stove-top grill over high heat, or preheat the oven to 500°F.

Cut the bread crosswise into slices about 1 inch thick. You will need 8 slices. Arrange the slices on the grill rack or stove-top grill and grill, turning once, until golden brown on both sides and just beginning to crisp, about 6 minutes total. Or, arrange in a single layer on a rimmed baking sheet, place in the oven, and toast, without turning, for about the same amount of time. The slices should be crunchy on the outside and slightly soft in the center.

Remove from the grill or oven and brush each bread slice on one side with 1 ½ teaspoons of the olive oil. Rub a tomato half over the oiled side of each bread slice, squeezing the tomato as you rub. Season with salt and pepper and serve.

SERVES 8

how do they do that?
. . . now you know.

BAKED HOMEMADE RICOTTA WITH HERBS — Most of the ricotta cheese sold in the United States is made from skim milk and whey. It pales in comparison with the traditional Italian ricotta I learned to make using only the whey left over from making mozzarella or provolone cheese. If you can find an artisanal ricotta, use it. Otherwise, make your own—it's easy—and you'll never return to store-bought.

COOKING NOTES: Ground spices lose their fragrance and flavor quickly on a cupboard shelf. That problem is easily solved when nutmeg is in the recipe. Always buy whole nutmegs and grate them on a specialized nutmeg grater or on the smallest rasps of a handheld grater.

ENTERTAINING NOTES: Fresh ricotta, by itself, is wonderful for brunch spread on grilled or toasted country-style bread with a little honey drizzled on top. This recipe for ricotta is one that I like to make in front of my guests. It adds a little theater to the gathering.

WINE NOTES: Serve a cool, crisp, tart Pinot Grigio.

---

2 quarts (8 cups) whole milk

2 cups heavy cream

1 tablespoon finely ground sea salt, preferably gray salt, dissolved in
   2 cups bottled spring water

Grated zest and juice of 2 lemons (about ⅓ cup juice)

1 tablespoon unsalted butter

1 tablespoon finely chopped fresh sage

1 teaspoon freshly grated nutmeg

6 tablespoons freshly grated Parmesan cheese

Freshly ground black pepper

3 tablespoons finely chopped fresh Italian (flat-leaf) parsley

Extra-virgin olive oil for drizzling

Toasted or grilled country-style bread slices

In a nonreactive saucepan, combine the milk, cream, and salted water over low heat and heat slowly until it boils. Add the lemon juice and stir with a wooden spoon until the mixture curdles; this will happen immediately. Remove from the heat and let the curds rest for a minute or two.

Using a slotted spoon or wire skimmer, skim the curds from the whey and place them in a colander lined with cheesecloth. Discard

the whey. Allow the curds to drain and cool for 15 minutes. You should have about ¾ pound ricotta cheese. Meanwhile, preheat the oven to 350°F.

Rub the butter on the sides and bottom of a 1-quart ovenproof glass (Pyrex, for example) bowl and sprinkle the sage and nutmeg evenly on the sides and bottom. Spoon one-third of the ricotta cheese into the prepared bowl. Sprinkle evenly with 2 tablespoons of the Parmesan cheese and ⅛ teaspoon pepper. Repeat twice, to create 3 ricotta cheese layers in all, ending with Parmesan and pepper.

Cover the dish with aluminum foil. Bake the cheese until set, about 10 minutes. Remove from the oven and let cool for 5 minutes. Run a spatula along the inside of the bowl to release the cheese from the bowl sides. Invert a round plate larger than the bowl on top of the bowl. Then, holding the plate and the bowl, invert them together. The cheese should release onto the plate. Lift off the bowl.

In a small bowl, stir together the lemon zest and parsley. Sprinkle three-fourths of the parsley-lemon mixture over the cheese. Drizzle a little olive oil on top and finish by sprinkling with black pepper. Accompany the cheese with the bread. Pass the remaining parsley-lemon mixture at the table.

SERVES 8 TO 10

CHOCOLATE PANINI—Warm, oozing chocolate sandwiches for dessert . . . need I say more? In the purest example of casual entertaining, I often host a *panini* party (see page 180). I put the press right on the counter with all the ingredients, pull out the wine and tumblers, and allow everyone to make their own sandwiches. Finish 'em off with this showstopper.

COOKING NOTES: Use the best-quality bittersweet chocolate you can afford. I like Scharffen Berger chocolate, which is manufactured in Berkeley, California, but you could use Callebaut, Valrhona, or another top-drawer brand.

ENTERTAINING NOTES: Try an all-dessert *panini* bar using Nutella and sliced bananas, orange marmalade and blue cheese, and sautéed apples, or Honey-Roasted Applesauce (page 153) and sharp Cheddar.

WINE NOTES: Chocolate-filled *panini* and tumblers of Chianti go together.

---

4 tablespoons (½ stick) unsalted butter, at room temperature

8 slices walnut or Italian country bread

8 ounces bittersweet chocolate, coarsely grated

2 teaspoons ground cinnamon

½ cup crème fraîche

Butter 1 side of each bread slice, then put 4 slices, buttered side down, on a work surface. Top the bread slices with the chocolate, distributing it evenly. Top the chocolate with a second slice of bread, buttered side up. Sprinkle both buttered sides of each sandwich with the cinnamon.

Preheat a sandwich press until hot, or preheat a grill pan or non-stick skillet on the stove top until hot. Lightly oil (with a neutral oil like canola) the surface if it is not nonstick. Place 2 sandwiches on the sandwich press, close, and cook until nicely browned, 3 to 4 minutes. If using a grill pan or skillet, place as many sandwiches in the pan as will fit without crowding, cover with a weight (a second

skillet works well; put a can of tomatoes in the skillet if it is not heavy enough), and cook until nicely browned on the first side, 2 to 3 minutes. Turn and cook until the second side is well browned, about 2 minutes longer. Repeat with the remaining sandwiches.

Cut the sandwiches in half and serve immediately. Pass the crème fraîche at the table. Each guest takes a small amount for dipping his or her sandwich.

SERVES 4

BRUNCH PIADINA WITH SPICY BASTED EGGS AND SPINACH—This *piadina* is my answer to the breakfast burrito. *Piadine*, pizzas smeared with a savory spread and folded over a green salad, were the midmorning snack of the Tra Vigne staff in the early days. This version is a terrific brunch item, not only because it looks great—two fried eggs and a spinach salad on top of a pizza—but also because who would have thought of it? Actually, our friends from Naples perfected a fried egg pizza, and I've always liked how slightly runny yolks mix with fresh greens.

COOKING NOTES: My mother taught me always to baste my eggs with olive oil. It makes the yolks and whites cook at the same time, and you get a great olive oil flavor in the eggs. You may need to bake the *piadina* in batches because they will not all fit on the baking sheets. Keep the already-baked ones warm until you have baked all of them, then assemble and serve them all at once.

ENTERTAINING NOTES: For a party, I recommend baking the dough halfway up to 1 hour in advance. When you are ready to eat, finish the dough in the oven (it is okay if the partially baked dough rounds overlap a little on the baking sheets), fry the eggs, dress the greens, and assemble the *piadina* in front of your guests. I have given a recipe for the dough, but you can go ahead and buy dough from your local pizzeria. It saves time and, of course, is foolproof. You will need 2 pounds.

WINE NOTES: Blanc de Blanc sparkling wine . . . what better for brunch?

Piadina Dough (page 22)

1 cup Calabrian Chili Paste (page 15)

Extra-virgin olive oil for cooking the eggs

16 large eggs

½ pound Fontina, Cheddar, or fresh goat cheese, coarsely shredded
   or crumbled

8 cups (about ½ pound) baby spinach leaves

2 to 3 tablespoons Whole-Citrus Vinaigrette (page 18)

Make the dough and let rise as directed, then punch down the dough, press into a rectangle, and divide into 8 equal pieces. Roll each piece into a ball, place on a lightly oiled baking sheet, cover with a clean kitchen towel, and let rise in a warm place until doubled in size, about 30 minutes.

Preheat the oven to 450°F.

On a lightly floured work surface, roll out each ball of dough into a circle 8 to 9 inches in diameter and about ⅛ inch thick. Arrange them in a single layer on 3 baking sheets. Spread 2 tablespoons of the chili paste over each dough circle. Bake until light brown and crispy, 8 to 12 minutes.

When the *piadine* are about half cooked, begin frying the eggs. Generously coat the bottom of 2 or 3 large skillets (preferably non-stick) with olive oil and place over medium heat. When the oil is hot, crack the eggs into the skillets. As the eggs cook, spoon the hot oil from the edges of the pan over the top of the eggs so the yolks cook as quickly as the whites. When the eggs are barely cooked, after 3 to 4 minutes, remove the skillets from the heat.

Remove the *piadine* from the oven and immediately divide the cheese evenly among them. Allow it to melt for about 1 minute. Arrange 2 eggs on the bottom half of each circle of dough. In a large bowl, lightly coat the spinach with the vinaigrette (you may not need all of it) and place 1 cup greens on each circle of dough, just above the eggs. Serve immediately. Guests may leave their *piadina* flat or fold it in half.

SERVES 8

GRILLED MANGOES WITH BLUE CHEESE AND HONEY — Grilling mangoes is something I learned how to do as a young chef working in Miami. The Jamaican cooks on the staff would often grill them up for salads, marinades, and vinaigrettes. They are wonderful alone with a squeeze of lime and sprinkle of gray salt, diced and tossed in chicken salad, or served alongside grilled pork. Or, simply serve them as I do here. When the mangoes are ripe, you don't need much more.

COOKING NOTES: The trick here is to have a smoky grilled flavor on the outside but cool fruit in the middle. My favorite blue cheese in the world is Point Reyes Original Blue from California, but you can use any good blue you like.

ENTERTAINING NOTES: Depending on the season and what looks good in the market, I trade out the mangoes for apricots, peaches, nectarines, pineapple, persimmon, apples, or pears. You can also put together a mixed-fruit grill, and then offer a variety of cheeses: put blue cheese on some, Brie on others, and shaved Parmesan on the rest.

WINE NOTES: Serve a rich sparkling wine like Blanche Noir.

3 large, ripe but not soft mangoes

2 tablespoons unsalted butter

1 teaspoon Toasted Spice Rub (page 16)

Finely ground sea salt, preferably gray salt

½ pound blue cheese, cut into 1-inch chunks

3 tablespoons honey, warmed slightly

2 limes, quartered

Ready a charcoal or gas grill for direct heat grilling over a medium-hot fire, and preheat the broiler.

Peel the mangoes with a paring knife. One at a time, set each mango on its side on a cutting board and cut the flesh away from either side of the large, flat seed in the center. Place these 2 large pieces from each mango in a bowl (cut away the remaining flesh and reserve for another use).

In a small skillet, melt the butter over medium heat and cook, without stirring, until it turns nut brown, 3 to 4 minutes. Add the spice mixture and ⅛ teaspoon salt and remove the skillet from the heat. Pour the butter mixture over the mangoes and toss to coat evenly.

Place the mango pieces, flat side down, on the grill and grill until nicely marked, 3 to 5 minutes. Remove the mango pieces, grilled sides up, to a rimmed baking sheet. Divide the cheese evenly among the mango pieces, arranging it on top. Place under the broiler for 30 seconds to weep the cheese. Be careful not to let the mango pieces get too hot.

Arrange the mangoes on a platter or divide among individual plates. Drizzle the warm honey evenly over the top. Squeeze the juice of ½ lime over the top and put the remaining quarters on the platter. Serve warm.

SERVES 6

GRILLED PIZZA WITH RICOTTA AND PESTO

GRILLED PIZZA WITH RICOTTA AND PESTO — Grilling pizzas is one of the best ways to create more than just a meal for your guests. You orchestrate a great experience by having your friends help you roll out, top, and grill the pizzas. They'll enjoy their just-off-the-grill warm crusts topped with soft cheese even more when they have been part of the cooking team. This creates a memory far greater than the food itself, just as a party should.

COOKING NOTES: Having cooked most of my professional life over a live fire (real wood), I am partial to the subtle but distinct flavor of wood. I do caution you, however, to make sure that you are cooking over a fire that has been allowed to burn down to the point that the coals are covered with white ash. If you cook over a just-started fire, your food will taste like raw bark.

ENTERTAINING NOTES: You don't need to make your own dough—not for a party for eight people. Buy it from a local pizzeria. To work ahead, roll the dough into rounds about a half hour before your guests arrive and stack the rounds, dusting each lightly with flour, between sheets of parchment paper. They'll keep fine at room temperature. Also, it's always important to keep the style of the party in mind from start to finish. That means choosing wineglasses based on the seriousness of the food. These appetizer-sized pizzas—serve just one pizza to each guest if you have other appetizers, or two if you don't—definitely call for tumblers or, better yet, jelly jars, the kind you see in small country trattorias across Italy.

WINE NOTES: Sauvignon Blanc, or Italian Vernaccia if you can find it.

¾ pound pizza dough, purchased from a local pizzeria

Extra-virgin olive oil for brushing

Finely ground sea salt, preferably gray salt

Freshly ground black pepper

½ cup basil pesto, homemade (page 21) or purchased

1 cup ricotta cheese, preferably whole milk

3 tablespoons freshly grated Parmesan cheese

Ready a charcoal or gas grill for direct heat grilling over a medium fire, or preheat a grill pan over medium heat.

Divide the pizza dough into 8 equal portions and shape each into a ball. On a lightly floured work surface, roll out each ball of dough into a circle 3 inches in diameter and about ⅛ inch thick. It's okay if the circles are a little misshapen (*deformata*). Your guests will appreciate that they are homemade. Lightly brush both sides of each dough circle with olive oil and season with salt and pepper.

Place the dough circles on the grill or grill pan and cook until the first side is nicely browned and the top is firm to the touch, 3 to 5 minutes. Turn the crusts over and spoon about 1 tablespoon pesto on each crust, spreading it to the edges. On top of each pizza, spoon 2 tablespoons ricotta cheese, in little balls. Cook until the ricotta just begins to melt, 3 to 5 minutes from the moment you turned the crusts.

Remove the pizzas from the grill or pan and sprinkle the Parmesan cheese evenly over the top of each pizza. Serve warm.

SERVES 4 OR 8

AUNT MARY'S PANETTONE CAKE—One of the great traits of growing up in an Italian family is that every cook in the family has a very particular way of making the family classics. One or two versions would be heralded as the best and all other renditions would be judged against them. This panettone recipe comes from my aunt Mary, the oldest sister of my beloved mother. I often say that the love you have for the people you cook for is a flavor more exotic than any your tongue can detect. I hope that you can taste the love I have for my aunt in every bite.

COOKING NOTES: Candied fruit and orange peels come in many grades. Recipes like this one require that cooks buy the best available. Toasting the aniseeds brings out their flavor; do it in a small, dry skillet on the stove top over low heat. If you have loaf pans that measure 8½ by 4½ by 2½ inches, use 3 pans; if you have the larger 9-by-5-by-3-inch pans, use 2 pans.

ENTERTAINING NOTES: Panettone cake is a holiday favorite, and we consume it many different ways at our house, including right out of the oven with a little butter; toasted for breakfast and dipped into caffe latte; fashioned into a Nutella sandwich, grilled, and served with ice cream; diced and toasted for bread stuffing for pork roast or turkey; and used for French—or should it be Italian?—toast. You are limited only by your imagination. These cakes make wonderful holiday gifts, too, so gather some friends, make a few batches, and wrap them up.

WINE NOTES: A little sherry or *vin santo* is perfect.

---

3 cups all-purpose flour, plus more for dusting

1 tablespoon baking powder

1 teaspoon finely ground sea salt, preferably gray salt

1 cup (2 sticks) unsalted butter, plus more for buttering the loaf pans, at room temperature

1 cup granulated sugar

3 large eggs, at room temperature

1 can (14 ounces) sweetened condensed milk

1 tablespoon aniseeds, lightly toasted

2 tablespoons dark rum

2 tablespoons brandy

2 teaspoons pure vanilla extract

1 cup chopped candied orange peel

1½ cups walnut pieces, lightly toasted

1¼ cups golden raisins

1 tablespoon confectioners' sugar

Preheat the oven to 325°F. Butter the loaf pans (see Cooking Notes for sizes), dust with flour, and tap out the excess.

In a bowl, sift together the flour, baking powder, and salt. Set the dry ingredients aside.

In a stand mixer fitted with the paddle attachment, cream together the butter and granulated sugar on medium speed until fluffy, 2 to 3 minutes. Stop, scrape down the sides of the bowl, and add the eggs. Mix on medium speed until the mixture is pale yellow and fluffy, about 4 minutes. Stop and scrape down the sides again.

Measure out 1 cup of the milk. With the mixer on low speed, alternately add the dry ingredients in 4 batches and the 1 cup milk in 3 batches, beginning and ending with the dry ingredients. Add the aniseeds, rum, brandy, and vanilla and mix just until incorporated. Add the orange peel, walnuts, and 1 cup of the raisins and mix just until combined.

Using a rubber spatula, spread the batter into the prepared pans. Sprinkle the remaining ¼ cup raisins evenly over the tops. Brush about half (about 6 tablespoons) of the remaining milk over the tops (save the rest for another use).

Bake the cakes until they start to pull away from the sides of the pans and a skewer inserted in the center comes out clean, about 1¼ hours, but start checking after 1 hour. Remove from the oven and let cool completely in the pans on racks.

Turn the cooled cakes out of the pans, turn upright on serving plates, and sift the confectioners' sugar over the tops. Gather your friends and family around and eat one right away!

MAKES 2 LARGE OR 3 MEDIUM LOAVES

goes great with
Roasted Tomato Soup

OPPOSITE: FRESH RICOTTA; ABOVE: PLT (PANCETTA, LETTUCE, AND TOMATO), PAGE 180

PANINI BAR—My daughter Giana likes card and board games, and when we have tablefuls of her friends in to play, we put together a sandwich bar. After all, the Earl of Sandwich invented the sandwich so that he would not have to stop for dinner while playing poker. Simply put, by doing nothing more than slipping a piece (in his case, probably a slab) of meat between two slices of bread, he could eat and continue his winning streak at the same time. With all the fixings set out on the counter and the sandwich press good and hot, everyone can jump up during a break in the action and return up by at least one sandwich. And you can stay in the game!

COOKING NOTES: When I am making a single variety of sandwich, I use a grill pan or skillet and set another pan on top for a weight. But for ease at parties where I am serving a few different kinds of *panini*, the electric sandwich press is best. It allows better control of the heat and you can easily cook a couple of sandwiches at once. Each sandwich recipe yields 4 sandwiches; if you make them all, you will have enough sandwiches to serve 8 to 10 guests.

ENTERTAINING NOTES: If you are serving everyone, rather than having guests serve themselves, make 2 sandwiches per person and keep them warm (uncut) in a 250°F oven for up to 30 minutes, then cut just before serving. For a larger grill-your-own party, ask a couple of friends to bring over their electric sandwich presses and set up three presses, with all the ingredients for a single type of sandwich next to each one.

WINE NOTES: Have sparkling cider on hand for the kids and a nice rosé for the adults.

PLT (PANCETTA, LETTUCE, AND TOMATO)

2 tablespoons extra-virgin olive oil
1 pound pancetta, sliced ¼ inch thick and then cut into ½-inch pieces
12 fresh basil leaves
½ cup mayonnaise
Freshly ground black pepper
3 tablespoons unsalted butter, at room temperature
8 slices country-style bread, each ½ inch thick
3 ripe tomatoes, thinly sliced
½ pound fresh mozzarella cheese, cut into 12 slices
3 cups baby arugula
Finely ground sea salt, preferably gray salt

In a sauté pan, heat the olive oil over medium heat. Add the pancetta and cook until crispy, 6 to 8 minutes. Pour the cooked pancetta with its fat into a bowl and let cool.

While the pancetta is cooking, place the basil leaves in a mini-processor and pulse until finely chopped. Add the mayonnaise and a little pepper and process until smooth.

Butter 1 side of each bread slice, then put 4 slices, buttered side down, on a work surface. Top the bread slices with the pancetta, distributing it evenly. (I use the pancetta and its fat; you can drain it if you are watching your fat intake.) Top the pancetta with a second slice of bread, buttered side up.

Preheat a sandwich press until hot, or preheat a grill pan or non-stick skillet on the stove top until hot. Lightly oil the surface if it is not nonstick. Place 2 sandwiches on the sandwich press, close, and cook until nicely browned, 3 to 4 minutes. If using a grill pan or skillet, place as many sandwiches in the pan as will fit without crowding, cover with a weight (a second skillet works well; put a can of tomatoes in the skillet if it is not heavy enough), and cook until nicely browned on the first side, 2 to 3 minutes. Turn and cook until the second side is well browned, about 2 minutes longer. Repeat with the remaining sandwiches.

Transfer the sandwiches to a work surface and remove the top slice of bread from each sandwich. Spread the underside of those slices with the basil mayonnaise (you may not need all the mayonnaise). Top the pancetta with the tomato slices, salt and pepper to taste, mozzarella, and arugula. Replace the top bread slice, cut the sandwiches in half, and serve immediately.

MAKES 4 SANDWICHES

MOZZARELLA IN CARROZZA

1 tablespoon extra-virgin olive oil

1 clove garlic, minced

2 large olive oil–packed anchovy fillets

¼ teaspoon red pepper flakes

Freshly ground black pepper

3 tablespoons unsalted butter, at room temperature

8 slices country-style bread, each ⅓-inch thick

½ pound fresh mozzarella cheese, thinly sliced

3 large eggs

Finely ground sea salt, preferably gray salt

1 cup all-purpose flour

In a large saucepan, heat the olive oil over medium heat. Add the garlic and sauté until light brown, about 1 minute. Add the anchovies and red pepper flakes, season with a little black pepper, and sauté for 1 minute. Remove from the heat and pour into a bowl.

Butter 1 side of each bread slice, then put 4 slices, buttered side down, on a work surface. Spread 1 side of 4 bread slices with the anchovy mixture, dividing it evenly. Top with the mozzarella, dividing it evenly. Top the mozzarella with a second slice of bread, buttered side up.

In a small bowl, whisk the eggs until blended, then season with salt and pepper. Spread the flour on a dinner plate and season with salt and pepper.

Preheat a sandwich press until hot, or a grill pan or nonstick skillet on the stove top until hot. Lightly oil the surface if it is not nonstick. One at a time, dip 2 sandwiches in the seasoned flour, coating well, and then in the egg bath. Place on the sandwich press, close, and cook until the bread is nicely browned and the cheese is molten, 3 to 5 minutes. If using a grill pan or skillet, coat the sandwiches as directed and place as many as will fit in the pan without crowding, cover with a weight (a second skillet works well; put a can of tomatoes in the skillet if it is not heavy enough), and cook until nicely browned on the first side and the cheese is molten, 2 to 3 minutes. Turn and cook until the second side is well browned and the cheese is molten, about 2 minutes longer. Repeat with the remaining sandwiches.

Cut the sandwiches in half or into quarters and serve immediately.

MAKES 4 SANDWICHES

HAM AND CHEESE "AS IT IS MEANT TO BE"

2 tablespoons butter

8 slices country-style bread

1 pound smoked ham, preferably apple wood smoked, sliced

½ pound Teleme or Brie cheese, thinly sliced

½ cup Dijon mustard

1 cup roasted peppers, purchased at a deli (optional)

Butter 1 side of each bread slice, then put 4 slices, buttered side down, on a work surface. Top the bread slices with the smoked ham and then the Teleme cheese, distributing them both evenly. Top the cheese with a second slice of bread, buttered side up.

Preheat a sandwich press until hot, or preheat a grill pan or nonstick skillet on the stove top until hot. Lightly oil the surface if it is not nonstick. Place 2 sandwiches on the sandwich press, close, and cook until nicely browned, 3 to 4 minutes. If using a grill pan or skillet, place as many sandwiches in the pan as will fit without crowding, cover with a weight (a second skillet works well; put a can of tomatoes in the skillet if it is not heavy enough), and cook until nicely browned on the first side, 2 to 3 minutes. Turn and cook until the second side is well browned, about 2 minutes longer. Repeat with the remaining sandwiches.

Transfer the sandwiches to a work surface and remove the top slice of bread from each sandwich. Spread the underside of those slices with the mustard. Top the cheese with roasted peppers, if desired. Replace the top bread slice, cut the sandwiches in half, and serve immediately.

MAKES 4 SANDWICHES

BREAKFAST PANZANOLA—Italians have *panzanella* (bread salad). Americans have granola. Combine elements of both and you have a fun way to serve the flavors everyone likes for breakfast. On a warm summer morning, I serve this for brunch with cured meats and cheeses.

COOKING NOTES: Once you have mastered the technique, try substituting other breads, such as raisin or walnut. The fruit you use should change with the season, and you can substitute plain yogurt for the whipped cream.

ENTERTAINING NOTES: You can hold this dish at room temperature for as long as an hour before serving. If any is left over, use it as a stuffing for Cornish game hens or small chickens.

WINE NOTES: A fruity sparkling wine is delicious with this morning dish.

¾ cup sliced almonds

FOR THE BROWN BUTTER SYRUP:
2 tablespoons unsalted butter
1 bay leaf
¼ cup firmly packed light brown sugar
1 tablespoon brandy
1 tablespoon fresh lemon juice
½ cup fresh orange juice
Finely ground sea salt, preferably gray salt

1 country-style Italian loaf, 1 pound
2 pints strawberries, stemmed and sliced lengthwise ¼ inch thick
¼ cup granulated sugar
1 tablespoon fresh lemon juice
1 tablespoon balsamic vinegar
Finely ground sea salt, preferably gray salt
¾ cup golden raisins
½ cup blueberries
½ cup lightly packed torn fresh mint leaves
1 cup heavy cream, whipped to soft peaks

Preheat the oven to 350°F. Spread the almonds on a baking sheet and toast in the oven until golden and fragrant, 8 to 10 minutes. Remove from the oven and pour into a small bowl. Leave the oven on.

While the almonds are in the oven, make the brown butter syrup: In a 10-inch skillet, melt the butter over high heat and cook, without stirring, until it browns, 3 to 4 minutes. Add the bay leaf and stand back (it might pop). Reduce the heat to medium, add the sugar, and stir. When the sugar has melted, add the brandy and stand back (it might flame). Add the lemon juice. Cook for 15 seconds, then add the orange juice and ¼ teaspoon salt. Stir and cook until the liquid has reduced by half and has a syrupy consistency, about 3 minutes. You should have about ½ cup. Remove and discard the bay leaf.

Using a serrated knife, shave off the thicker parts of the crust from the bread loaf. Cut the bread into ½-inch cubes. You should have about 8 cups. Place the bread in a large bowl, add ¼ cup of the brown butter syrup, and toss to coat evenly. Spread the bread cubes in a single layer on a rimmed baking sheet. Bake the bread cubes, turning occasionally for even coloring, until golden and crispy on the outside and still chewy inside, 15 to 20 minutes. Remove from the oven and let cool.

While the bread cubes are cooling, in a bowl, combine the strawberries, granulated sugar, lemon juice, vinegar, and ½ teaspoon salt and mix well. Allow to macerate for 5 to 10 minutes. In a small bowl, combine the raisins with hot water to cover. Allow the raisins to plump for 8 to 10 minutes, then drain well.

Place the toasted bread in a large bowl. Add the remaining ¼ cup brown butter syrup, the toasted almonds, raisins, blueberries, and mint and toss well.

To serve, spoon some strawberries in each bowl. Spoon some of the bread mixture alongside the berries, and spoon some whipped cream over the strawberries.

SERVES 6 TO 8

PIADINA SALAD WITH BLUE CHEESE AND APPLES—I created this dish for a show on the Food Network that celebrated the Giacomini family of Northern California, makers of one of the state's great artisanal cheeses, Point Reyes Original Blue. The cool, tart mix of apples and greens tucked inside a warm, crisp savory pizzalike bread is pure pleasure.

COOKING NOTES: You can use other fruits in place of the apples, such as Fuyu persimmons and pears in the fall, or tomatoes in the heat of the summer. If you have a mandoline, use it for slicing the apples. You will get thinner, more uniform slices.

ENTERTAINING NOTES: To save time, buy the dough from your local pizza parlor; you will need 2 pounds. If you have dough in the freezer, remember to begin thawing it 2 hours before you plan to use it.

WINE NOTES: A New World rosé is perfect with this dish. One of my favorites is Solo Rosa from Sonoma.

Piadina Dough (page 22)

FOR THE VINAIGRETTE:
2 tablespoons cider vinegar
2 tablespoons honey
1 tablespoon minced shallot
½ teaspoon finely ground sea salt, preferably gray salt
⅛ teaspoon freshly ground black pepper
¼ cup extra-virgin olive oil

12 cups (about ¾ pound) lightly packed frisée leaves
    (from about 2 heads)
2 cups thinly sliced Granny Smith apples (about 3 apples),
    tossed with juice of 1 lemon
1 cup roughly chopped Spiced Candied Walnuts (page 23)
Extra-virgin olive oil for brushing
Finely ground sea salt, preferably gray salt
¼ pound Point Reyes Original Blue or other
    good-quality blue cheese, crumbled

Make the dough and let rise as directed, then punch down the dough, press into a rectangle, and divide into 8 equal pieces. Roll each piece into a ball, place on a lightly oiled baking sheet, cover with a clean kitchen towel, and let rise in a warm place until doubled in size, about 30 minutes.

Preheat the oven to 250°F. Ready a charcoal or gas grill for direct heat grilling over a medium-hot fire. You can also cook the *piadine* on a grill pan preheated over medium-high heat on the stove top. You can start preheating the pan about 5 minutes before you will begin cooking.

Make the vinaigrette: In a small bowl, whisk together the vinegar, honey, shallots, ½ teaspoon salt, and ⅛ teaspoon pepper until the salt dissolves. Slowly whisk in the olive oil to form an emulsion. Set aside.

In a large bowl, combine the frisée, apples, and walnuts. Set aside.

Lightly dust a work surface with flour. One at a time, roll out each ball of dough into a round 8 inches in diameter and ⅛ inch thick. Lightly brush each round on both sides with olive oil and season with a pinch of salt.

Place as many rounds as will fit comfortably on the hot grill or grill pan. After about 3 minutes, when the underside is browned, turn each round over and sprinkle an equal amount of the blue cheese on each grilled side to melt. Continue to grill until golden brown on the second side, 3 to 4 minutes longer. As the rounds are done, transfer them to 2 large rimmed baking sheets and keep them warm in the oven.

Toss the apple mixture with the vinaigrette. Place a *piadina* on each plate. Divide the apple mixture evenly among the still-warm *piadine*, arranging it on half of each round. Fold the uncovered half over the apple mixture and serve at once.

SERVES 8

SAVORY FRENCH TOAST WITH PROSCIUTTO, MOZZARELLA, AND BALSAMIC SYRUP—

These French toast–inspired sandwiches can also be a stunning hors d'oeuvre or nibble at a cocktail party if you cut them into small pieces. Your guests will immediately be curious about the little "French toasts" as you pass them on a tray. With the first bite, however, everyone will be sold on the crispy bread, salty prosciutto, creamy mozzarella, and a little dip into balsamic vinegar to seal the deal.

COOKING NOTES: If you feel like a decadent splurge, try serving a twelve-year-old balsamic vinegar in place of the syrup. It will be a real treat.

ENTERTAINING NOTES: You can cook these toasts on the griddle, and then hold them in a 200°F oven for up to 1 hour before serving. These sandwiches are also good served alongside salads for a light supper.

WINE NOTES: Prosecco, the light sparkling wine of Italy, is an ideal match.

¾ cup balsamic vinegar

1 loaf country-style bread, 1 pound, preferably a day old

1 pound fresh mozzarella cheese, cut into ¼-inch-thick slices

Finely ground sea salt, preferably gray salt

3 tablespoons extra-virgin olive oil

16 large fresh basil leaves

½ pound prosciutto, sliced paper-thin

6 large eggs

⅓ cup freshly grated Parmesan cheese

Freshly ground black pepper

2 tablespoons unsalted butter

In a small saucepan, bring the vinegar to a simmer over medium heat and simmer until slightly thickened and reduced to about ¼ cup, about 10 minutes. Remove from the heat and pour into a small bowl. Set aside.

Using a serrated knife, trim off about half of the thickness of the hard crust from all sides of the bread loaf. Cut the loaf in half lengthwise, trim off the ends, and then cut each half crosswise into ½-inch-thick slices. You should have 16 slices.

Arrange half of the bread slices on a work surface and divide the mozzarella slices evenly among them. Season the mozzarella slices with about ½ teaspoon salt and drizzle evenly with the olive oil. Place the basil leaves and then the prosciutto slices on top of the mozzarella slices, dividing them both evenly. Place the remaining bread slices on top. Press down on each sandwich with your hand to compress slightly. Arrange the 8 sandwiches in a single layer in a 9-by-13-inch baking dish.

In a bowl, whisk together the eggs, Parmesan cheese, ½ teaspoon salt, and ¼ teaspoon pepper. Pour the egg mixture over the sandwiches. Turn the sandwiches over and allow them to sit in the egg mixture for 5 minutes, turning once after a couple of minutes.

Preheat a griddle over medium heat. Melt the butter on the hot griddle. Working in batches if necessary, place the sandwiches on the griddle and press down on each one with a spatula. Cook, continuing to press down with the spatula and turning once, until browned on both sides, 4 to 6 minutes total.

Remove the sandwiches to a cutting board. Cut the sandwiches into halves or quarters. Serve warm with the reduced balsamic vinegar for dipping.

SERVES 8

RHUBARB COMPOTE WITH PARMESAN AND CHEDDAR FRICCO CUPS—Nothing beats the combination of strawberry and rhubarb . . . unless, of course, you make a two-cheese *fricco* cup (think the best part of a grilled cheese sandwich—the part that has oozed out and gotten crispy on the griddle) and serve the compote right inside.

COOKING NOTES: You can make an apple, pear, or cherry compote using the same method you use for rhubarb. For information on the origin of the *fricco*, see Tricolor Salad with Fricco Crackers and Caesar "Vinaigrette" (page 72).

ENTERTAINING NOTES: You can make the rhubarb compote the day before serving, cover, and refrigerate it; bring it to room temperature before serving. You can also make the *fricco* cups a day in advance, wrap them in plastic wrap, and keep them at room temperature. Serve this dish in place of a cheese plate and a dessert, satisfying two courses with just one recipe.

WINE NOTES: Pour a sparkling wine or a Moscato.

FOR THE RHUBARB COMPOTE:

4 tablespoons (½ stick) unsalted butter

1 cup firmly packed light brown sugar

2 tablespoons fresh lemon juice

1 cup fresh orange juice

Finely ground sea salt, preferably gray salt

Freshly ground black pepper

2 pounds rhubarb, trimmed and cut into ¾-inch dice

FOR THE FRICCO CUPS:

3 cups (¾ pound) grated Cheddar cheese

1½ cups (6 ounces) freshly grated Parmesan cheese

6 large, ripe strawberries, stemmed and thinly sliced lengthwise

6 small fresh rosemary sprigs

Make the compote: In a 12-inch skillet, melt the butter over high heat and cook, without stirring, until it browns, 3 to 4 minutes. Reduce the heat to medium, add the sugar, and stir. When the sugar has melted, add the lemon juice. Cook for 15 seconds, then add the orange juice, ½ teaspoon salt, and ¼ teaspoon pepper. Add the rhubarb, stir, and cook, stirring occasionally, until tender, about 10 minutes. Transfer the rhubarb mixture to a small bowl and set the bowl inside a larger bowl filled with ice water. Stir occasionally until the mixture stops steaming. Cover and refrigerate until needed. Bring to room temperature before serving.

Make the *fricco* cups: Heat an 8-inch nonstick skillet over medium heat. Sprinkle ½ cup of the Cheddar cheese and ¼ cup of the Parmesan cheese into the pan, creating an even, lace-thin layer that covers the bottom of the skillet. Cook for 6 to 7 minutes; the cheese will melt and bubble. Using a fork or tongs to lift up an edge, look for the moment when the bottom of the cheese begins to turn dark orange. Carefully turn the *fricco* over and cook for 1 minute on the second side. Remove the *fricco* from the pan and place it on top of an overturned coffee cup, shaping it into a little bowl. Allow it to cool and firm up for about 1 minute, then remove and set aside on a platter or an individual plate. Wipe the skillet clean with paper towels. Repeat with the remaining Cheddar and Parmesan cheeses to make 5 more *fricco* cups.

Spoon some of the rhubarb compote into each cup and arrange the strawberry slices on top of the compote. Garnish with the rosemary sprigs. Serve at room temperature.

SERVES 6

SWEET FOCACCIA WITH GOLDEN RAISINS AND ROSEMARY—Foccacia is one of the easiest of all breads

to make. I love taking the base dough and turning it into different flavor combinations to suit the entertaining theme. This raisin-topped sweet version is perfect on a fruit and cheese platter that is served for a snack or after a main course. It is also an irresistible addition to a brunch menu.

COOKING NOTES: You may be tempted to reduce the amount of olive oil, but I encourage you to try this recipe at least once with the full amount. All of the golden richness bakes right into the dough, and the oil is critical to achieving the authentic flavor I want in this bread.

ENTERTAINING NOTES: You can easily transform this crisp and golden bread into an hors d'oeuvre. Cut it into small triangles, dot each one with some blue cheese, and serve warm.

WINE NOTES: Moscato is a wonderfully aromatic wine with a hint of sweetness . . . perfect here.

FOR THE SPONGE:

2¼ teaspoons (1 envelope) active dry yeast

2 cups lukewarm whole milk

2 tablespoons mild honey, preferably orange blossom

1 cup all-purpose flour

1 cup golden raisins, plumped in hot water to cover for 8 to 10 minutes, drained, and patted dry

¾ cup plus 2 tablespoons extra-virgin olive oil, plus more for oiling bowl

2 teaspoons finely ground sea salt, preferably gray salt

About 3½ cups all-purpose flour, plus more for dusting

2 tablespoons light-colored honey, preferably orange blossom

1 tablespoon coarsely chopped fresh rosemary

1 tablespoon crystal sugar

Make the sponge: In the bowl of a stand mixer fitted with the paddle attachment, combine the yeast, lukewarm milk, and 2 tablespoons honey. Add 1 cup flour and mix on low speed until the ingredients are well incorporated. Cover the bowl with a kitchen towel and let the dough rise in a warm place for 20 to 25 minutes.

Uncover the bowl and attach the dough hook to the mixer. With the mixer on low speed, add ½ cup of the raisins. When the raisins are incorporated, add 2 tablespoons of the olive oil, 1½ teaspoons of the salt, and 2 cups of the flour and mix until incorporated. Continue to add the remaining 1½ cups flour in ½ cup increments until the dough wraps itself around the hook; you may not need all of the final ½ cup. The dough will be sticky but should be well combined. Continue to knead on low to medium speed until the dough is smooth and elastic, 5 to 7 minutes.

Move the dough to a lightly floured work surface and knead by hand for 1 to 2 minutes to disperse any raisins that may have clumped on the bottom. Lightly grease a bowl with oil. Shape the dough into a ball, flatten slightly, and place in the oiled bowl. Turn the ball to coat on all sides with the oil. Cover the bowl with a kitchen towel and let the dough rise in a warm place until doubled in size, about 1 hour.

Cover the bottom of an 11-by-17-inch rimmed baking sheet with

5 tablespoons of the olive oil. Punch down the dough, turn it out onto a lightly floured work surface, and flatten it into a disk. Using a lightly dusted rolling pin, roll out the dough into a sheet the same size as the prepared baking sheet. Carefully move the dough sheet to the baking sheet. Using your palms, work the dough into the corners. Brush the top with 1 tablespoon of the olive oil. Cover the pan with a kitchen towel and let the dough rise until it has doubled in thickness, about 45 minutes.

Preheat the oven to 400°F. In a small bowl, combine the remaining ½ cup raisins with the 2 tablespoons honey and the remaining 6 tablespoons olive oil.

Once the dough has doubled in thickness, evenly dimple the surface with your fingertips, pressing firmly. The dimples should be about 1 inch apart, and deep but not breaking through the bottom. Bake for 15 minutes. Remove from the oven and spread the raisin mixture evenly over the top. Sprinkle the remaining ½ teaspoon salt, the rosemary, and the sugar on top. Return to the oven and bake until the top is golden, 12 to 15 minutes.

Remove from the oven and let cool in the pan on a rack. Cut the focaccia into narrow rectangles the width and length of your index finger to serve.

SERVES 12

BLUE CHEESE FONDUE—When it's cold and blustery outside, there's almost nothing better than having a handful of friends inside, gathered around a fondue pot, enjoying one another's company. Dishes like this inevitably encourage great storytelling, which adds just the right spark to the evening.

COOKING NOTES: You can make the fondue sauce a couple of hours in advance, but you must reheat it very slowly to prevent separation. Cambozola is a triple-cream, blue-veined cheese that originated in Germany in the 1970s. You can substitute other cheeses, such as Brie, aged English Cheddar, or another creamy blue. The sauce can also be used as a base for lasagna, tossed with pasta and steamed asparagus, or spooned over grilled steak.

ENTERTAINING NOTES: Fondue parties are great retro-style get-togethers. Try serving an all-fondue meal, such as four different fondues with four different wines. Make the first three savory and the last one sweet. For two savory fondues to go along with the blue cheese one here, put Bolognese sauce (see Potato Cakes with Quick Bolognese Sauce, page 144) in one pot with bread cubes for dipping, and steak cubes (see Grilled Gaucho Steak with Blue Cheese and Pita, page 126) in another pot with a bowl of *chimichurri* sauce on the side. Your guests will travel from pot to pot, catching up with old friends as they sample something at each stop. Everyone finishes around a pot of bittersweet chocolate fondue (1 pound bittersweet chocolate, chopped; ¼ cup heavy cream, and 1 tablespoon unsalted butter) with small cubes of pound cake for dipping. *Bellissimo!*

WINE NOTES: Contrast is called for here. I like to pour a crisp, clean Sauvignon Blanc. The rich, creamy fondue highlights the bright acid and the fruitiness of the wine.

---

1 pound small yellow creamer potatoes, halved or quartered, depending on their size

Finely ground sea salt, preferably gray salt

1 pound broccoli crowns, cut into florets

½-pound piece cooked ham, cut into ¾-inch cubes

2 Granny Smith apples, quartered, cored, cut into ½-inch-wide wedges, and then tossed with 2 teaspoons fresh lemon juice

½ slender baguette, cut into slices ¾ inch thick

FOR THE FONDUE SAUCE:

1 tablespoon unsalted butter

1½ teaspoons finely chopped fresh thyme

1 teaspoon minced garlic

2 cups heavy cream

½ pound Cambozola cheese, crumbled

Freshly ground black pepper

In a saucepan, combine the potatoes with water to cover by 1 inch. Add 1 tablespoon salt and bring to a boil over high heat. Reduce the heat to medium and simmer until the potatoes are tender, 6 to 8 minutes. Using a slotted spoon, transfer the potatoes to a colander to drain and let cool completely. Return the water to a boil, drop in the broccoli, and cook the florets until barely tender, about 2 minutes. Drain the florets into a colander and rinse them under cold water to stop the cooking. Pat the potatoes and broccoli dry, then arrange them attractively on a platter with the ham, apples, and bread.

Make the sauce: In a small saucepan, combine the butter, thyme, and garlic over medium-low heat. Cook, stirring to prevent the garlic from browning, for 2 minutes. Add the cream, raise the heat to medium, bring to a simmer, and cook until the cream is reduced by one-third, about 2 minutes, reducing the heat as needed to maintain a slow simmer. Add the cheese and stir until the cheese melts and the mixture is smooth. Season to taste with pepper.

Pour the sauce into a fondue pot set over an alcohol burner or candle to keep it hot. Place the platter of potatoes, broccoli, and other items alongside. Serve at once.

SERVES 6 TO 8

ARTISANAL WINE AND CHEESE PARTY— The single most important element of serving a great cheese course, beyond buying good cheese, is the temperature of the cheese when you serve it. It needs to be only one temperature: room temperature! Set the cheese out a few hours before serving time. It really is true that a five-dollar cheese will taste like a twenty-dollar cheese at the right temperature and a twenty-dollar cheese will taste like a five-dollar cheese at the wrong temperature. When you offer it to your guests, your Brie should be weeping, your blue stinking, and your Parmigiano-Reggiano glistening with a whisper of its oil.

COOKING NOTES: Be sure to rely on a first-rate cheese purveyor. The best merchants should be able to walk you through the various cheeses and, if necessary, through any substitutes. Use any mild artisanal honey, such as lavender or chestnut, for drizzling on the blue cheese.

ENTERTAINING NOTES: I like to add interest to the presentation of the cheeses and their accompaniments, such as using a retired barrel top as a serving platter. You can also serve the cheeses as a plated course by simply cutting them into small portions and arranging them on individual plates. The most elegant thing you can serve with a cheese course is a bowl of warm pistachios. They nicely occupy hand and mouth while you're sitting around the table talking with friends and finishing a bottle of great red wine.

WINE NOTES: As a general rule, the cheeses you choose should match the flavor and intensity of the wine. If you are drinking a big, intense wine, choose a big, intense cheese. For example, if you've chosen a Petite Sirah, which is typically deep colored and full bodied, choose a Gorgonzola, the creamy Italian cow's milk blue cheese that comes in two varieties, *naturale* or mountain (aged, firm textured, and pungent) and *dolcelatte* or sweet (young, softer, and milder). If you are serving a Sauvignon Blanc, which tends to be crisp and medium bodied, pair it with a delightfully tart or tangy medium-aged goat cheese. Robert Mondavi Fumé Blanc Reserve or Luna Pinot Grigio, two fruity, tart wines, go well with young, fresh goat cheeses. Or, try the same wines with Port-Salut, a smooth, mildly tangy cow's milk cheese originally made only by monks. Its lesser cousin, Saint Paulin, is yet another option with these wines. A top-caliber Chardonnay pairs well with a well-aged Brie or Camembert, because it has the acid needed to balance the creamier cheeses, while a full-flavored Zinfandel is a good match for Parmesan and blue cheese. Of course, contrasting flavors can also guide you toward great cheese-course combinations, so from time to time I like to serve a crisp, fruity sparkling wine with Parmigiano-Reggiano—a true contrast for the palate.

For the cheeses:

½ pound fresh goat cheese

½ pound aged goat's or sheep's milk cheese

½ pound Teleme cheese

½ pound Camembert or Brie cheese

½ pound Gorgonzola or other blue cheese

½ pound Parmigiano-Reggiano or aged pecorino cheese

½ pound pistachios

3 tablespoons artisanal honey

12 almond biscotti

1 loaf walnut bread or other dark, dense bread, sliced

2 cups candied almonds (see Cooking Notes for Spiced
   Candied Walnuts, page 23)

3 pounds assorted fruits such as figs, cherries, nectarines, plums,
   persimmons, apples, and pears, in any seasonal combination

60 crackers, 20 each of 3 different types

At least 3 hours before your guests arrive, remove the cheeses from the refrigerator. Place them on a large, round tray, arranging them clockwise, starting at 6 o'clock, and moving from the sweetest to the strongest cheese: fresh goat, aged goat, Teleme, Camembert, Gorgonzola, and Parmigiano-Reggiano. Leave enough space between the cheeses for adding the accompaniments later. Cover loosely with plastic wrap.

Put the white wines in the refrigerator to chill for 3 hours, and the red wines in to chill for 20 minutes before serving. When the red wine goes in the refrigerator, finish assembling the cheese tray: Preheat the oven to 325°F, spread the pistachios on a rimmed baking sheet, and warm in the oven for 8 minutes. Transfer to a serving bowl. Drizzle the honey over the blue cheese and set some biscotti and walnut bread slices nearby. Set a pile of candied almonds next to the fresh goat cheese, and finish the platter by arranging the fruits, whole or cut up, in the middle and crackers all around.

Pour the wine and serve the cheese tray and pistachios.

SERVES 10 TO 12

BLOOD ORANGE WHITE SANGRIA—A lot of the sangria I have been served made with red wine seems too heavy. My favorite version of the classic Spanish beverage is made with a crisp white wine and exotic citrus. Give this recipe a try, but be sure to warn your guests that its effects can creep up on them.

COOKING NOTES: You can use any citrus for the sangria, but it is worth it to spend a couple of extra dollars for organic fruits and less common varieties, such as Meyer lemons, satsuma tangerines, and blood oranges.

ENTERTAINING NOTES: Of course, this sangria is a natural partner to a paella feast, but it is also great with a lobster bake (page 104) or with a meal made up of antipasti. For a little drama, try mixing a batch in a large, beautiful pitcher or vase from which you ladle it into goblets.

3 bottles (750 ml each) Pinot Grigio or Sauvignon Blanc, chilled

1½ cups brandy

¾ cup orange liqueur such as Cointreau or triple sec

½ cup superfine sugar

1 orange, thinly sliced

1 blood orange, thinly sliced

3 kumquats, thinly sliced

1 lime, thinly sliced

Ice cubes (optional)

In a large pitcher, combine the wine, brandy, and orange liqueur. Pour in the sugar and stir to mix all the ingredients and dissolve the sugar. Add all the citrus slices at once. Cover and refrigerate for 1 hour to allow the citrus flavors to come through. Serve over ice, if desired.

SERVES 10 TO 12

"DRINKING" CHOCOLATE—Before there was a Starbucks on every corner or even coffeehouses in Europe, there were chocolate houses where Europe's elite would gather and consume frothy chocolate drinks to stimulate conversation and well-being. One sip of this rich drink and you and your guests will know why the upper class was hooked.

COOKING NOTES: The quality of chocolate you pick for this drink is imperative. I like Scharffen Berger bittersweet (70 percent cacao) or semisweet (62 percent cacao), but any superior chocolate will do. Use semisweet if you like your hot chocolate a little sweeter.

ENTERTAINING NOTES: I love to serve this hot chocolate topped with a sprinkle of pure chili powder and the Biscotti "One Time" (page 206) or Molten Flourless Chocolate Cupcakes (page 209) alongside. During the holiday seasoning, you can help your guests watch their calories and cholesterol by making the chocolate with nonfat milk and serving it in place of the traditional eggnog.

6 ounces best-quality bittersweet or semisweet chocolate

1 quart (4 cups) milk (nonfat, skim, or whole) or half-and-half

Softly whipped cream (optional)

Cognac, rum, Irish whiskey, or brandy (optional)

Chop or break up the chocolate into small pieces and place in a small, heavy saucepan. Add 1 cup of the milk, place over medium-low heat, and melt while stirring constantly. Once the chocolate has melted, raise the heat to medium and add the remainder of the milk while whisking rapidly so that it will froth slightly. Heat until very hot, but do not allow to boil.

Divide the chocolate among small cups. Top with a dollop of cream or fortify with a little Cognac, rum, Irish whiskey, or brandy, if desired.

SERVES 8

bloody mary brunch

libations

Two thousand years ago, a libation was the ritual pouring of a drink as an offering to a god. Over time, the rituals have changed, but the premise has remained the same, except today it is an offering to a friend or family member. Welcoming your guests with a creative drink served in a fun glass is a delightful way to have your first course standing up. A big pitcher of jet-cold Blood Orange White Sangria (page 194) followed by a festive Italian-influenced paella (page 90) in the cool days of autumn is nothing less than spectacular. A Fresh Tomato Bloody Mary (page 202) made with vine-ripened, peak-of-the-season tomatoes will launch any brunch with style and flavor. And I don't think life gets any better than sipping a cool, refreshing Mint Julep (page 199) made with just-picked mint leaves before the last barbecue of summer.

Purchase high-quality liquor and your drinks will taste twice as good. We often neglect a stellar drink as an integral part of entertaining . . . but not any more!

OPPOSITE: FRESH TOMATO BLOODY MARY, PAGE 202; BLOOD ORANGE WHITE SANGRIA, PAGE 194

WHOLE-CITRUS MARGARITA—All the flavor of citrus is locked up in the skins. This method extracts every bit of it for a once-in-a-lifetime margarita.

COOKING NOTES: Farm freshness is the key here. Look for the citrus, preferably organic, that is at its height of season and adjust the recipe. Tangerines, Meyer lemons, and Key limes all have amazing flavor and any one of them would be good here.

ENTERTAINING NOTES: Serve these tangy margaritas with Seafood Gazpacho Cocktail with Flavored Popcorn (page 57) or your favorite Mexican dishes.

Finely ground sea salt, preferably gray salt, for coating glass rims
   (optional)
2 navel oranges, cut into ¾-inch pieces
1 lemon, cut into ¾-inch pieces
1 lime, cut into ¾-inch pieces
¼ cup superfine sugar
6 tablespoons Cointreau
¼ cup triple sec
¾ cup best-quality tequila
6 cups ice cubes

If you want to coat the glass rims with salt, spread some salt on a flat plate. Have ready 8 margarita glasses. Working with 1 glass at a time, dip the glass in water, dip the rim in the salt, and place the glass in the freezer to frost, about 30 minutes. If you are not using the salt, simply dip the glass in water and place in the freezer to frost.

Pass the oranges, lemon, and lime through a heavy-duty juicer, capturing the juice in a bowl or pitcher. Whisk the sugar into the juice until dissolved. Add the Cointreau, triple sec, and tequila and mix well. You should have about 2 cups.

In a blender, combine the citrus-tequila juice with 3 cups of the ice and process on high speed until a slushy consistency forms, about 1 minute. Add the remaining 3 cups ice and continue to process until smooth, about 2 minutes.

Divide evenly among the frosted glasses. Serve at once.

SERVES 8

LIMONCELLO—I fell in love with this easy-to-make drink while traveling along southern Italy's Amalfi coast, where lemon groves flourish. It is the perfect way to end a perfect evening—jet-cold and citrusy!

COOKING NOTES: You can make this with any citrus. The key is the best and freshest citrus possible. Fruit that has been in storage for a long time will give the drink a muddy taste. The lavender sprigs are optional, but they give the drink a lovely floral edge.

ENTERTAINING NOTES: Generally, I serve this drink in small aperitif glasses at the very end of a meal, though it is also refreshing before a big lobster bake (page 104). Because it is sweet and tart, it tastes best ice cold, so keep it stored in the freezer, ready for capping any feast.

12 Meyer lemons or a mixture of lemons and limes, preferably organic
4 fresh lavender sprigs
2 liters light rum or vodka
6 cups granulated sugar
3 cups water

Using a vegetable peeler, remove the zest—no pith—from the lemons in strips. In a glass container, combine the lemon zest, lavender, and rum, cover tightly, and let stand in a cool, dark place for 4 weeks.

Strain the rum mixture through a fine-mesh sieve into a pitcher, then pour through a funnel into 1 or more glass bottles of the same size, dividing it evenly if using more than a single bottle. In a saucepan, combine the sugar and water and bring to a boil over high heat, stirring to dissolve the sugar. Reduce the heat to medium and simmer, stirring, until the sugar is fully dissolved. Remove from the heat and let cool completely.

Pour the sugar syrup into the strained rum, dividing it evenly if you have used 2 or more bottles. Serve immediately in small aperitif glasses, if desired, or cap and store in the freezer for up to 1 year. Serve directly from the freezer.

MAKES ABOUT 2¾ QUARTS

OPPOSITE: WHOLE-CITRUS MARGARITA, PAGE 195; ABOVE: LIMONCELLO, PAGE 195

TOMATO WATER MARTINI—Back in my restaurant days, there were always buckets of freshly peeled and chopped tomatoes in the kitchen. When I would come into work in the morning, a pool of gin-clear tomato-infused water would be standing on the top of the tomatoes. A glass of that would start my day, and a glass of this would end it.

COOKING NOTES: To cut the basil chiffonade, stack 8 to 10 fresh basil leaves, roll up lengthwise, and finely cut crosswise with a sharp knife.

ENTERTAINING NOTES: Imagine a steamy hot summer day and your guests arriving weary and parched. Have a tray of these martinis ready to both cool them off and get the party started.

4 pounds ripe tomatoes, cored and cut into chunks

1 cup vodka

Finely ground sea salt, preferably gray salt

16 Sweet 100 or other small cherry tomatoes, stemmed

¼ pound fresh mozzarella cheese, cut into eight ¾-inch cubes, using a thin sharp knife

1 tablespoon fresh basil chiffonade

Freshly ground black pepper

Working in batches, process the tomatoes in a food processor until pureed. Slowly pour the juice through a fine-mesh sieve placed over a large measuring pitcher. (If you want a very clear juice, line the sieve with cheesecloth.) You should have about 4 cups liquid. Add the vodka and 1 teaspoon salt to the juice and mix well. Cover and refrigerate until very cold, about 2 hours. At the same time, dip 8 martini glasses in water and place them in the freezer to frost.

Meanwhile, thread 2 cherry tomatoes and 1 mozzarella cube on each of 8 toothpicks, placing the mozzarella between the tomatoes.

When the tomato-vodka mixture is well chilled, divide it evenly among the frosted glasses. Rest a mozzarella-tomato toothpick inside each glass. Garnish with the basil and a little pepper. Serve at once.

SERVES 8

MINT JULEP — There is something magical about a slow afternoon spent sipping mint juleps under a big old magnolia tree . . . a very Clark Gable–like moment.

COOKING NOTES: You can use other herbs in place of the mint, such as lemon verbena and lavender, to create juleps of another flavor. My favorite bourbon whiskey for this southern drink is Maker's Mark.

ENTERTAINING NOTES: This iconic drink hits the spot whether you are watching the Kentucky Derby or the World Series.

3 bunches fresh mint

⅓ cup water

⅔ cup granulated sugar, plus more for garnish

1 fifth bourbon whiskey

1 egg white

Fresh mint or lavender sprigs for garnish

Remove the leaves from 2 bunches of the mint sprigs, roughly tear the leaves, and then bruise them by squeezing them into a ball. In a saucepan, combine the water, ⅔ cup sugar, and the torn mint and bring to a boil over medium-high heat, stirring to dissolve the sugar. Continue to stir until the sugar dissolves completely, then immediately remove from the heat. Let cool completely.

Pour the cooled light mint syrup through a fine-mesh sieve into a large pitcher. Open the bottle of whiskey and pour it into the pitcher of mint syrup, then stir to mix. Stuff the empty whiskey bottle with the whole sprigs of the remaining bunch of mint, and then pour the whiskey-syrup mixture into the bottle. Cap and place in the freezer overnight. It will freeze to a slushy consistency.

About 30 minutes before serving, in a small bowl, whisk the egg white just until loosened. Spread a little sugar on a flat plate. Have ready 10 to 12 martini glasses. One at a time, dip the rim of each glass in the egg white and then in the sugar to coat evenly. Place the glasses in the freezer to chill for 30 minutes.

To serve, fill the glasses with the whiskey-mint mixture straight from the bottle and garnish with a mint or lavender sprig. Serve at once.

SERVES 10 TO 12

NAPA SUNSET—My dear friends Rich and Connie Frank of Frank Family Vineyards make this Champagne cocktail, complete with a distinct Napa twist—grenadine—to welcome their friends to the winery.

COOKING NOTES: It is worthwhile to squeeze the oranges yourself for the ultimate freshness. The Tiziano, a similar drink, calls for 1 part chilled grape juice (you can find good-quality nonsparkling grape juice at a specialty grocer) and 3 parts sparkling wine.

ENTERTAINING NOTES: Champagne and fruit juices have been combined for decades to create a super-flavorful, low-alcohol *aperitivo.* Try a variety of juices for your own version: fresh grape juice, peach puree, raspberry puree—the list is endless.

2 cups fresh orange juice, well chilled
½ cup grenadine
1 bottle (750 ml) rosé sparkling wine, well chilled

For each serving, pour ¼ cup orange juice in the bottom of a Champagne flute, being careful not to dirty the sides of the glass. Drizzle 1 tablespoon grenadine on top, then very slowly pour the wine in the middle of the glass.

SERVES 8

RASPBERRY FRAPPÉ—Welcoming your brunch or lunch guests to your home with a garden-fresh frappé is a great way to set the tone for the meal. These are nonalcoholic drinks for adults, but my kids love them, too.

COOKING NOTES: The raspberries must be perfectly ripe and harvested at the peak of their season. If the market doesn't have good raspberries, consider strawberries, mangoes, peaches, or other soft fruits. They, too, must be the best.

ENTERTAINING NOTES: Try the raspberry ice cubes in iced tea, lemonade, or a cocktail. They both look good and taste good.

2 pints raspberries
3 tablespoons superfine sugar
1 cup water
1½ cups vanilla yogurt
2 tablespoons honey
1 tablespoon fresh lemon juice

In a food processor, process the raspberries until a smooth puree forms. Strain the puree through a fine-mesh sieve into a 4-cup measuring pitcher. Add water as needed to total 3 cups. Add the sugar and stir to dissolve. Pour the raspberry mixture into 2 ice-cube trays. Place in the freezer until frozen, about 2 hours or longer.

In a blender, combine the water, yogurt, honey, lemon juice, and half the raspberry ice cubes. Process on high speed until the ice cubes are broken up into fine crystals. Add the remaining ice cubes and continue to process until the mixture has the consistency of a milk shake.

Pour into small juice glasses. Serve immediately.

SERVES 8

HOMEMADE APERITIVO—Imagine yourself sitting at a bar in Florence watching the sun set and sipping an *aperitivo* just like this one. I guarantee that this simple concoction will deliver the warm and festive spirit of Italia!

COOKING NOTES: You can mix the ingredients together in a large pitcher in advance, but don't measure out more than 2 drinks into the martini shaker at a time.

ENTERTAINING NOTES: Serve as a companion to Toasted Marcona Almonds (page 49), Giant Crostini (page 42), or Potato and Sage Fritters (page 43).

1 cup Italian sweet vermouth

1 cup Italian dry vermouth

2 cups Campari

2 tablespoons fresh orange juice

1 teaspoon aromatic bitters, preferably Angostura

8 cups lightly crushed ice

8 thin orange slices

In a large pitcher, mix together the sweet vermouth, dry vermouth, Campari, orange juice, and bitters.

Place 2 cups of the ice in a martini shaker. Add 1 cup of the liquor mixture to the shaker, cap the shaker, and shake for a few seconds to chill the contents. Strain into 2 martini glasses. Garnish each glass with an orange slice. Serve at once and repeat the process with the remaining ingredients.

SERVES 8

ICED VERBENA COFFEE—I am from a family of iced-coffee drinkers. Come summertime, any coffee that was left over from the morning would be sweetened and put in the refrigerator until the afternoon. I can still remember having iced coffee on the patio with my mother as we took a break from our garden work.

COOKING NOTES: Lemon verbena, which has narrow, deep green leaves and a bright, sharp lemon flavor, has long been used for its medicinal properties, easing everything from poor digestion to stress. You can use fresh mint or thyme sprigs in its place.

ENTERTAINING NOTES: Add a shot of whiskey and top with a dollop of barely sweetened softly whipped cream for a refreshing—and different—end-of-the-meal treat.

2 cups tightly packed fresh lemon verbena sprigs

6 cups hot, freshly brewed strong coffee, sweetened to taste

Ice cubes

Place the verbena in a heatproof pitcher and pour the hot coffee over it. Let steep for 5 minutes, then strain through a fine-mesh sieve into a clean container, discarding the herbs. Let cool to room temperature, then cover and refrigerate until well chilled, about 2 hours.

Fill tall, narrow glasses with ice, pour the coffee over the ice, and serve.

SERVES 8

FRESH TOMATO BLOODY MARY — You have not had a bloody Mary until you have had one made from juice squeezed from ripe, midsummer tomatoes just off the vine. It's time to pull out that juicer in the closet from your wheatgrass days and put it to work.

COOKING NOTES: If you don't have a juicer or you're short of time, you can ask your natural-foods grocer to juice up this combo for you. It will also save you cleanup time.

ENTERTAINING NOTES: You can juice the ingredients 1 day in advance of serving. Cover tightly and refrigerate until serving. This is a good drink to accompany Brunch Piadina with Spicy Basted Eggs and Spinach (page 174).

4 pounds ripe tomatoes, cored and cut into ¾-inch pieces

2 cups ¾-inch-long celery pieces, preferably inner stalks

1 to 2 jalapeño chilies, cut into ½-inch-pieces

1 lemon, cut into ¾-inch pieces and seeds removed, plus 1 or 2 lemon
    wedges for dampening glass rims

1 tablespoon Worcestershire sauce

1 tablespoon hot-pepper sauce such as Crystal or Tabasco brand

Finely ground sea salt, preferably gray salt

Fennel Spice Rub (page 16) or finely ground sea salt, preferably gray salt,
    for coating glass rims

Ice cubes

Vodka or gin, preferably kept in the freezer

Celery heart stalks, lemon wedges, or Spanish queen olives for garnish

In a bowl, toss together the tomatoes, celery pieces, jalapeños, lemon, Worcestershire sauce, hot-pepper sauce, and 1 teaspoon gray salt. Pass the contents of the bowl through a heavy-duty juicer. You should have about 3½ cups.

Have ready 8 to 10 collins glasses. Spread some spice mixture on a small plate. One at a time, run a lemon wedge around the rim of each glass, then dip the rim into the spice mixture. Fill all the glasses with ice. Pour ¼ cup vodka into each glass, followed by 6 to 8 ounces of the tomato mix. Garnish each glass with a celery stalk and serve at once.

SERVES 8 TO 10

is my drink getting spicier?
It could be if you used Jalapeño ice cubes for a zesty surprise.

dessert buffet

desserts

Ending the meal with something showy is all important. Dessert is the final chance to leave a lasting impression on your guests. Blow their minds with a two-tier stand of Molten Flourless Chocolate Cupcakes (page 209) and leak to someone at the table that there is mayonnaise in the batter. Serve warm freeform Doughnuts (page 213) that will make your friends forget about Krispy Kreme. Or, roll up your sleeves and deliver an herb-scented Olive Oil Cake (page 218) crowned with a little marmalade to finish off an already-memorable feast.

You don't have to be an accomplished baker to make creative desserts. These recipes are simple to prepare and even simpler to enjoy.

OPPOSITE: MOLTEN FLOURLESS CHOCOLATE CUPCAKES, PAGE 209

BISCOTTI "ONE TIME" — The *bi* in biscotti refers to baking the cookies twice. Like a lot of people these days, I barely have time to cook something once, let alone twice, so I developed this approach. It makes soft, warm cookies, not to mention a story that begs to be told and retold.

COOKING NOTES: Crystal sugar, also known as coarse or decorating sugar, is large grained and is available both white and in colors. It gives these cookies a lighter, moister texture than you would get using granulated sugar. Use white crystal sugar here. If you cannot find it, use granulated sugar; the results are still very good.

ENTERTAINING NOTES: Wrap the uncooked log of dough in plastic wrap and freeze it, then slice and bake the cookies as you need them. I like to serve them alongside a bowl of strawberries or cherries. If leftover cookies get a little dry, pulverize them in a food processor and use the crumbs to make the bottom layer of a cheesecake.

WINE NOTES: Serve the cookies after dinner with a glass of Moscato or an espresso.

---

1 ¾ cups all-purpose flour, plus more for dusting

¾ teaspoon baking powder

¾ teaspoon finely ground sea salt, preferably gray salt

4 tablespoons (½ stick) unsalted butter, at room temperature

⅓ cup crystal sugar, plus more for decorating

3 tablespoons firmly packed light brown sugar

4 large eggs

3 tablespoons aniseeds

½ cup whole almonds, lightly toasted and coarsely chopped

In a bowl, sift together the flour, baking powder, and salt; set aside.

In the bowl of a stand mixer fitted with the paddle attachment, combine the butter, crystal sugar, and brown sugar and beat on high speed until light and fluffy, about 5 minutes. Reduce the speed to low, add 3 of the eggs, the flour mixture, and the aniseeds, and beat just until the dough begins to come together. Add the almonds and continue to mix just until evenly distributed. Do not overwork the dough.

Remove the dough from the mixer. On a piece of waxed paper, shape the dough into 2 logs, each about 1 inch in diameter. Cover the logs with plastic wrap and refrigerate for 2 hours or longer, to make them easier to cut.

Preheat the oven to 350°F. Line 2 baking sheets with parchment paper.

In a small bowl, lightly beat the remaining egg. Cut the logs crosswise into rounds about ½ inch thick and arrange them on the prepared baking sheets, spacing them 1 inch apart. Lightly brush the tops of the cookies with the beaten egg. Sprinkle a pinch of crystal sugar on top of each cookie.

Bake the cookies until golden on the bottom and light brown on top, 20 to 25 minutes. Remove the baking sheets from the oven and transfer the cookies to racks to cool. Store them in an airtight container at room temperature for up to 2 weeks.

MAKES 4 TO 5 DOZEN COOKIES

CANTALOUPE GRANITA—You need search no further than this classic Italian ice for refreshing relief in the heat of the summer. The flavors of ripe cantaloupe come through perfectly in this granita, and you send your guests home full of flavor but free of the classic dinner-party food "hangover" brought on by a heavy dessert.

COOKING NOTES: This works best in 2 glass loaf pans or one 7-by-12-inch glass baking dish. The only critical point here is *not* to stir it past the almost frozen state or the ice crystals will become too fine and hard to scrape.

ENTERTAINING NOTES: The finished granita can be transferred to a container with a tight-fitting lid and stored in the freezer for up to 1 week. Place the container in the refrigerator 30 to 45 minutes prior to serving so the granita will soften slightly. To serve, find interesting-looking clear-glass glasses or bowls, dip in cold water, and put in the freezer for 15 minutes. Dip them a second time and return them to the freezer for at least 30 minutes. The result will be frosted vessels that look great and provide just the right backdrop for the granita.

WINE NOTES: Pour sparkling wine or Moscato.

1¼ cups superfine sugar

½ cup water

¼ cup lightly packed fresh mint leaves

2 cantaloupes, about 4 pounds each, halved, seeded, peeled, and cut into 1-inch chunks

1 teaspoon finely ground sea salt, preferably gray salt

In a small saucepan, combine the sugar and water over low heat and stir until the sugar dissolves. Add the mint, remove from the heat, and let cool completely.

Working in batches, process the melon chunks in a food processor until a smooth puree forms. Pour the sugar syrup through a fine-mesh sieve held over the melon puree, discarding the mint. Add the salt and stir to mix well.

Pour the cantaloupe mixture into a 7-by-12-inch baking dish. Place uncovered in the freezer. Every 30 minutes, remove the dish from the freezer and scrape the contents with a fork, forming shaved ice crystals. Repeat until the mixture is almost completely frozen but still grainy, 3 to 4 hours.

Spoon into small glass bowls or stemmed glasses and serve.

SERVES 6 TO 8

HAZELNUT SEMIFREDDO—This is a version of one of the most popular summer desserts I made at Tra Vigne. The hot and cold makes for a wonderful combination.

COOKING NOTES: Frangelico is a hazelnut liqueur. Look for it in better liquor stores.

ENTERTAINING NOTES: If you are making the *semifreddo* for a larger party, you can put the scoops of ice cream right into the bowls or glasses, cover them, and put them in the freezer. This dessert looks particularly inviting served in large, clear-glass coffee mugs.

1 pint vanilla ice cream

1 pint hazelnut ice cream

½ cup hazelnuts

1½ cups heavy cream

2 tablespoons granulated sugar

½ cup plus 2 tablespoons Frangelico

2 cups hot, freshly brewed espresso

1 ounce bittersweet chocolate, thinly shaved with a vegetable peeler

---

Let the vanilla and hazelnut ice creams sit at room temperature for several minutes to soften slightly so they will be easier to scoop. Then scoop the vanilla ice cream into 8 equal-sized balls and arrange in a single layer in a dish lined with plastic wrap. Repeat with the hazelnut ice cream. Cover the dish with plastic wrap and freeze again until firm.

Preheat the oven to 375°F. Spread the hazelnuts on a rimmed baking sheet and toast in the oven until they take on color and are fragrant and crisp, about 5 minutes. Remove from the oven and let cool. Wrap the nuts in a textured kitchen towel and rub vigorously to remove the skins. Transfer to a food processor and pulse until finely ground. Do not overgrind or you will end up with hazelnut butter.

In a bowl, using a mixer or a whisk, whip together the cream, sugar, and 2 tablespoons Frangelico until stiff peaks form. Do not overbeat.

To serve, place 1 scoop each of vanilla and hazelnut ice cream into each bowl or glass. Add 1 tablespoon Frangelico and 2 tablespoons hazelnuts to the top of each serving. Pour ¼ cup hot espresso into each bowl. Top the ice cream with a dollop of the whipped cream and some chocolate shavings. Serve immediately.

SERVES 8

chocoholic?

Try buying some cocoa mulch from your progressive garden shop and serve right on it. The smell will fill the room with the suggestion of what's to come.

MOLTEN FLOURLESS CHOCOLATE CUPCAKES—It is wonderfully childlike to eat a cupcake. Make that cupcake out of this sophisticated chocolate cake batter and it grows up to be just plain wonderful. For a showy presentation, arrange a big batch on a two-tier dessert stand and dust the entire pyramid with confectioners' sugar.

COOKING NOTES: Select muffin pans with cups that hold about 6 tablespoons batter. Be sure to add the chocolate chunk to each cupcake while it's still hot from the oven; otherwise, the crust will form and you will damage the appearance. The mayonnaise is here to add moisture to the cupcakes. You could omit it without adjusting the recipe, but it has an amazing effect. Again, as with any chocolate-based recipe, the quality of the main ingredient makes the difference between a good result and a great result. Scharffen Berger bittersweet chocolate is my first choice, but any first-class bittersweet chocolate will do. Check the packaging for a high cacao content, an indication of quality; bittersweet chocolate by Scharffen Berger has a cacao content of 70 percent.

ENTERTAINING NOTES: These cupcakes are perfect for a buffet dinner, as all you need to provide is napkins—no plates—to catch the drop of oozing chocolate that may run down a chin. You can serve the cupcakes as a plated dessert by removing them from the paper cups and adding Warm Bananas with Brown Sugar and Bay (page 211) to the plates.

WINE NOTES: This is one of the few desserts I love with red wine. Pour a very ripe Zinfandel, preferably an old-vine Zinfandel if you can find one.

Nonstick cooking spray for greasing the muffin cups and paper liners

¼ cup unsweetened cocoa powder

½ cup (1 stick) unsalted butter

1 cup heavy cream

8 ounces bittersweet chocolate, preferably Scharffen Berger

4 large eggs, at room temperature

1⅓ cups granulated sugar

½ cup mayonnaise

½ teaspoon finely ground sea salt, preferably gray salt

½ cup cornstarch

½ teaspoon ground cinnamon

Confectioners' sugar for dusting

Preheat the oven to 300°F. Line a 12-cup standard muffin pan (or use two 6-cup pans) with nonstick cooking spray. Line the cups with paper liners, preferably gold ones. Spray the papers with nonstick cooking spray and dust them with the cocoa powder, tapping out the excess.

In a small saucepan, combine the butter and cream over medium-high heat. While the mixture is heating, thinly shave 5 ounces of the chocolate with a large knife into a heatproof bowl. When the cream mixture reaches a simmer, pour it over the chocolate and mix gently to combine the ingredients and to melt the chocolate.

In a bowl, whisk together the eggs, sugar, mayonnaise, salt, cornstarch, and cinnamon just until the sugar has dissolved. Pour the chocolate mixture into the egg mixture and gently mix just until combined. Do not overmix, or you will prevent the eggs from rising in the oven. Scoop about ¼ cup of the batter into each muffin cup; it should reach about three-fourths of the way up the sides.

Bake the cupcakes just until a toothpick inserted in the center comes out clean, 40 to 45 minutes. Meanwhile, cut the remaining 3 ounces chocolate into 12 equal chunks. Remove the cupcakes from the oven, quickly add a chunk of the chocolate to the center of each cake, and, using a small spoon, gently push it through the top. Let the cupcakes cool in the pan(s) on a rack for 10 minutes and then unmold them.

Arrange the cupcakes warm on a pedestal plate or a platter, stacked in a pyramid if possible. Dust with confectioners' sugar and serve at room temperature.

MAKES 12 CUPCAKES

CHOCOLATE MOUSSE CANNOLI—I live in a houseful of certified chocoholics. Pass a platter of these cannoli, and forget about the candied-fruit version your grandmother bought for you in Little Italy. These are guaranteed to be a crowd pleaser.

COOKING NOTES: You can use ³/₄-inch wooden dowels, cut into 5-inch lengths, in place of the cannoli molds. The mousse and the shells (store the latter in an airtight container at room temperature) can be made a few days ahead. Just whip the mousse again before piping, and don't let them sit around long once the shells have been filled.

ENTERTAINING NOTES: I like to serve these in a cigar box or a paper-lined humidor.

WINE NOTES: Cabernet Sauvignon and chocolate make a great combination, so serve them together and enjoy.

½ cup hazelnuts

5 ounces bittersweet chocolate, cut into pieces

¾ cup heavy cream, at room temperature

1 cup mascarpone cheese, at room temperature

6 tablespoons dark rum

2 large egg yolks, at room temperature, lightly beaten

¼ cup granulated sugar

Pinch of finely ground sea salt, preferably gray salt

FOR THE CANNOLI SHELLS:

2 cups all-purpose flour, plus more for dusting

2 teaspoons granulated sugar

¼ teaspoon finely ground sea salt, preferably gray salt

3 tablespoons white wine vinegar

3 tablespoons water

3 large eggs

2 tablespoons unsalted butter, melted, plus more for buttering the molds

Canola oil for deep-frying

Confectioners' sugar for dusting

Preheat the oven to 375°F. Spread the hazelnuts on a rimmed baking sheet and toast in the oven until they take on color and are fragrant and crisp, about 5 minutes. Remove from the oven and let cool. Wrap the nuts in a textured kitchen towel and rub vigorously to remove the skins. Coarsely chop the nuts and set aside.

Pour water to a depth of about 2 inches into a saucepan and bring to a bare simmer. In a large stainless-steel or other heatproof bowl, combine the chocolate and cream. Set the bowl over—but not touching—the simmering water and heat, stirring occasionally, until the chocolate is melted, smooth, and shiny. Remove the bowl from the heat and set aside.

In the bowl of a stand mixer fitted with the whip attachment, beat the mascarpone on medium speed until soft and creamy. Stop to scrape down the sides of the bowl as necessary. Add the rum and mix until incorporated. Add the chocolate mixture and half the hazelnuts and beat until smooth.

In another stainless-steel bowl, whisk together the eggs, sugar, and salt until the mixture is pale yellow. Add one-third of the chocolate mixture to the egg mixture and whisk until incorporated. With a rubber spatula, fold in the remaining chocolate mixture, being careful not to deflate the mousse. You should have about 4 cups. Cover the bowl and refrigerate until cold.

Make the cannoli shells: Sift the flour into the bowl of a stand mixer fitted with the paddle attachment. Add the sugar and salt. In a small bowl, whisk together the vinegar, water, and 2 of the eggs just until blended. With the mixer on low speed, pour the vinegar mixture into the flour mixture. Add the melted butter in a thin stream. Stop the mixer and scrape down the sides of the bowl and the paddle as necessary. Continue to mix on low speed for about 3 minutes. The dough should be soft, slightly sticky, and smooth.

Transfer the dough to a clean work surface, dust it lightly with flour, form it into a ball, and flatten slightly. Wrap in plastic wrap and chill for at least 2 hours or up to overnight.

In a small bowl or cup, beat the remaining egg just until blended. Lightly butter 16 cannoli molds each 5 inches long and ¾ inch in diameter. On a lightly floured surface, roll out the dough about ¹⁄₁₆ inch thick. (You can instead roll out the dough on a hand-cranked pasta machine, as you would fresh pasta dough.) Using a 4-inch plate or other template as a guide, cut out 16 circles. Wrap each dough circle around a prepared cannoli mold. Brush a little of the beaten egg between the 2 edges of the circle where they meet and overlap, then press together to seal.

Pour the canola oil to a depth of at least 3 inches into a deep fryer or a heavy, 8-inch-deep stockpot and heat to 375°F. Add the cannoli shells, a few at a time, and fry until lightly browned, about 1 minute. Using tongs, transfer to paper towels to drain. Before the shells cool, pick each one up with a clean towel and gently knock the mold out from the shell. Set the shells aside on a tray to cool completely.

Put the reserved chopped hazelnuts in a small bowl. Spoon the mousse into a pastry bag fitted with a ½ inch plain tip. Fill the cannoli shells by piping the filling into both ends of each shell. Gently dip both ends of the cannoli in the nuts to coat lightly. Arrange on a platter and dust with the confectioners' sugar.

SERVES 8

WARM BANANAS WITH BROWN SUGAR AND BAY

I have always loved the combination of sweet, tart, and rich flavors. When I was a chef in Miami, I made this dessert with a mix of bananas and mangoes and served it with basil gelato.

COOKING NOTES: I cook the butter according to the season. The colder the temperature outside, the browner I want the butter to be. The rule is that the intensity of the flavor should match the intensity of the weather.

ENTERTAINING NOTES: You can make the brown butter sauce several hours ahead of time, and then reheat the sauce to a simmer and add the bananas. The fruit should remain a little cool inside. You can serve bananas and sauce as they are, or you can spoon them over wedges of a good store-bought chocolate cake or your favorite vanilla or chocolate gelato.

WINE NOTES: Serve a cool, crisp Moscato.

4 tablespoons (½ stick) unsalted butter

1 bay leaf

1 cup firmly packed light brown sugar

2 tablespoons brandy

2 tablespoons fresh lemon juice

1 cup fresh orange juice

¼ teaspoon finely ground sea salt, preferably gray salt

6 ripe bananas, peeled and cut on the diagonal into ⅓-inch-thick slices (about 4 cups)

¼ to ½ teaspoon freshly ground coarse black pepper

In a large skillet, melt the butter over high heat and cook, without stirring, until it browns, 3 to 4 minutes. Add the bay leaf and stand back (it might pop). Add the sugar, reduce the heat to medium, and stir. When the sugar has melted, add the brandy and stand back (it might flame). Add the lemon juice. Cook for 15 seconds, then add the orange juice and salt. Stir and cook until the liquid has reduced by half and has a syrupy consistency, about 5 minutes. Remove the pan from the heat.

Add the bananas and pepper to the browned butter and stir gently to coat the banana slices evenly. Serve immediately.

SERVES 6 TO 8

gather around

After years of being force-fed dessert directly after dinner, I have grown fond of a half-hour break. Taking time to fry up hot doughnuts and then stand around the kitchen island and eat them while they are still warm is a wonderful way to end a meal.

COFFEE AND DOUGHNUTS—I grew up in California's Central Valley town of Turlock alongside a large population of Portuguese whose roots were in the Azores. They held a number of different annual *festas* to celebrate the seasons—and still do. No matter what time of year, these doughnuts are always the center of attention. Here is my version of a childhood favorite.

COOKING NOTES: At first glance, these doughnuts seem like they take a while to make, but almost all of the time is spent waiting for the dough to rise. You can leave out the ground coffee, and simply coat the doughnuts with confectioners' sugar and omit the pinch of coffee on top.

WINE NOTES: Take your choice—sherry or Champagne, cappuccino or *caffè corretto* (espresso with a little grappa or other liquor).

FOR THE DOUGH:
2¼ teaspoons (1 package) active dried yeast
2 tablespoons warm water
¾ cup whole milk
3 tablespoons unsalted butter
1 large egg
¼ cup granulated sugar
2¾ cups all-purpose flour, plus more for dusting

1 teaspoon finely ground sea salt, preferably gray salt
¾ teaspoon freshly grated nutmeg
Nonstick cooking spray for baking sheets

Peanut oil for deep-frying
1 cup confectioners' sugar
5 tablespoons finely ground espresso roast or other dark roast coffee

Make the dough: In a bowl, combine the yeast and warm water. In a saucepan, combine the milk and butter over medium-high heat and heat until the milk is warm but not simmering and the butter has melted. Add the warm milk mixture to the yeast mixture. In another large bowl, whisk together the egg and granulated sugar until the sugar dissolves. Add the milk mixture to the egg mixture and whisk to combine. Add the flour, salt, and nutmeg and, using a wooden spoon or a mixer on low speed, beat until all the ingredients are well combined into a soft dough, 1 to 2 minutes. Cover the bowl with a kitchen towel and let the dough rise in a warm place until doubled in size, 1½ to 2 hours.

Line 2 rimmed baking sheets with parchment waxed paper and spray the paper with nonstick cooking spray. Punch down the dough and turn out onto a lightly floured work surface. Roll out into a rectangle about 18 by 10 inches and ½ inch thick. Cut the dough into 30 small rectangles, each about 2 by 3 inches. Space the rectangles about 2 inches apart on the prepared baking sheets. Cover with a clean kitchen towel and let the dough rise in a warm place until doubled in size, about 2 hours.

Pour the peanut oil to a depth of at least 3 inches into a deep fryer or a heavy, 8-inch-deep stockpot and heat to 350°F. In a small bowl, stir together the confectioners' sugar and 3 tablespoons of the ground coffee.

Working in batches, add the doughnuts to the hot oil and fry, turning occasionally with tongs, until golden brown, about 3 minutes. Using the tongs, transfer to paper towels to drain.

Slip half of the hot doughnuts into a brown-paper shopping bag. Add half of the sugar-coffee mixture and shake the bag to coat the doughnuts evenly. Move the first doughnuts to a serving platter and sprinkle the top of each one with a pinch of the remaining 2 tablespoons ground coffee. Repeat the process with the remaining doughnuts and sugar-coffee mixture and the remaining ground coffee. Serve hot, warm, or at room temperature.

MAKES ABOUT 30 DOUGHNUTS

FREEFORM CHEESECAKE POURED OVER FRESH FRUIT — This is a flip-flop recipe. Typically the cheesecake is the star and the fruit rides on the top. Here, the fruit is the star and the cheesecake rides on top. I seldom have the extra two hours needed to make a traditional cheesecake for a casual get-together. But by reworking the classic, I have both added whimsy and saved time.

COOKING NOTES: I favor firm, fleshy fruits for this dessert, such as mango, banana, or Fuyu persimmon. Be careful if using fruits with a higher water content, like strawberries. You must cut them *just* before serving to reduce puddling. This is a good recipe to play around with, adding extra flavors to suit your taste. You can use any nut-flavored liqueur, for example, in place of the amaretto. Experiment and make this recipe your own.

ENTERTAINING NOTES: Try serving this dessert in unexpected vessels, like martini glasses. Or, set out bowls of fruit and the cheesecake mixture, and let your guests build their own desserts.

WINE NOTES: Serve a small glass of amaretto over ice.

6 ounces cream cheese, at room temperature

Pinch of finely ground sea salt, preferably gray salt

½ cup granulated sugar

2 large eggs, at room temperature

2 tablespoons fresh lemon juice

1 teaspoon grated lemon zest

1 pound mascarpone cheese, at room temperature

2 tablespoons amaretto

6 cups bite-sized, peeled fresh fruit of choice (see Cooking Notes)

In a stand mixer fitted with the paddle attachment, beat the cream cheese and salt on medium-high speed until smooth. Gradually add the sugar and beat until completely blended. Add the eggs one at a time, beating well after each addition and stopping to scrape down the sides of the bowl once or twice. Add the lemon juice and zest, and then add the mascarpone and liqueur and beat until smooth.

Pour water to a depth of about 2 inches into a saucepan and bring to a bare simmer. Transfer the cream cheese mixture to a stainless-steel or other heatproof bowl. Set the bowl over—but not touching—the simmering water and heat, stirring occasionally, until the mixture registers 170°F on a candy thermometer, 25 to 30 minutes. The temperature rises quickly in the final minutes, so at that point stir almost constantly to prevent lumps. When the mixture is at 170°F, remove the saucepan with the bowl still inside from the heat. Allow to stand for 15 to 30 minutes. The temperature will continue to rise to 180°F and then cool gradually.

If desired, strain the cheesecake mixture through a fine-mesh sieve. You should have about 3 cups. Let cool to room temperature. You can serve the cheesecake mixture at room temperature, or cover and refrigerate until chilled.

Arrange the fruit in individual bowls. Spoon ½ cup of the sauce into each bowl. Serve immediately.

SERVES 6

"SPEED SCRATCH" NEAPOLITAN ICE CREAM WITH FORK-SMASHED STRAWBERRIES—

I grew up eating Neapolitan ice cream out of half-gallon containers. Turning that idea into a dessert is half the fun . . . the other half is eating it. My childhood ice-cream experiences went beyond store-bought cartons, however. Whenever we had a big family reunion, my family would make peach ice cream in our old hand-crank White Mountain ice cream freezer. A touch of salt is added here to give the ice cream the salt-churned flavor you got when you were a kid and a little salt spilled over into the canister as you turned the crank.

COOKING NOTES: Be sure to smash the berries with a fork. The flavor and texture will change dramatically if you put them in a food processor. Buy the best ice cream you can afford for this recipe, or even use a trio of Italian gelati.

ENTERTAINING NOTES: Freezing the plates along with the ice cream will prevent the ice cream from melting too quickly once it is served. If this dessert caps a fairly sophisticated menu, you may want to vary the ice cream flavors to match the savory dishes better. Just be sure to adjust the sauce to go with the new flavors. You could make the ice creams yourself, but I say save the time and enjoy your company.

WINE NOTES: Make a batch of "Drinking" Chocolate (page 194).

---

1 pint strawberry ice cream

1 pint chocolate ice cream

1 pint vanilla ice cream

Finely ground sea salt, preferably gray salt

2 pints strawberries

$\frac{1}{2}$ cup granulated sugar

Freshly ground black pepper

Remove all the ice creams from the freezer and leave on the counter-top for 15 to 20 minutes to soften. Line an 8½-by-4½-by-2½-inch loaf pan with two 18-inch-long pieces of plastic wrap, one going lengthwise and the other crosswise.

Spoon out the chocolate ice cream into the bottom of the loaf pan and spread it evenly with the back of the spoon. Lightly sprinkle the top with salt. Spoon the strawberry ice cream on top of the chocolate layer and again lightly sprinkle the top with salt. Repeat with the vanilla ice cream. Bring the overhanging plastic wrap over the top of the pan, first the sides and then the ends. Place the pan in the freezer for at least 3 hours or up to overnight. Put 8 to 10 individual plates in the freezer at the same time.

Remove the stems from the strawberries and place the berries in a wide bowl. Using a fork, smash the berries into ½-inch pieces. Stir in the sugar, 3 twists of the pepper mill, and a pinch of salt. Cover and refrigerate.

Remove the pan and the plates from the freezer. Uncover the top of the ice cream and invert the pan onto a cutting board. Lift off the pan and peel away the plastic wrap. Run the blade of a large, sharp knife under hot water for a moment, wipe it dry, and then cut the ice cream crosswise into slices ¾ to 1 inch thick. Place a slice in the middle of each plate. Spoon about ¼ cup of the smashed strawberries on top of each slice. Serve at once.

SERVES 8 TO 10

---

2 days before	1 day before	morning of	1 hour before	service
shop	*make neapolitan*	*rest*	*remove ice cream from freezer to refrigerator to soften, mash berries*	*open spumante*

goes great with . . .

Crumbly shortbreads are good alongside your favorite gelato,

or make an interesting addition to your iced verbena coffee;

even sneak a few in bed with a good book.

ABOVE: SHORTBREAD WITH FLEUR DE SEL, PAGE 221

OPPOSITE: OLIVE OIL CAKE, PAGE 218

OLIVE OIL CAKE—When I was a kid, I seldom ate gooey, sticky desserts. When my family did indulge, it was with simple cakes like this one—no frosting, just a little marmalade on top. Serve it without telling your guests what's in it for the first few minutes. They will be talking about this superb and unusual cake for a long time.

COOKING NOTES: This cake takes on a whole new character when you use a deep green early harvest oil. Buy the best-quality marmalade you can find. Meyer lemon or Seville orange is a good choice.

ENTERTAINING NOTES: I sometimes like to use two different marmalades or preserves when serving these cakes side by side. I am fond of topping one with Meyer lemon marmalade and the other with huckleberry preserves. If you do this, cut each cake into 8 wedges, so that guests can sample a wedge of each.

WINE NOTES: Go old world with a small glass of *vin santo*.

1 ½ cups extra-virgin olive oil, plus more for oiling pans	2 cups granulated sugar
1 cup fresh orange juice	1 ¼ cups whole milk
1 teaspoon finely ground sea salt, preferably gray salt	¼ cup orange liqueur, dark rum, brandy, or whiskey
2 cups all-purpose flour	1 tablespoon grated lemon zest
½ teaspoon baking soda	1 teaspoon aniseeds
½ teaspoon baking powder	2 teaspoons finely chopped fresh rosemary, plus 2 sprigs for garnish
3 large eggs, at room temperature	6 tablespoons lemon or orange marmalade

Preheat the oven to 350°F. Oil two 10-inch round cake pans with olive oil.

Pour the orange juice into a small saucepan, bring to a simmer over medium heat, and cook until reduced to ¼ cup, 5 to 7 minutes. Remove from the heat, stir in the salt, and let cool to room temperature.

In a bowl, sift together the flour, baking soda, and baking powder. Set aside. In a stand mixer fitted with the paddle attachment, beat the eggs on medium speed just until blended. Add the sugar, olive oil, milk, liqueur, lemon zest, aniseeds, and 1 teaspoon of the rosemary. Mix on medium speed until well blended, about 1 minute. Add the flour mixture and mix until well blended.

Divide the batter evenly between the prepared cake pans. Place in the oven and bake until firmly set, medium brown, and a toothpick inserted in the center comes out clean, about 1 hour. Remove from the oven and place on racks. Let cool to room temperature.

Run a knife blade around the inside edge of each pan to loosen the sides of the cake. Turn the cakes out of the pans, then turn upright and place on flat serving plates. Using an icing spatula, spread 3 tablespoons of the marmalade evenly over the top of each cake. Sprinkle the remaining 1 teaspoon rosemary over the cakes, dividing it evenly. Garnish the center of each cake with a rosemary sprig. To serve, cut each cake into 4 wedges.

SERVES 8

2 days before	1 day before	morning of	1 hour before	service
shop	*bake cake*	*rest*	*top with preserves*	*slice and enjoy*

PEACHES WITH BALSAMIC-CARAMEL SAUCE — This is one of the most amazing dessert sauces I have ever made. I love recipes that rely on simple, evocative ingredients put together in interesting ways. Once you taste this sauce, you will be making it by the gallon and passing it out to your friends.

COOKING NOTES: You won't use all the sauce for this recipe, but it's so good you will want to use it whenever you would normally use caramel sauce. This recipe easily shifts with the seasons. Simply substitute berries, figs, cherries, or baked apples for the peaches.

ENTERTAINING NOTES: The sauce can be made several weeks ahead, covered with plastic wrap, and stored in the refrigerator. If time is short, warm gently on the stove top or in a microwave oven to room temperature before using.

WINE NOTES: I love Moscato, as it is really fruity, a little sweet and generally much lower in alcohol, which is better at the end of a meal.

2 ½ cups heavy cream	½ teaspoon finely ground sea salt, preferably gray salt
1 cup plus 2 tablespoons granulated sugar	8 large, ripe peaches, halved, pitted, peeled if desired,
3 tablespoons water	and cut into ½-inch-wide wedges
2 tablespoons balsamic vinegar	1 tablespoon fresh lemon juice

Pour 1 cup of the cream into a small saucepan, bring to a boil over high heat, and then reduce the heat to low to keep the cream hot.

In a large, deep, heavy saucepan, combine 1 cup of the sugar with 3 tablespoons of the water and place over medium-high heat. Heat the mixture, tilting and swirling the pan in a circular motion every now and again, until the sugar dissolves. As the sugar mixture begins to bubble, watch for crystals developing on the inside of the pan just above the liquid. Using a pastry brush dipped in water, brush the inside of the pan right above the crystals, so the water drips down and dissolves the crystals back into the liquid. When the sugar begins to brown, occasionally move the pan to swirl the liquid gently and cook it evenly. Continue to cook, without stirring, until the mixture is a dark golden brown. The total cooking time will be 12 to 15 minutes. Remove the pan from the heat.

Very carefully add the hot cream to the sugar mixture a few tablespoons at a time. The liquid will bubble up dramatically, so watch for splatters. Stir the sauce, place over medium heat, and cook for 1 minute. Pour into a heatproof bowl. Add the vinegar and ¼ teaspoon of the salt and mix well. You should have about 1 ¼ cups sauce. You will only need ½ cup for this recipe; cover and reserve the remainder for another use.

Put the peaches in a bowl. Add the lemon juice and the remaining ¼ teaspoon salt and toss lightly to coat evenly. Divide the peaches evenly among individual glass bowls. Cover and refrigerate to chill the fruit and frost the bowls, about 1 hour.

In a bowl, using a mixer or a whisk, whip the remaining 1 ½ cups cream with the remaining 2 tablespoons sugar until stiff peaks form. Cover and refrigerate until serving.

To serve, plop a large spoonful of whipped cream into each bowl of peaches. Drizzle 1 tablespoon of the sauce over each bowl. Serve immediately.

SERVES 8

RASPBERRY GRATIN—I love desserts for cooks. There are some of us (me for instance) who are better cooks than bakers. This supersimple, sexy dessert is for the cook in all of us. It is perfect for entertaining, as the zabaglione will hold for hours. The biscotti give taste and texture. The raspberries are bright and zingy and the sauce is sensual.

COOKING NOTES: I like to use almond biscotti for the base, but you can use whatever flavor—anise, hazelnut, pistachio—you like.

ENTERTAINING NOTES: You can make the zabaglione up to 3 hours in advance and refrigerate it in the same bowl you cooked it in for easy cleanup. The individual gratins can be baked an hour before serving. If you want to serve this recipe restaurant style, you can make single gratins in 4- to 5-inch ring molds (omitting the topping of confectioners' sugar); they will bake in the same amount of time. Remove the gratins from the oven and let rest for 3 to 5 minutes, then unmold and serve warm with a simple fruit puree flavored with a touch each of salt and sugar.

WINE NOTES: Open a bottle of Champagne or Prosecco.

FOR THE ZABAGLIONE:

8 large egg yolks

¼ cup honey

¼ cup Marsala

1 cup heavy cream

1 teaspoon granulated sugar

½ pound biscotti, broken into ½-inch pieces

1 pint raspberries

1 tablespoon fresh lemon juice

¼ teaspoon finely ground sea salt, preferably gray salt

2 tablespoons confectioners' sugar

Make the zabaglione: Pour water to a depth of about 2 inches into a saucepan or the bottom pan of a double boiler and bring to a bare simmer. In a large stainless-steel or other heatproof bowl or the top pan of the double boiler, whisk together the egg yolks and honey until well blended. Set the bowl or pan over—but not touching—the simmering water and whisk vigorously until the mixture lightens in color and thickens and the whisk leaves a trail, 3 to 5 minutes. To test, draw the whisk through the center of the mixture; it should leave a clean trail on the bottom of the bowl or pan. Add the wine and continue whisking constantly until the mixture is pale, thick, and greatly expanded in volume, about 10 minutes. Do not let the mixture boil or the eggs may curdle. If it is getting too hot, remove the bowl or pan from over the water for a few seconds and continue to whisk. When the zabaglione is light and fluffy and capable of holding a soft peak, remove the bowl or pan from the heat and let cool at room temperature for 10 minutes, whisking occasionally.

Meanwhile, preheat the oven to 425°F. In a bowl, using a mixer or a whisk, whip the cream with the granulated sugar until stiff peaks form.

When the egg mixture has cooled for 10 minutes, using a rubber spatula, fold the whipped cream into the zabaglione, being careful not to deflate the mixture. You should have 3 to 3½ cups.

Divide the biscotti evenly among six 5-inch gratin dishes. In a small bowl, combine the raspberries, lemon juice, and salt and toss lightly to coat the berries evenly. Arrange the raspberries over the biscotti, dividing them evenly. With a large kitchen spoon, scoop up the zabaglione (about ½ cup per portion) and spoon it over the raspberries. Sift the confectioners' sugar over the tops of the gratins.

Arrange the gratin dishes on a rimmed baking sheet and slip it into the oven. Bake the gratins until the tops are golden brown in spots, 10 to 12 minutes. Remove from the oven and let stand for 5 minutes, then serve warm.

SERVES 6

SHORTBREAD WITH FLEUR DE SEL—Who else but a salt fanatic would have thought of salt as a hero on top of a sweet cookie? Guilty as charged, but the flavor is to die for: rich butter cut by the mouthfeel of crystals and a mild saline taste. The result is not salty, but it is amazingly good.

COOKING NOTES: *Fleur de sel*, highly prized French sea salt made up of only the light crystals that form on the surface of coastal salt beds in Brittany, has a more delicate flavor than gray salt, so if you want to use the latter, use about one-third less. Using an herb like rosemary in a dessert is a practice from ancient times that deserves to be renewed (see also Olive Oil Cake on page 218). You can also use 1 tablespoon orange-flower water or 1 teaspoon fennel pollen (a Tuscan-inspired addition) in place of the rosemary.

WINE NOTES: Single-malt scotch is my favorite "wine" with shortbread.

2 cups all-purpose flour

½ cup granulated sugar

1 teaspoon grated lemon zest

½ teaspoon finely chopped fresh rosemary

1 teaspoon *fleur de sel*

½ pound (2 sticks) cold unsalted butter, cut into tablespoon-sized pieces

---

In a stand mixer fitted with the paddle attachment, combine the flour, sugar, lemon zest, rosemary, and ½ teaspoon of the *fleur de sel* and mix on low speed just to combine. Add the butter and continue to mix on low speed just until the dough begins to come together, 2 to 3 minutes.

Move the dough to a lightly floured work surface. Knead for just a few seconds to bring the dough together. Cover with plastic wrap and refrigerate for at least 1 hour or up to 24 hours.

Preheat the oven to 250°F. Line a rimmed baking sheet with parchment paper.

On a lightly floured work surface, roll out the dough into an 8-inch square about ½ inch thick. Evenly sprinkle the remaining ½ teaspoon *fleur de sel* over the dough, then gently press the crystals into the surface. Cut the dough into sixteen 2-inch squares. Arrange the squares on the prepared baking sheet, spacing them evenly apart.

Bake the squares until light golden brown on the edges, 50 to 60 minutes. Remove from the oven and let cool to room temperature on the baking sheet on a rack. Serve at once or store in an airtight container at room temperature for up to 2 weeks.

MAKES 16 COOKIES

STRAWBERRY TIRAMISÙ CONES—In Italian, *tiramisù* means "pick-me-up," and it is typically made with mascarpone cream, lady fingers, espresso, and shaved chocolate. I borrowed the espresso, chocolate, and mascarpone from that beloved dessert and turned it into a cone your friends will never forget.

COOKING NOTES: The idea here is to create little discoveries that your guests will make as they eat their way down the cones. You can vary what they find, such as trading out the espresso beans for toasted hazelnuts or the strawberries for rhubarb compote (page 187). I have melted the chocolate over simmering water, but a microwave oven can be used instead.

ENTERTAINING NOTES: If you have an art supply store nearby, pick up a painter's palette, cut more holes in it, and set the cones in the holes for a dramatic presentation.

WINE NOTES: Pour small glasses of ice-cold Limoncello (page 195).

8 ounces bittersweet chocolate, chopped

30 espresso roast or other dark roast beans, finely chopped, or ¼ cup
    finely ground espresso roast or other dark roast coffee

8 dark brown sugar cones

FOR THE CREAM AND GARNISH:

3 pints strawberries

3 tablespoons fresh lemon juice

7 tablespoons granulated sugar

1 cup heavy cream

1 cup mascarpone cheese

1 ounce bittersweet chocolate

Pour water to a depth of about 2 inches into a saucepan and bring to a bare simmer. Place the chocolate in a heatproof glass bowl. Set the bowl over—but not touching—the simmering water and heat, stirring occasionally, until the chocolate is melted and smooth. Remove the bowl from the heat.

Put the chopped espresso in a small bowl. Line a large plate with waxed paper. Turn a cone upside down and dip the top 1 inch into the melted chocolate and then dip the chocolate-coated part into the chopped espresso. Place the cone, chocolate side up, on the prepared plate. Repeat with the remaining cones and refrigerate until the chocolate is firm, about 5 minutes.

When the chocolate has set, remove the cones from the refrigerator and place each cone in a juice glass. Divide the remaining melted chocolate among the cones, carefully spooning it into the bottom. Return the cones, still in the juice glasses, to the refrigerator.

Make the cream: Set aside 1 pint strawberries for garnish. Remove the stems from the remaining 2 pints berries, quarter the berries lengthwise, and place in a food processor. Add 2 tablespoons of the lemon juice and 6 tablespoons of the sugar and process until a smooth puree forms. Strain the puree through a fine-mesh sieve placed over a measuring pitcher. You should have about 2 cups.

Pour the puree into a small saucepan, place over medium-high heat, and heat, stirring frequently, until reduced to 1 cup, 20 to 30 minutes. Remove from the heat, let cool, cover, and refrigerate until well chilled, about 1 hour.

In a stand mixer fitted with the whip attachment, combine the chilled puree, cream, and mascarpone and beat on high speed until stiff peaks form, 3 to 5 minutes. Cover and refrigerate until set sufficiently to be scooped like a soft ice cream, 1 to 2 hours.

Just before serving, remove the stems from the remaining 1 pint strawberries and cut the berries lengthwise into ¼-inch-wide strips. Place the cut berries in a bowl, add the remaining 1 tablespoon each lemon juice and sugar, and toss to coat the berries evenly.

To serve, spoon the strawberries into the cones (still in the glasses), dividing the berries evenly and filling the cones about halfway. Using an ice-cream scoop that has been dipped in warm water, scoop up about ½ cup of the cream and place in each cone. Using a vegetable peeler, shave the chocolate evenly over the tops of the filled cones. Serve in the glasses.

SERVES 8

the kid in all of us . . .

loves a strawberry ice cream cone.

The adult in all of us dreams of tiramisù.

entertaining 101

CHOOSING A DINING AREA

Where and how you set the table can sometimes be as important as the food you put on it. Location helps to define the mood and spirit of the party. Experiment on using the entire house, especially areas you would not normally think of as suitable, such as a den for a night of cards or a child's room for a kids' party. Such breaks with convention can add a wonderful sense of drama to a meal. Here are three new locations to get you started on relocating your dinner party.

THE KITCHEN—The center island is an ideal dining spot. Spread out your nice linens right on the butcher block. I love using tablecloths in unexpected areas. Yes, the site is definitely casual, but that doesn't mean that you should use paper towels for napkins. Put cushions on your bar stools to turn them into dining chairs, bring out your better plates, and dine by candlelight.

THE LIVING ROOM—You can set your coffee table in a fashion similar to the kitchen-island idea. Most coffee tables are relatively small, so I suggest serving a plated meal. A few extra pillows on the floor will help your guests feel right at home. A fireplace makes this plan even better. A number of fireplace grills are now on the market, so you might consider cooking part of the meal directly in the fire.

In the bleak winter months, you can dispense with the table and host an indoor picnic. Move the furniture out of the way, lay out your picnic blanket, fill your picnic basket, build a fire in the fireplace, and throw on a pair of shorts!

THE GARDEN—Moving your party outdoors opens up a world of possibilities. My daughter Giana and my wife, Eileen, love to drag our television set out onto the lawn and set a table in front of it for Summer Dinner Theater. Serve a menu that matches your movie rental: dessert on the lawn with *Chocolat*, an Italian feast with *Big Night*, a menu that can be eaten with your fingers with *Star Wars*, or barbecued steaks with a John Wayne western.

Try a twist on the traditional tailgate party: host it in your driveway. Invite over a couple of friends who have pick-up trucks or 4x4s for the big game. Bring out the television set and the grill, and fire up both of them. One obvious plus? Win or lose, it's much easier to get out of the parking lot when it's all over.

Set your dining table in the vegetable garden, next to one of the stars of the menu. Imagine an all-tomato meal enjoyed right alongside the tomato patch. The smell alone of the fruits on the vine will make everything taste twice as good.

EQUIPMENT

Cooking for four requires a much different array of equipment than cooking for twenty. Over the years, I have collected a number of must-haves for both cooking and serving. You will no doubt add to and subtract from the list, depending on how you entertain and how much of a gadget junkie you are. I generally prefer items, usually manual, that can be used in a variety of different ways, rather than things like a bagel slicer, which is basically limited to a single use. Putting together the right collection for creative entertaining can be almost as much fun as entertaining itself.

THE KITCHEN

POTS AND PANS—What you have or what you buy depends on your skill level. High-gauge nonstick aluminum (look for anodized aluminum) is right for the novice because it is affordable and easy

to clean. Stainless steel, which delivers better caramelization but requires a little more technique, is ideal for the enthusiast. Finally, more pricy cladded cookware—aluminum or carbon core sandwiched between two sheets of stainless steel—is for the serious cook who appreciates superior heat distribution and retention. If you are shopping, I recommend that you buy a relatively small set of 10 to 12 pieces (for the value) and then add specific specialty pieces that you are likely to use often. Most important, add two 12-inch or 14-inch sauté pans, a roasting pan with a rack, and a 12-quart stockpot.

BAKING SHEETS—These sheets are like cookie sheets but with sides. You should have 8 rimmed baking sheets, all of them heavy gauge to prevent buckling in the heat of the oven. I know that sounds like a lot, but they come in handy for holding prepped foods for individual dishes and are regularly used for baking. Buy them at a restaurant-supply store for good value and quality. Look for large ones—11 by 17 inches or 13 by 18 inches.

BLENDER—My favorite blender model does not have a dozen buttons for a dozen different speeds. Instead, it has a simple knob that goes from very low speed to very high speed. This feature helps to prevent blowing the lid to the ceiling when you are moving from one speed to another.

FOOD PROCESSOR AND STAND MIXER—I use both of these appliances regularly. If you don't already own them, wait until they go on sale and buy more powerful versions than you would normally be able to afford.

OVENS—Countertop ovens, or toaster ovens, come in handy for baking small dishes and keeping things warm. With luck, you also have a friendly neighbor with a large oven when you need extra roasting room.

VERTICAL CHICKEN ROASTER—I have sung the praises of this fantastic tool in my recipe for Vertical Roasted Chicken Cocorico (page 116). Enough said.

PIZZA STONE—Yes, the pizza stone lives up to its reputation. It delivers pizza crusts and breads with better lift and crispier crusts.

KNIVES, KNIFE SHARPENER, AND CUTTING BOARDS—You need an assortment of good-quality knives—chef's knife, paring knife, carving knife, slicing knife, bread knife—preferably made of a carbon–stainless steel alloy, and you need to keep them sharpened. A whetstone or rod-type sharpener embedded with diamond dust will help you maintain a good edge. And once a year, take your knives to a professional sharpener to reset the angle of the blades. Make sure you have a couple of large wooden cutting boards, too.

BOWLS—You should have at least 8 different-sized stainless-steel bowls, ranging from small to large, with doubles of all the smaller bowls. I like the ones with rubber bottoms because they don't slip around on the countertop. I also have glass bowls in various sizes, but especially 4-ounce ones for holding small amounts of prepped ingredients such as chopped herbs or garlic. I primarily use the stainless-steel bowls for mixing and making sauces like zabaglione, while the glass ones, in addition to holding ingredients, are good for marinating foods and for working with tomatoes and other acidic ingredients.

STACKABLE STORAGE CONTAINERS—Usually made of high-density plastic, these practical containers are good for both storing any prepped items or completed dishes the day before the party and storing any leftovers once the guests have gone. Square containers can be stored more efficiently than round ones. You can buy excellent containers at good prices at restaurant-supply stores.

SMALL WARES AND GADGETS—At least 2 slotted spoons, a wire skimmer, 3 pairs of professional-grade tongs in different sizes, 2 or 3 ladles in different sizes, a few wooden spoons (some round, some with a flat edge) in different sizes, a few wooden and silicone rubber spatulas in different sizes, assorted whisks (elongated French, flat roux, and balloon), a mortar and a pestle, a large and a medium-sized colander, fine- and coarse-mesh sieves in different sizes, an instant-read thermometer and a deep-frying (candy) thermometer, a food mill, a scale, a mandoline, a Japanese spiral vegetable slicer, a Microplane grater (fantastic superfine grater for hard cheeses and citrus zest) and a box grater-shredder, a citrus reamer, and a couple of nonstick baking liners (Silpat is a good brand).

LARGE ICE CHEST—When your refrigerator is too small to hold everything you need, a large ice chest will handle the overflow nicely.

BUS BINS—These are those large, usually gray or black rectangular bins that restaurant workers use for bussing tables. They are great for storing any dirty kitchen stuff you haven't had the time to clean. Just empty the sink into the bins and store them out of sight.

PLASTIC WRAP, ALUMINUM FOIL, AND PARCH-
MENT PAPER—Buy these indispensable kitchen helpers at a restaurant-supply store. The quality is better, the boxes are bigger, and you'll save money.

KITCHEN TOWELS—Have 20 high-quality white terry-cloth towels on hand. Believe me, you can never have enough.

ICE—You always need lots of ice when throwing a party—usually more than you think you will need. Have an extra 10 or 20 pounds in an ice chest for insurance.

FIRST AID KIT—Just in case.

MUSIC—To keep you in the mood while you are cooking. Pick something you love with a beat that motivates you.

THE DINING ROOM

TABLE SETTINGS—This is up to you. Just know that you need to have enough place settings—in rustic pottery or fine china or both, matched or not—for whatever size sit-down dinner you typically host. You want to have all the elements, from soup bowls to dinner plates to water glasses to flatware. And you need the linens, too.

COCKTAIL PLATES—Plates 6 to 8 inches in diameter are usually just the right size, and you need lots of them. Cocktail plates with a wineglass holder attached are a Napa Valley favorite.

FORKS—Figure out how many forks you need, and then double the number. Guests will set down their forks for a moment and walk away, forgetting them, or they will decide they are finished eating and then change their minds. In other words, you always need more than you think.

COCKTAIL NAPKINS—Have both cloth and paper. Cloth ones are a little more work, but wow, what a difference. And have more on hand than you think you will need. Guests go through paper ones quickly, and sometimes misplace cloth ones.

GLASSES—You want a nice assortment of cocktail glasses and wineglasses. In the case of the latter, you'll need both stemware and tumblers, so you can match the glassware to the style of the party. As with most party items, you need more glasses than the number of guests, who regularly forget where they left their wine-filled tumbler while they were grazing at the buffet table.

BUFFET PLATES—Buffets demand lots of serving plates. Sometimes you will want to arrange more than one plate of the same item, such as roasted peppers or salami and other cured meals, so you can immediately replace an emptied plate with a full one. You should have a minimum of 20 plates, each 10 to 12 inches in diameter.

SERVING UTENSILS—A pair or two of salad tongs; 1 or 2 ladles, assorted serving spoons (both slotted and solid); cheese knives, slicers (outfitted with a taut wire), and/or planes and wooden and/or marble cheese boards; stainless-steel cocktail picks for drinks and hors d'oeuvres; Chinese porcelain soup spoons for serving hors d'oeuvres; extra sauceboats or pitchers.

PROPS—These can make the difference between a good-looking party and a memorable one. If you are a traveler, collect props on the road. Look for things unique to the area you are visiting that you can serve food in or on, such as an earthenware *tagine* in Morocco or a paella pan in Spain. What you choose does not even have to be for food—it only has to look great for serving. Use your imagination here, but always remember to ask the sales clerk if what you are buying is safe to use for food service. Other ideas? I am a retired altar boy, so I love to shop at religious-articles stores for Sunday offering baskets that I can use for passing appetizers, but nearly any kind of attractive basket will work. Look for interesting platter-like objects for serving hors d'oeuvres, too, such as a great picture frame outfitted with Plexiglas or a pizza peel. Or, clean up a chunk of broken marble or granite and press it into service.

STEAK KNIVES—This may seem like a fussy inclusion here, but I always seem to struggle through a piece of meat at parties when I am saddled with one of those typical flatware knives with a serrated edge. Some beautiful and sharp looking—and sharp edged—steak knives are on the market. I recommend them if you serve steak often.

Take notes when you are entertaining, and if you see something come up more than twice on your I-don't-have-that list, buy it. Try not to get too specific, however, as tastes change, and that special short-grain rice cooker might end up in the garage-sale pile in a couple of months.

OLD-FASHIONED CLEANING TIPS

This is an ode to Mrs. Isabella Beeton, the British home guru of the nineteenth century. I found myself growing tired of sending everything out to be cleaned whenever it was stained. Because I grew up with a frugal mother, I witnessed firsthand, how, with nothing more than a handful of everyday household items, you can clean just about anything.

My wife and daughters and I love to entertain at home, but it does cause wear and tear on the house. Below are some ideas on how to deal with various stains and other cleanup problems. First, I have listed my five favorite cleaning agents. Following them you'll find some common cleaning headaches with their solutions.

TOP FIVE CLEANING AGENTS

CLUB SODA—This is my go-to stain fighter, whether I am at home or in a restaurant. Back in my restaurant days, a bottle of club soda was kept in every server station, in case the second—or third—bottle of wine ordered at a customer's table resulted in some spillage. Use club soda on any fabric (if it's a fabric that must be dry cleaned, do a small test on an inside seam first to be sure it's okay) or surface that can be treated with water—just dab it on and blot it off. Club soda keeps spills from becoming stains and brings the offending spill to the surface so it can be easily removed. It's totally safe. I always have a bottle on hand when I am entertaining—and every other time, too.

CREAM OF TARTAR—A little cream of tartar mixed with lemon juice acts as an immediate bleach for white clothes stained with food.

DENTURE-CLEANING TABLETS—This is probably the funniest agent, but when you think about it, these tablets make perfect sense. After all, they are designed to be cleaners. Dissolve the tablets in cold water, using 1 tablet for $\frac{1}{2}$ cup water, and pour directly onto the stain or spot. The tablets work particularly well for cleaning food and wine stains off white linen tablecloths and napkins.

DISHWASHING LIQUID—This is a wonderful spotter. Use it undiluted on tough stains.

MEAT TENDERIZER—A combination of a powdered meat tenderizer (plain) and cold water will remove stains caused by meat juices, milk, or any other protein. Dissolve 1 teaspoon of the tenderizer in $\frac{1}{4}$ to $\frac{1}{2}$ cup water, depending on the seriousness of the stain.

COMMON CLEANING HEADACHES AND SOLUTIONS

CAST-IRON PAN—Rub out stains with a ball of aluminum foil and then wipe with a soft cloth.

COFFEE—Dampen a soft cloth with club soda and dab it on the stain.

COOKING GREASE ON HANDS—Go outside, grab a handful of dirt, rub it into your hands well, and then wash with soap—an old farmer's trick.

FRUIT JUICE—Avoid using detergent. Instead, try loosening the stain with cold water and then dab set stains with distilled white vinegar.

GARLIC SMELL ON HANDS—Rub your wet hands on stainless steel, such as on a kitchen faucet.

KETCHUP OR TOMATO SAUCE ON CLOTHES—Make a thick paste from powdered laundry detergent and cold water and work the paste into the stain.

RED FRUIT JUICE OR RED WINE ON CARPETS—Sprinkle salt liberally on the stain and let it absorb the juice, then scrape or vacuum the salt and stain away.

SILVER—Cover the bottom of a heavy-duty plastic bucket with a large piece of aluminum foil and place the tarnished silver on top. Bring 2 quarts water to a boil, add $\frac{1}{2}$ cup baking soda (the baking soda will foam), and pour the mixture over the silver to submerge completely. Let sit for 20 minutes, then remove, rinse, and let dry.

STAINLESS-STEEL SINK—Mix 3 parts cream of tartar and 1 part hydrogen peroxide. Apply with a damp cloth to the stain, rubbing well. Let dry completely, then wipe clean with a damp cloth.

STAINS ON HANDS—To clean stains caused by everything from raspberries to grass, rub vigorously with a peeled raw potato.

FOOD SMELLS IN THE KITCHEN—It's supposed to smell like food . . . it's a kitchen!

SCALING RECIPES

Sometimes you will find a recipe you want to make, but it doesn't yield the number of servings you need for the occasion. In many cases, you can follow a general rule to increase or decrease a yield. The following guidelines are not absolutes, of course, but they are what I consider when I need to adjust a yield. Always use your good judgment as backup.

COOKING TIME—If you are doubling a sauce recipe and the original cooking time is 20 minutes, you will likely need to cook it for 30 minutes to achieve the same flavor. If you are halving the recipe, then you should reduce the cooking time to 15 minutes. In other words, the volume has a positive or negative effect on the time needed to realize the same end result.

MEATS—I plan on about 6 ounces meat per person for boneless cuts. The days are gone of trying to impress someone by serving a 1-pound steak. Simply multiply the number of portions you need by 6, then divide by 16 to arrive at the number of pounds of meat you need to buy. Remember to ask your butcher to trim the meat for you. He or she will weigh it before trimming, so ask that any weight lost in the trimming process be figured into the total you need. If you end up trimming the meat yourself, allow an extra ounce per portion.

FISH—As with meat, I plan on 6 ounces fish fillet per person. When serving bone-in whole fish, like trout, I figure on 12 to 16 ounces per person.

SALADS—Generally speaking, salads can be successfully scaled up or down in the same proportions.

SAUCES—All ingredients should be scaled up or down in the same proportions except the amount of wine. The amount of wine should follow the rules described in the wine entry, following, while cooking time should follow the rules outlined in the cooking time entry, above.

WINE—If I am doubling a recipe that calls for wine, I add only one and a half times the amount of wine. Conversely, if I am halving a recipe calling for wine, I use only two-thirds the original amount.

YEAST—If I am doubling a recipe that calls for 1 envelope active dry yeast (2¼ teaspoons), I use 1½ envelopes. If I am halving a recipe that calls for 1 envelope, I use ¾ envelope.

WINE DO'S AND DON'TS

For many people, me among them, wine and entertaining are nearly inseparable. The following tips on serving will guarantee that your wines live up to their starring role.

THE RIGHT TEMPERATURE—The single most important thing you can do for your wine, besides picking a good one, is to serve it at the right temperature.

WHITE WINES AND SPARKLING WINES—Nothing beats a cool glass of white wine. Notice that I said *cool*, not *cold*. In general, I don't serve white wines or sparkling wines straight from my 34°F refrigerator. Wine that cold can't show off all its flavor and nuance. Of course, if you have a cheap wine, there may be some off flavors that are best left hidden, and pouring it cold from the refrigerator is probably a good idea. But if you are opening a decent wine, serve it at 45° to 50°F. You will be pleasantly rewarded.

RED WINES—For some reason, many of us were taught to serve red wine at room temperature. That's fine if your room is the cellar at 60°F, and not so fine if your room is under the stairs at 80°F. My simple rule is a $10 wine served at 60°F tastes like a $20 wine. But a $100 wine served at 85°F tastes like a $10 wine. A cool red wine is a little thicker in your mouth and tends to linger a lot longer, allowing you to taste its character. Once the wine is headed for the table, my trick for keeping it at the right temperature is to decant it into a Chianti cooler. Remember those old-fashioned flasks that have a little place to set an ice cube or two? Perfect.

CHOOSING GLASSES—Don't get me wrong. I appreciate a fine piece of crystal stemware as much as any other vintner does. But if I'm eating a pizza or a simple pasta with tomato sauce, I want my wine in a jelly jar or tumbler. Simply put, the wine experience needs to match the food. Of course, there is something to be said for crystal. When you swirl wine in crystal stemware, the shape and quality of the glass help to aerate it, bringing out its full flavor. The Reidel company, a European glass maker, actually makes specific glasses for specific wines, with the idea that a specially designed glass will deliver the wine to the area of the tongue than can best appreciate the different characteristics of that varietal. Because I am a vintner and I am tasting wines all the time, I can attest to a small increase in appreciation when using a Reidel glass, but I would venture to say that 98 percent of the wine-drinking public would not be able to detect the difference. At the same time, I admit that I am guilty of pouring a fine Cabernet Sauvignon into a gigantic crystal wineglass simply for the drama of it.

HOW TO DEAL WITH A BROKEN CORK—If a cork breaks while you are opening a bottle, welcome to the club. It happens to all of us. If you angle the corkscrew, you usually can get the remaining cork out. If not, push the cork fragment into the bottle. Then, holding the bottle over the sink, flick your wrist. Little bits of floating cork should flow out with just a tiny bit of the wine.

WHEN TO DECANT—If you're opening an expensive, top-drawer red wine that is meant to age, and you're serving it young, giving it some air will oxidize it, thus accelerating the aging process. In other words, you will bring it a bit closer to what it might be ten years down the road. This is the main reason why people decant red wine, that is, spill it out of its bottle and into a glass pitcher. Pouring exposes the wine to maximum oxygen; some servers even pour it back and forth between two decanters, thereby increasing the oxygen exposure. You may want to try this if you have a very young, very tannic red—say, a Cabernet from Bordeaux or California that's no more than a year or two old.

STAIN-FREE POURING—One little trick can prevent a lot of stained tablecloths: as you are about to stop pouring wine into a glass, give the bottle a sharp little twist of only about twenty degrees and immediately return it to a vertical position. This simple action helps to ensure the drip-free pour. You can also purchase inexpensive pour spouts, commonly used at large wine tastings, at your local jug shop. They work great.

HOW MUCH SHOULD WINE COST?—Typically, I do not spend more on a bottle of wine than the cost of two dinners, whether I am in a restaurant or at home. So, if it costs you $20 to entertain two friends, then buy a $20 bottle of wine.

WHAT TO DRINK WITH WHAT—Listen closely: drink what you like and like what you drink. If Chardonnay tastes great with your steak, then pour it and enjoy it. Over time you will develop a taste for certain wines, but when you are just starting out, the only way you can learn what to drink with what is through practice.

HOW TO PICK THE RIGHT WINE—Frequent a reputable local wine merchant often and he or she will learn your tastes and keep a record of what you have purchased in the past. Knowledgeable wine sellers are guideposts on the wine journey, so use them wisely. You may sometimes spend a couple of extra dollars at a good shop, but in the long run you will save money by avoiding costly trial and error.

ACKNOWLEDGMENTS

At Home with Michael Chiarello is not just a cookbook, but rather my collective thoughts after a recent epiphany. I realized that so many home cooks were sticking to curiously strict recipe and ingredient guidelines, seldom veering off the beaten path to create the experience they envisioned and worked toward when entertaining. I knew a fresh viewpoint would come in quite handy to those of you in that camp. I truly hope you are as inspired by using this book as I was while writing it. I salute you and support your need to have those you love and care for gathered around your table, enjoying the pleasures of great food and spectacular company. Please remember this rule: "Make it twice and the recipe is yours," then give credit to the cook . . . you!

I consider myself a very lucky man to have met my life's partner whose brilliance shines through all that she touches. Eileen Gordon Chiarello . . . thank you from the bottom (and top) of my heart for helping me bring my feelings to life in this book. Your belief that it is never too late to make it better pushed this book to the next level. Your encouragement and help in keeping my voice real was masterful. As with all brilliant artists your ability to help another craftsman achieve their vision is a true gift, for which I am very thankful. Here's to many more collaborations!

To Bill LeBlond and Chronicle Books, an enormous thanks for your patience and knowing that a little more time will get the job done in a more spectacular way. Thank you for the opportunity to write this one myself—a pure pleasure—and where I stumbled, the masterful editing of Jan Hughes and Amy Treadwell picked up my pace and voice beautifully. Is an editor really supposed to know so darn much about food?

Having the wonderful opportunity to work with Karl Petzke again (we did the *Tra Vigne Cookbook* together) was a dream come true. Your evolution as both a photographer and visionary is astounding. Thank you for your even and inspired spirit, your jokes and can-do attitude. I have always believed that the positive feelings felt while creating a book are held forever in the work. This book is a testament to Karl's influence on the set (i.e., my kitchen).

Stylists tend to take real food and turn it inside out for the convenience of photography. Dan Becker, stylist extraordinaire, your ability to not only cook my food as I do but present it in a way I haven't yet thought of was a wonderful gift to this book. Your talents will serve you well in all your work and our future work together. Thanks for being you.

Alessandra Mortolla, whose props and discoveries are as big a part of this book as the food itself . . . thank you for seeing the voice and searching out those pieces that best represent the spirit of the book.

Dave Hughes, of Level Design, once again our book looks fantastic. It's fun, whimsical, and easy to chew. Your collaboration made the process of designing this book a real joy and accomplished with ease. I love your I-think-we-can-do-that manner. Cliff, you are sorely missed on the planet but rest assured Dave is keeping your spirit alive in all that he touches.

I am blessed to have all of my recipes and entertaining tips come to life on television. Very warm and special thanks to Bob Tushman and the Food Network for believing in me. Natalie Gustafson, my producer and friend, for helping shape and capture these visions. Thanks for working so hard with me to create our beautifully shot *Easy Entertaining* show. Fine Living Network's Ken Solomon and Charles Seagars for understanding that entertaining is more than just food, it's a lifestyle. Steve Kroopnick of Triage for producing our *NapaStyle* show with nothing less than brilliance. Producer Melody Shafer for creating with me in your own special way. You carry with you a wonderful gift!

My NapaStyle family for believing that media and great unique products really do belong together. Wayne Badovinus, my surrogate father, you are a gift in my life that I will always cherish. And you may be right . . . the shows in which you and Nancy are guests may be my best ever. John Hansen for believing in my vision of something larger, always being there when I most need you and giving me the room to learn and grow when I don't. Tara Voorhis for your amazing skill to see what is just beyond my vision. Michael Laukert, you have always been there to bring my food ideas to life. Karlene Cranston, who makes the web of my life maneuverable. And of course the rest of my NapaStyle family . . . Ben Covone for the big change; Eileen Ferrari Grady, welcome to the family; Christy Stritter for lasting creativity; "Get it Done" Greg; "In Stock" Alan; "Web Maven" Terra; "Customer Queen" Robyn; "Get it on the Road" Honore; "With a Smile" Christine; "The Joy" of merchandise; and the rest of the brilliant team.

And there are those whose belief that we can make a better mouse trap allowed us to grow our vision into appliances, cookware, cutlery, and tabletop. David Sabin and Leon Dreimann (Salton), you have been there with me through PBS and now our products. Your friendship and support is a great gift. Stanley Cheng (Meyer Cookware) for seeing that cookware is about the experience as much as the performance. I promise to all of you . . . we have only just begun.

To my mentor and Mom . . . I miss you every day but our love lives on in each dish I cook. My father, Fortunato, by gracing our table you keep the magic of our family alive. My brothers, Ron, remember the kitchen is where the heart is, and Kevin, I promise there will be a life's supply of chili paste. My in-laws, Denis and Judi, brother in-law Tim, thank you for opening your arms and making me feel so welcomed and loved.

SOURCES

FOR COOKWARE, PROPS, SERVING PLATTERS, DINNERWARE, GLASSWARE, LINENS, SPECIALTY SALTS, SPICES, CHEESES, FLAVORED OILS, AND OTHER ARTISANAL FOOD PRODUCTS:
www.napastyle.com
866.827.6836
You can shop online, through the catalog, or at one of the many stores in Northern California that carry NapaStyle products in their housewares departments.

FOR GREAT NATURAL BEEF:
www.longmeadowranch.com

FOR PAELLA PANS:
www.paellapans.com

FOR SCHARFFEN BERGER CHOCOLATE:
www.scharffenberger.com

FOR SPANISH PAPRIKA (*PIMENTÓN DE LA VERA*) AND OTHER SPICES:
www.worldspice.com

FOR WINES AND WINE-TASTING NOTES:
www.chiarellovineyards.com
You can find information on wines from Chiarello Family Vineyards through this site.

www.winespectator.com
This is a good source of information on wines from California and around the world.

INDEX

TABLE OF EQUIVALENTS — The exact equivalents in the following tables have been rounded for convenience.

LIQUID/DRY MEASURES

U.S.	METRIC
¼ teaspoon	1.25 milliliters
½ teaspoon	2.5 milliliters
1 teaspoon	5 milliliters
1 tablespoon (3 teaspoons)	15 milliliters
1 fluid ounce (2 tablespoons)	30 milliliters
¼ cup	60 milliliters
⅓ cup	80 milliliters
½ cup	120 milliliters
1 cup	240 milliliters
1 pint (2 cups)	480 milliliters
1 quart (4 cups, 32 ounces)	960 milliliters
1 gallon (4 quarts)	3.84 liters
1 ounce (by weight)	28 grams
1 pound	454 grams
2.2 pounds	1 kilogram

LENGTH

U.S.	METRIC
⅛ inch	3 millimeters
¼ inch	6 millimeters
½ inch	12 millimeters
1 inch	2.5 centimeters

OVEN TEMPERATURE

FAHRENHEIT	CELSIUS	GAS
250	120	½
275	140	1
300	150	2
325	160	3
350	180	4
375	190	5
400	200	6
425	220	7
450	230	8
475	240	9
500	260	10